RE-IMAGINING JAPAN AFTER
FUKUSHIMA

RE-IMAGINING JAPAN AFTER
FUKUSHIMA

-TAMAKI MIHIC-

PRESS

ASIAN STUDIES SERIES MONOGRAPH 13

Published by ANU Press
The Australian National University
Acton ACT 2601, Australia
Email: anupress@anu.edu.au

Available to download for free at press.anu.edu.au

ISBN (print): 9781760463533
ISBN (online): 9781760463540

WorldCat (print): 1140933891
WorldCat (online): 1140933873

DOI: 10.22459/RJF.2020

This title is published under a Creative Commons Attribution-NonCommercial-NoDerivatives 4.0 International (CC BY-NC-ND 4.0).

The full licence terms are available at
creativecommons.org/licenses/by-nc-nd/4.0/legalcode

Cover design and layout by ANU Press. Cover artwork by Viart Studios, 2019.

This edition © 2020 ANU Press

CONTENTS

Acknowledgements vii
Note on Names and Terms. ix
Introduction 1
1. Japan after Fukushima. 11
2. Sustainable Japan 35
3. Oppressive Japan 51
4. Heterogenous Japan 71
5. (Still) Cool Japan. 87
6. Exotic Japan 117
Conclusion 139
References 145

ACKNOWLEDGEMENTS

This book started as a PhD project under the supervision of Dr Rebecca Suter at the School of Languages and Cultures, University of Sydney, from 2013 to 2016. Although I am responsible for the arguments presented in this book, Dr Suter's insightful feedback and guidance throughout the years were indispensable in its creation. From when I arrived at her office as a 20-year-old, she has been a constant source of academic inspiration and career mentoring. I cannot thank her enough.

I would also like to thank my three thesis examiners, Dr Marc Yamada, Dr Fabien Arribert-Narce and Dr Christophe Thouny, who went over and beyond their task by making suggestions for how to turn my thesis into a book. My PhD was generously funded by an Australian Postgraduate Award and was also supported by two grants from the School of Languages and Cultures, through the Postgraduate Research Support Scheme.

From 2017 to 2019, I significantly revised my manuscript by thematically re-organising my material. I also added sections on two 2016 films, *Kimi no na wa* and *Shin Gojira*, which are discussed in Chapters 3 and 5, respectively. I was able to work on this manuscript using the research time given to me by the University of Sydney as a full-time employee. During this process, I received detailed and insightful guidance from two anonymous reviewers, as well as the editor of the ANU Press Asian Studies Series, Professor Craig Reynolds. I was also fortunate to receive a Capstone Editing Early Career Academic Research Grant for Women in 2018, which paid for copyediting costs. Many thanks to Dr Lisa Lines from Capstone Editing and Emily Tinker from ANU Press for their meticulous attention to detail and editing work.

Parts of Chapters 1 and 2 have appeared in the *Asia-Pacific Journal: Japan Focus*, under the title 'The Post-3/11 Quest for True *Kizuna—Shi no tsubute* by Wagō Ryōichi and *Kamisama 2011* by Kawakami Hiromi' (2015). I am very grateful to the two anonymous reviewers as well as the journal editor, Dr Laura Hein, for their valuable feedback. Another part of Chapter 4 has been published in the *Japanese Studies* journal and I would like to thank the three anonymous reviewers for this paper as well as the journal editor, Dr Carolyn Stevens, for their well-informed comments.

Last, but definitely not least, I would like to thank Sava for his endless support and encouragement. If you are a non-Japanese speaker or a non-academic, you have him to thank for the numerous English-language definitions and explanations I have added following his reading of the manuscript.

NOTE ON NAMES AND TERMS

Foreign words from the Japanese or French languages have been indicated in italics, with translations provided in square brackets. Word-to-word translations of foreign-language titles in the reference list have also been provided in this way. In the case of books already translated into English, I have placed the title of the English-language publication in the square brackets, using italics to indicate this. For foreign terms (identified by italics), square brackets are used to provide English equivalents, while round brackets are generally used when the term does not have a close equivalent in English, to provide explanations or translations that are contextually most appropriate.

The Hepburn system of romanisation is used throughout for Japanese terms, with long vowels indicated by macrons, except for words that have been appropriated into the English language, such as 'Tokyo' or 'Kyoto', or when referring to characters whose names appear without macrons in the original text. I have avoided the use of Japanese characters in the main text unless necessary.

Throughout the main body of this book, the Japanese convention that the surname precedes the first name is respected with regards to Japanese authors who publish primarily in Japan. Uncertainty may be resolved by referring to the reference list, in which all authors are listed by their surnames, regardless of their cultural heritage.

All quotations from texts in foreign languages are my translations unless otherwise identified.

INTRODUCTION

The Tōhoku earthquake and tsunami that hit Japan on 11 March 2011 (3.11) was an event of unforeseen proportions. A magnitude 9.0 earthquake was followed by 9.3-metre-high tsunami waves over the coast of north-eastern Japan, which claimed the lives of nearly 20,000 people and obliterated communities. The earthquake began at 2.46 pm, which meant that most children were at school and were guided to higher ground in anticipation of a tsunami. Over 240 children were orphaned as a result. Numerous medical and administrative institutions were destroyed when they were most needed and 160,000 people were forced to move to temporary shelters.[1] However, the disaster did not end there—nearly 700 aftershocks of magnitude 5 or greater were recorded within a year of 3.11 (Ministry of Economy, Trade and Industry, 2012). Further, 3.11 developed into a triple disaster, with the subsequent meltdown of three nuclear reactors at the Fukushima Daiichi power plant, which caused 344,000 people to evacuate from the affected areas (Reconstruction Agency, 2012). Many continue to suffer, especially from the effects of the nuclear disaster, while the rest of the nation attempts to move on. There is no doubt that 3.11 has left a permanent scar on the lives of many—even if they did not lose their friends and loved ones, they lost their livelihood, their homes and their lifestyles.

In the foreign media, perhaps the most memorable images from the disaster were Japanese people calmly lining up to receive supplies or waiting for the public transport system to resume without any outward display of stress or anguish, despite the shock of the disaster. Perhaps they were the pictures of the widescale debris removal that was accomplished one year on, which has often been compared to the state of reconstruction in post-quake Haiti. These images reinforced age-old foreign stereotypes of

---

1 All figures taken from Samuels (2013, p. 3).

the hardworking, resilient and orderly Japanese and were widely accepted by Western audiences. However, did the Japanese feel the same way? Some Japanese were inspired by these foreign images to live up to this ideal and restore their pride in a country that had been ageing and slowly dwindling in global economic and technological influence, while their Asian neighbours seemed to prosper. Conversely, many Japanese felt that this portrayal masked the real issues of the disaster: the ongoing nuclear disaster and radiation damage, the discrimination against Fukushima residents, fishermen and farmers that resulted from it, the socioeconomic gap between the disaster-hit northern areas versus Tokyo and the insularity and secrecy of the nuclear power industry.

For optimists, the disaster resulted in a *Nihon raisan*, or 'Japan-praising' boom, in which the Japanese consumed cultural products to regain confidence in their identity. Books containing positive portrayals of Japan experienced a surge in popularity. For example, a book that explained 'why Japanese people are the most popular in the world' by pro-royal family commentator Takeda Tsuneyasu was fortuitously published a few months before 3.11 and sold 47,000 copies. Takeda published two other books in the same vein and the series sold 81,000 copies in total (Oguni, 2013). Television programs featuring Japanophile foreigners gushing over the country and its culture became the norm. However, the fact that these cultural products were in high demand illustrated how much the triple disaster shook the Japanese to their core.

The Fukushima disaster and the response of the authorities forced many Japanese to question fundamental post-war Japanese values: the country's heavy dependence on nuclear power, despite its history of being a victim of nuclear bombings and its status as a technologically advanced nation that achieved the economic miracle of the 1960s–1980s, despite having virtually no resources of its own. A desire to reconstruct Japanese identity rather than to praise it can be observed in the birth of an anti-nuclear environmentalist movement that blames the Japanese system for the ongoing nuclear incident. Those in this movement criticise the 'typically Japanese' lack of transparency on the part of authorities in dealing with the Fukushima nuclear disasters and their attempt to suppress dissenting voices through a uniting official discourse. Whether change comes in the form of reactionary nationalism or a reconsideration of post-war values, 3.11 may be a major historical turning point for Japan, akin to the Meiji Restoration of 1868 or the end of World War II (WWII). In David Pilling's (2014) words:

> It has become a cliché of Japanese scholarship that big external shocks have produced decisive changes in direction. The threat of being colonized in the nineteenth century led Japan to jettison feudalism almost overnight in the Meiji Restoration of 1868. Defeat in the Second World War caused it to pursue 'greatness' by economic, rather than military, means (p. 303).

If the Meiji Restoration was the catalyst for Japan's economic and military development and the end of WWII led the country to abandon the latter and exclusively focus on the former, then the result of 3.11 could be considered to be a more complex mix, polarised between the complete abandonment of any ambition, as observed in the debates arguing for 'degrowth' in an ageing Japan, and, at the other extreme, enthusiastic support for a 're-militarised' and stronger Japan, which has been encouraged by the policies of Prime Minister Abe Shinzō.

What can be relied upon to find new directions in such situations of national confusion? A major source of inspiration in Japan is literature; through their works, authors and intellectuals of the Meiji period prepared readers for a new Japan that accepted Western influence but still stood on its own two feet. They did this by introducing the West to Japanese readers through mass translations of foreign works and by endeavouring to create a new, modern Japanese literature using these influences. Similarly, contemporary Japanese writing offers a glimpse into potential forms that the country may take following the disaster. Despite the physical and emotional turmoil caused by the disaster, many Japanese authors chose to immediately respond to the disaster and its impact in their writing. Important works that reflect on future directions for the country have been published by some of Japan's best-known authors, such as Kawakami Hiromi, Tawada Yōko and Takahashi Gen'ichirō.

These works provided a refreshingly different and imaginative way of representing Japan at a time when television programs repeated the same information on every channel day after day in their focus on the devastation of the disaster-hit areas. Many Japanese who did not have any direct experience of the disaster suffered from Post-Traumatic Stress Disorder (PTSD) following 3.11 because they were constantly exposed to these shocking images in the immediate aftermath of the disaster. A study funded by the Japan Science and Technology Agency (Nishi et al., 2012) found that those who watched TV a month following the disaster for more than four hours a day were at significantly higher risk of developing PTSD. In this situation, in which the mainstream media were a constant source of fear and suffering, cultural responses provided those who were ready with a more forward-looking way of re-imagining their country. It was often said following 3.11 that nuclear power experts lacked the imagination to foresee and prepare for large disasters and were only able to provide the excuse that such an event was *sōteigai* [unforeseeable; beyond imagination].[2] The freedom for imaginative visions in post-3.11 fiction allows it to contribute to the debate regarding how Japan should move forward from the disaster in ways that are not possible in factual discourse.

Following 3.11, literary critic Saitō Minako (2011) claimed that there was an attitude that authors should concentrate on purely literary activities and should not be influenced by the earthquake. She argued that this attitude was created by a group of influential Japanese literary figures, which she termed *bungaku mura* (literature village) for its similarity to *genshiryoku mura* (nuclear village, which refers to the lack of transparency and groupism in the Japanese nuclear energy industry). Published immediately following 3.11 on 27 April 2011, her article was a call for authors to pluck up their courage to stand up to the *bungaku mura* and express their 3.11 experiences through literature. Authors responded to this call, producing literary works and exploring the role and purpose of literature in post-3.11 society. For example, Tanikawa Shuntarō's (2012) poem, *Words*, which opens the 3.11 anthology *March Was Made of Yarn*, evokes the resilience and power of literary expression: 'Losing everything/ We even lost our words/But words did not break/Were not washed from the depths/Of our individual hearts' (Tanikawa, 2012, p. 7, trans. Jeffrey Angles). Meanwhile, other authors and poets sought to disseminate social messages through their words (e.g. Henmi Yō and Genyū Sōkyu), in their paper publications and online platforms.

These cultural responses went far beyond the scope of the kind of memoirs that are typically produced after a disaster. Unlike memoirs, which are typically written by direct victims of the disaster (although the concept of victim is difficult to define following a nuclear incident like 3.11),[3] fictional responses to disaster are not always created by insiders. Most of the authors selected for this study did not experience the event in the most affected areas and responses were not limited to those by Japanese authors. There is a significant body of responses to the disaster in languages other

---

2   See Yanagida (2013, pp. 150–151).
3   See Chapter 1 in DiNitto (2019) for an in-depth exploration of who the 'victims' are in 3.11 and for nuclear disasters in general.

than Japanese, which is testament to the fact that, as a national and international disaster, 3.11 influenced not only how the Japanese view themselves (what I call 'self-images'), but also how non-Japanese view the Japanese (I use the term 'hetero-images').

Due to the scale of the disaster and that the world was able to watch as it unfolded through extensive coverage on television and the internet, the response to 3.11 has been global. There were large-scale anti-nuclear protests in France and Germany and there was an overwhelming response from overseas governments in the form of donations and disaster relief operations, such as the US *Operation Tomodachi* and the Australian *Operation Pacific Assist*. Artists and authors worldwide organised charity publications, such as *March was Made of Yarn* (an anthology of 17 works, all written within three months from the quake by both Japanese and non-Japanese authors and published simultaneously in Japan, the UK and the US) and *2:46: Aftershocks: Stories from the Japan Earthquake* (a collection of various written pieces and artworks, including contributions from William Gibson and Ono Yōko). As Anderson (2012, p. 211) argued, 'there is a growing sense that 3.11 was not an isolated incident … people saw the Great Eastern Japan Earthquake and thought about the natural disaster that would impact them in their respective countries' (p. 211). Jimenez (2018) also noted that 'the event has received attention on such a worldwide scale … that it in fact constitutes a global trauma' and that 'the implications of the disaster itself … also extend beyond the scale of the national and have influenced global public opinion to the extent that we cannot consider 3.11 to be isolable to Japan' (p. 276).

Foreign interest in Japan has historically had a tendency to increase when the country enjoyed a relatively successful political and socioeconomic period or when it suffered through a crisis, which was the case for 3.11. Following 3.11, many foreign publications attempted to describe the country and capitalised on increased reader interest in Japan. Examples include British author David Pilling's (2014) *Bending Adversity: Japan and the Art of Survival*, as well as French publications, such as *Japon: d'Hiroshima à Fukushima* [Japan: from Hiroshima to Fukushima] by Philippe Pons (2013) and *Atlas du Japon: après Fukushima, une société fragilisée* [An Atlas of Japan: After Fukushima, a Weakened Society] by Philippe Pelletier (2012). Cultures are often studied when they are going through crises because it is believed that emergency situations tend to reveal psychological and behavioural characteristics that do not otherwise surface in everyday life. In French historian Bloch's (1961) words, 'just as the progress of a disease shows a doctor the secret life of a body, the progress of a great calamity yields valuable information about the nature of a society' (p. 152). Given that 'disasters unmask the nature of a society's social structure, including ties of resilience and kinship and other alliances' (Oliver-Smith & Hoffman, 2002, p. 9), it is natural that post-3.11 media attention on Japan has focused on these areas.

Disasters are also highly televised and broadcast occasions in which heightened foreign interest in the country leads to an increase in the circulation of national images, in which new images may be produced or existing ones reinforced. Moreover, many of these foreign images have made their way back into domestic discourse and influenced Japanese self-images. The present study examined post-3.11 texts written in English, French and Japanese, to gain an understanding of how they represented post-3.11 Japan. Below, I explain why English-language and French-language texts were important to analyse.

The disaster raised unusually high public interest in the US because some parts of the US were affected by the earthquake. For example, one man died after being swept out to sea in northern California, where 8.1-foot tsunami waves were observed and 6-foot waves reached the Hawaiian islands.[4] A survey conducted in the US found that more than half of the population was following the story 'very closely' in the few days following the initial earthquake and the media devoted more than half of news coverage to the disaster on the first day (Pew Research Center, 2011).

A notable characteristic of US news stories regarding the earthquake in Japan was that there was high interest in the lack of 'looting' following the disaster, especially in comparison to the perceived breakdown of law and order in Haiti following the 2010 earthquake or New Orleans following Hurricane Katrina in 2005.[5] American news media also reported extensively on the Fukushima nuclear incident. The US had reason to be interested, having the largest number of nuclear reactors in the world and a vivid memory of the Three Mile Island incident, as well as a long history of anti-nuclear activism. This was also evidenced by the press conference held by President Obama on 17 March 2011 (Bo, 2011, p. 53), following

---

4   'As U.S. damage measured, emergency declared in California counties' (2011).
5   See James and Goldman (2011) and Flax (2011). I use quotation marks for 'looting' here because it is debatable whether the act of taking bare necesseties during a disaster situation can be classified as being illegal.

the multiple explosions at the Fukushima Daiichi power plant, which updated the American people on 'what we're doing to support American citizens and the safety of our own nuclear energy'.

Perhaps due to this heightened interest, English-language authors began to produce cultural responses to the disaster simultaneously to their Japanese counterparts. For example, *2:46: Aftershocks: Stories from the Japan Earthquake*—a publication containing essays, artwork and photographs, by both Japanese and non-Japanese authors—was created within a week of the disaster through collaboration on Twitter. This was followed by responses by North American-based authors with extensive knowledge of Japanese culture, such as Ruth Ozeki, Gretel Ehrlich and Marie Mutsuki Mockett, whose works are explored in this book.

The main difference between US and French reporting on the triple disaster was that initial media stories in France were mostly focused on the nuclear incident and not the earthquake or the tsunami. This is not surprising, given that while the US has the largest number of nuclear reactors in the world, France has the highest dependence on nuclear power, with 75 per cent of its energy coming from 58 active nuclear power plants (Bo, 2011, p. 52). The French interest in the nuclear disasters was brought to the attention of the Japanese audience when satirical newspaper *Le Canard enchaîné* notoriously published a cartoon by Cabu, which portrayed sumo wrestlers with extra limbs fighting in the 2020 Olympics, with the ruins of the Fukushima nuclear power plant in the background.[6] Because of this high level of interest in the nuclear aspect of the disaster, French texts may provide a different perspective to English-language texts.

The French were also unique in their active cultural response to the disaster. Artists and authors in particular have been quick to respond. For example, Michaël Ferrier (2012) published his essay *Fukushima: Récit d'un désastre* [Fukushima: The tale of a disaster] and a collection of essays by Japanese authors translated into French, *L'Archipel des séismes* [The archipelago of earthquakes], was published in February 2012. Emmanuel Lepage, a comic artist known for his *Un printemps à Tchernobyl* [A spring in Chernobyl], produced his *Les Plaies de Fukushima* [The wounds of Fukushima] for the Winter 2013–2014 edition of *La Revue dessinée* [The illustrated review] and it was also French comic

---

6   'Japan to protest Fukushima-Olympics cartoons in French weekly' (2013).

creators Jean-David Morvan and Sylvain Runberg who edited the volume *Magnitude 9—Des images pour le Japon* [Magnitude 9—images for Japan], which gathered 250 artworks by comic artists from all over the world in response to the disaster. Additionally, Japan was the guest country at the 2012 *Salon du Livre* in Paris, for the second time since 1997, with 21 authors (including Ōe Kenzaburō, Azuma Hiroki and Hagio Moto) invited from Japan.[7] Takahashi Gen'ichirō's (2011a) *Koisuru genpatsu* [A nuclear reactor in love], one of the main works of 3.11 literature that is examined in Chapter 4, has been translated into French but not into English at the time of writing, which is a testament to the high level of cultural interest in the disaster from the French public.

As a manifestation of collective consciousness, these cultural responses to the disaster, which I have tentatively named '3.11 literature',[8] provide useful insight into how Japan and the rest of the world responded to 3.11. These responses are rich sources of creative future visions for the country. However, if such a literary subgenre exists post-3.11, what are its boundaries? Should any text produced in the current Japanese post-disaster climate be treated as 3.11 literature? Does 3.11 literature need to explicitly mention 3.11? Is it possible for an author to completely ignore a mega-disaster like 3.11 and carry on writing in the same style, unaffected by the events? There are no clear answers to these questions—even if an author does not intend to write about the disaster, its influences can subconsciously creep into the text. Ultimately, it is up to the reader to decide whether to read any piece of writing as 3.11 literature. For example, it is possible to read influences of the disaster in Murakami Haruki's *Colourless Tsukuru Tazaki and His Years of Pilgrimage*, even though the novel itself makes no explicit mention of 3.11 because the events of the novel unfold between 1995 and 2011.[9] There are also authors, such as Hirano Kei'ichirō (2013), who have publicly spoken about the disaster being an inspiration for their post-3.11 works, even though they do not directly explore the disaster.

---

7   The full list of authors is available in the 'Press release official announcement of Japanese authors', dated 18 January 2012, on the *Salon du Livre* website (www.salondulivreparis.com/GB/HomePro/Press/Press-Agency--Releases.htm).
8   Although the term *shinsai bungaku* [earthquake literature] has gained currency in Japan as a term to describe these works, which specifically represent the 3.11 disaster, the term '3.11 literature' is proposed in English for this literary subgenre, due to the potential association of the term 'earthquake literature', with an apocalyptic depiction of earthquakes designed for entertainment, in a similar way to 'disaster novels' or 'disaster film'. Further, 3.11 literature is not only about the earthquake, as the term *shinsai bungaku* would imply. Most of the works selected for this study also deal with the nuclear incident.
9   For an exploration of how writing introspective stories of individuals such as *Shikisai* is Murakami's way of engaging with society, see Suter (2016).

Defining this genre at this moment in time is made difficult by the fact that the genre still has the potential to develop in many different ways. However, 3.11 literature has been characterised by extremely efficient publication processes, rapid responses on the part of authors, as well as the use of new technologies. Some examples of this phenomenon that are covered in this study include Kawakami Hiromi's (2011) *Kamisama 2011*, which was published six months after 3.11, and the Twitter poetry of Wagō Ryōichi, who started writing and publishing his works online six days after the quake.

This book focuses on such early literary reactions to the disaster, by examining a corpus of texts published within a six-year period following 3.11, while keeping in mind that future responses to the disaster may be different to these immediate responses. The present work is not an exhaustive study of 3.11 literature, even within the time period examined.[10] Instead, the selected texts are designed to provide a small sample of the wide range of texts available, from a variety of different genres.

This monograph examines imaginative responses to the 2011 triple disaster to gain an understanding of how authors, both in Japan and abroad, imagined the future of Japan in the aftermath of the disaster. By focusing on cultural responses, I bring to light the creative discourse surrounding the disaster, beyond hard facts and numbers. The texts analysed include two blockbuster films, *Shin Gojira* [*Shin Godzilla*] and *Kimi no na wa* [*Your Name*], which were released in 2016, Twitter poetry, manga and a wide range of novels and short stories, written by Japanese and non-Japanese authors.

It is important to note here that my approach to these responses is inspired by the imagological method, proposed by Leerssen (2007), who defined imagology as 'a critical study of national characterization' (p. 21) in literary texts (e.g. a study of how the Japanese were portrayed in American literature in the post-war period). Imagologists take as their starting point the presupposition that these characterisations are a valuable object of study in themselves and that it is not the imagologist's task to verify them. The imagologist does not focus on how 'true' these characterisations are, but rather on how they were formed and how they compare to characterisations in other texts (e.g. from different time periods, authors or cultures). In this book, I do not make any claims regarding real-life Japan and how it may or may not have changed following the triple disaster.

---

10 For a more comprehensive exploration of 3.11 literature, see Kimura (2013, 2018), who prefers to use the term *shinsaigo bungaku* (post-earthquake literature).

In talking about images of Japan, it is inevitable to touch upon the concept of *Nihonjinron* (discussions about the Japanese), which makes Japan a particularly interesting case for imagological study. Most scholars agree that Nihonjinron is the discourse within a corpus of literary texts that portrays Japanese identity as being homogenous, unique and static, such as Ruth Benedict's (1946) *The Chrysanthemum and the Sword* or Ezra Vogel's (1979) *Japan as Number One*. Nihonjinron is produced by both Japanese and foreign writers and typically reiterates preconceived notions relating to the Japanese, such as harmony, sympathy and an emphasis on the group rather than the individual (portrayed as a positive or negative characteristic depending on the author) and attempts to find historical, geographical and even genetic explanations for how these national characteristics came about. Nihonjinron is also characterised by dichotomous comparisons with Western culture, in which the Japanese are said to be group-oriented and driven by shame, whereas Westerners are considered to be individualistic and driven by guilt. I refer to the concept of Nihonjinron occasionally because many of the future visions for the country that are explored in this book are based upon these preconceived images of the Japanese.

This book is divided into five parts. This first chapter has established the background for the literary analysis to follow by examining the post-3.11 discourse surrounding Japanese identity created by various authors and intellectuals. Chapters 2 to 5 present analyses of 3.11 literature, which are divided thematically. The first two chapters contain works by Japanese authors only. Chapter 2, 'Sustainable Japan', deals with how traditional values, especially with regards to relationships with nature, were brought to the forefront by authors in the vision for a new Japan, whereas Chapter 3, 'Oppressive Japan', examines the ways in which authors imagined a potential future Japan that was lacking in intellectual freedom. The last three chapters contain a mix of both Japanese and non-Japanese authors and film-makers. Chapter 4, 'Heterogenous Japan', examines the disaster as a catalyst for destroying the myth of a homogenous Japan and explores the future of rural Japan. Chapter 5, '(Still) Cool Japan', focuses on those responses that portrayed the continuing appeal of the Japanese brand on the global stage. Chapter 6, 'Exotic Japan', considers the writings of foreign authors, who focused on Japan's exotic beauty as the unwavering core of its culture, although with some unexpected twists. What is clear from the large variety of images produced is that the Fukushima disaster was an opportunity for many to reimagine Japan, for reasons that I clarify in the next chapter.

1
JAPAN AFTER FUKUSHIMA

Cultural images in literature and film do not exist in a vacuum, so it is necessary to examine what kind of non-literary commentary was being produced by both Japanese and non-Japanese authors and public intellectuals on the subject of post-3.11 Japanese society. This brief overview of non-literary expressions guides the analysis of the selected cultural responses in the following chapters by giving a general background to how people began to reimagine Japan following the disaster. It is important to emphasise that the focus of this chapter is on revealing imaginations and visions for Japan's future in the immediate aftermath of the disaster, rather than determining the true state of post-3.11 Japanese society.

The discourse produced on post-3.11 Japanese society was not homogenous by any means. Heightened emotions as a result of the disaster had a polarising effect on Japanese society, dividing both public and expert opinion on political and social matters from long-term energy options to issues of national security. The 2014 gubernatorial election of Tokyo was a testament to this continued polarisation in the country, with the candidates' policies on nuclear power receiving greater voter scrutiny than other issues, such as the 2020 Tokyo Olympics and welfare policy.[1] The gubernatorial race had seven candidates, but in the end the pro-nuclear Masuzoe Yōichi was elected. However, when all the votes were tallied, there was a relatively even split between those who had supported pro-nuclear versus anti-nuclear candidates.[2]

---

1 '"Nuclear power" cited the Most in Tokyo Governor Election Tweets' (2014).
2 There were approximately 2,700,000 votes for Masuzoe and Tamogami Toshio combined and 1,900,000 for Utsunomiya Kenji and Hosokawa Morihiro combined (Tokyo Metropolitan Government Election Administration Commission, 2014).

These two opposing camps have painted post-3.11 Japanese society in diametrically opposite ways. Although simplistic, writer Tachibana Akira's (2012) summary of these two main views can be used as a starting point for my discussion: 'Japanese disaster victims moved the world and Japanese politics drove citizens to despair' (p. 5). Tachibana's description of disaster victims roughly corresponds to the discussion on disaster nationalism in the section 'Putting the Group Before the Self' below, whereas his description of Japanese politics corresponds to my discussion of the 'anti-nuclear left-wing' presented in 'A Disaster "Made in Japan"'. The pro-nuclear right-wing is a more recent development, which is partially derived from disaster nationalism and is explored in 'Japan as (Still) Number One'. This analysis is followed by the discussion of non-fictional responses from the literary world. Although real-life ideological divisions are not as clear-cut as this summary implies, it is useful to first paint a broad picture of the discourse emerging from these main camps, to demonstrate the full spectrum of images that are being produced.

In both journalism and commentaries from intellectuals, the discourse on 3.11 has crossed Japanese borders in many ways, not only in the sense that today's big names in the Japanese literary world, such as Murakami Haruki, Ōe Kenzaburō, Karatani Kōjin and Tawada Yōko have global renown and influence, but that they chose to deliberately express themselves on international platforms, perhaps because they felt that their views would be disseminated more widely if published outside of Japan. Much of the commentary on 3.11 by these Japanese authors was published exclusively in foreign languages. For example, Murakami Haruki's interview with Judith Brandner was not published in the Japanese edition of her book, whereas Ōe wrote a special contribution for *The New Yorker* and gave an interview to French newspaper *Le Monde*. Foreign-language news stories and texts were also enthusiastically received and circulated within Japan, with translations made available by avid readers on the internet. This coexistence of and, to some extent, convergence between self-images and hetero-images is an integral part of understanding post-3.11 Japan.

Putting the Group Before the Self

As one would expect from a nation facing an unprecedented natural disaster, the government focused on a nationalistic narrative of a united and strong nation, harking back to traditional ideas and myths of Japanese-ness. In particular, authorities emphasised the bond, or *kizuna*, between citizens in the reconstruction efforts. As psychiatrist and critic Saitō Tamaki (2011) argued, the term *kizuna* was originally used to describe various types of intimate and personal bonds involving people and places, such as the love for one's family or hometown, rather than public relationships. Conversely, following 3.11, *kizuna* has also been used to sentimentalise and standardise positive and heart-warming bonds or relationships between Japanese people today—an attitude that may be summed up simply as 'caring for others and working together', which is almost synonymous with Nihonjinron keywords such as 'group-oriented' and 'community'. This broadened conceptualisation is especially useful for the Japanese authorities, who wish to unite Japanese people in the effort to reconstruct the nation. Post-3.11, the authorities have succeeded in incorporating *kizuna* into the Nihonjinron discourse, to make it seem as though prioritising reconstruction is part of the natural disposition of Japanese citizens. It is implied that this prioritisation is carried out, if necessary, at the expense of more personal and familial goals, which is a complete departure from the original uses of the term, albeit a popular one.

The state has been so successful in disseminating this ideology that the concept of *kizuna* has become inseparable from the disaster. The term, which was publicly recognised as one of the vogue words of the year,[3] was voted *kanji* of the year in 2011, ahead of other *kanji* such as 災 (sai) or 震 (shin), meaning 'disaster' and 'quake', respectively. *Kizuna* has been used as a keyword by numerous projects set up to support the disaster-hit areas, such as Ken Watanabe's 'Kizuna 311', Japan News Network (JNN)'s 'Kizuna Project' and Japan Foundation's 'Kizuna (Bond) Project', which sent high school and college students from Asia/Oceania and North America to the Tōhoku region. The concept of *kizuna* was also evoked indirectly in the ubiquitous Advertising Council Japan television advertisements, which replaced withdrawn commercials, such as the one featuring soccer player Uchida Atsuto's message: 'Japan is all one big team'. Even a centre-left 'Kizuna Party' was formed in January 2012 by former members of the Democratic Party of Japan. The state took advantage of this to promote the country to the world. As early as a month after the quake, the term was disseminated internationally as Prime Minister Kan Naoto's words of gratitude for international aid, 'Kizuna—the bonds of

---

3   This was for a *shingo ryūkōgo taishō* award. Established in 1984, the *shingo ryūkōgo taishō* awards are awarded to the top 10 vogue words of the year, which are chosen by a committee of seven judges from a pool of public nominations.

friendship', were printed as a three-quarter page advertisement in major international newspapers, including the *International Herald Tribune*, the *Wall Street Journal*, the *Financial Times*, *Le Figaro*, Russian newspaper *Kommersant* and South Korea's *Chosun Ilbo*, as well as China's leading newspaper, *People's Daily* (Tsuruoka, 2011).

However, one question remains unanswered: why did the concept become so widespread and popular in the first place? Although it is clear from the examples given above that *kizuna* has been actively promoted through Japanese official discourse, it is also true that foreign-language news stories on 3.11 played an equally important role. For example, anglophone news media including *The Japan Times*, *The Telegraph* and ABC News *20/20* carried numerous stories on the behaviour of Japanese people in the disaster-hit areas, such as the absence of looting. They related this to Japanese national stereotypes, such as group-orientation and a high level of social order (Chavez, 2011; James and Goldman, 2011; West, 2011). This evoked the concept of *kizuna*, albeit indirectly. Since before the disaster, Japanese citizens had been able to watch foreign news on the NHK's BS2 channel, which runs programs from various countries with Japanese simultaneous translation. What was interesting in the case of 3.11, was that these stories were widely discussed by internet users, who posted and viewed these stories on social media, where they were accompanied by translated comments written by users from other countries.[4] These posts glorified what are seen as typically 'Japanese' values of unity and cooperation. Through the activities of these netizens, the international perception that Japan was a country that was calm, collected and united in the face of disaster was made known to many Japanese people. These values came to be seen as national characteristics to be proud of and *kizuna* was linked to them. This may serve as a partial explanation for why this form of disaster nationalism was so readily accepted by ordinary Japanese citizens.

Another important example is American-born Japanologist Donald Keene (2012, p. 275), who praised the unique ability of the Japanese people to stay calm, humble and respectful towards others in a disaster of this scale. Keene was so impressed that he decided to show his support towards the disaster victims by moving to Japan permanently

---

4 An example of this is 'Kaigai 'Nihonjin ni kokoro kara no keii wo': shinsai ji no 'Nihon no tamashii' ni gaikokujin kandō' [The world sends their heartfelt respect to Japanese people: foreigners are touched by the 'Japanese spirit' displayed after the earthquake] (2013).

and obtaining Japanese citizenship, in a time when many foreigners were fleeing the country (Keene, 2012, pp. 274–81). This decision was announced at a news conference in Tokyo's Kita Ward and reported by media outlets both in Japan and overseas, including *Asahi Shimbun*, *The New York Times* and *The Japan Times* (Arita, 2012; Fackler, 2012). As popular culture critic and novelist Azuma Hiroki (2011b) observed five days after the disaster, these positive foreign reactions were 'a surprise to the Japanese themselves', which led to the sentiment that 'we aren't so bad as a whole nation after all'. According to Azuma (2011b), this came as a welcome change for Japan, which was 'a timid nation worrying about its eventual decline' prior to the earthquake. These positive images of Japan, or at least the Japanese perception of them, played an important role in helping Japanese people to define the future of their country.

Although many Japanese people view *kizuna* as a positive concept, it is also true that some have expressed discomfort at the mindless repetition of the term, which carries the risk of masking other serious issues of 3.11. For example, Saitō Tamaki (2011) warned that *kizuna* is not something that can be strengthened through effort, but rather is a product of time. Further, he feared the spread of what he calls '*kizuna* bias'—a tendency to become blind to the shortcomings of society as a whole, as a result of excessive groupism. In Saitō's (2011) view, '*kizuna* bias' suppresses dissent and encourages people to work together towards local and national goals rather than thinking about how to make changes in society. He also believed that this bias has the potential danger of letting the government place the full burden of the care of the weak and vulnerable, including disaster victims, on the shoulders of their families, in the name of *kizuna*.

Another related term that was observed frequently in the media was *gaman* (persevering in the face of adversity, often by putting others before yourself), although it was often generalised to describe the behaviour of all Japanese people rather than just the Tōhoku people.[5] Starting with an article by Nicholas Kristof (2011) in *The New York Times* on the day of the quake, *gaman* was a term especially favoured by foreign journalists in the immediate aftermath of the disaster.[6] However, an article in *The Economist* on 20 April 2011, 'Silenced by Gaman', pointed out the negative side of this *gaman* mentality, in a similar way to the criticism directed at *kizuna*

---

5   See Burgess (2011) for a detailed exploration of the use of the term in the international media.
6   Also seen in Roan (2011), Beech (2011) and 'Crushed, but True to Law of "Gaman"' in *The Australian*, 16 March 2011.

within Japan. The article, which refers to *gaman* as a typically Tōhoku characteristic, observed that 'people in Tohoku are beginning to resent the phrase, because it sounds like a demand to endure even more'.⁷

Some commentators questioned the assumption that there was any increase in *kizuna* following 3.11. In her Fukushima reportage, Ogino Anna (2011, pp. 73, 181, 214) argued that although altruistic behaviour could be observed, it was also true that large amounts of cash were being stolen from safes and some disaster victims were hoarding or even stealing emergency supplies. An important loss of intergenerational *kizuna* was observed in Minami-Soma city. While it was previously common for two or three generations to live under one roof, many young people had made the decision to move and start a separate household to escape potential radiation (Yanagida, 2013, p. 13). Japanologist Richard J. Samuels (2013) is one of many who remarked on the 'shallowness of local identities' due to the large-scale municipal mergers that concluded a year prior to the disaster (*heisei-no-daigappei*: 'the great Heisei mergers'). According to Samuels (2013), 'reports of distrust among the new neighbours were reflected in choices of temporary shelters and undercut the ideals of community that were being spun by political leaders and editorialists' (p. 40). Further, despite his previous optimism, Azuma Hiroki (2011a, p. 12) observed in September 2011 that 3.11 served to reveal the lack of solidarity in Japanese society. The earthquake demonstrated that, despite the illusion of homogeneity and equality, personal circumstances such as income, place of residence and age translated directly to undeniable differences in the ability to deal with such disasters (p. 14). According to Azuma (2011a), Japanese people were coming to terms with the depressing realisation that they were on their own and that even their government could not be relied on in the case of such disasters, which is a far cry from the image of social cohesion evoked by *kizuna*.

Apart from *kizuna*, there are many other examples of Japanese national myths being evoked in the immediate aftermath of the disaster. The talk between Fujiwara Masahiko, author of *Kokka no hinkaku* [The dignity of a state] and journalist and ex-TV presenter Sakurai Yoshiko in the 20 May 2011 issue of the *Shūkan Post* is one example. In this talk, Fujiwara

---

7   Another phrase that the article refers to is *ganbarō* [let's hang in there], which is 'a phrase that smacks of heads-down endurance, rather than the hope of better things to come'. The phrase '*ganbarō nippon*' [hang in there, Japan] was even described as a 'tool of violence' by philosopher Nakajima Yoshimichi (2011, p. 134), for reasons similar to Saitō's idea of '*kizuna* bias'—the individual is forgotten in the pursuit of larger national goals.

tells the story of a firefighter who messaged his wife before departing on a life-risking mission to water and cool down the Fukushima power plants and received as a reply: 'Please become Japan's saviour'. This unselfish wife was praised by Fujiwara as a true 'samurai wife' and the couple as an embodiment of the values of *bushido*, which are written into Japanese genes since the Yayoi or even Jōmon period. Similarly, Fujiwara also gave the example of his acquaintance, who was Emeritus Professor at Tōhoku University and the director of the Red Cross hospital at Ishinomaki, whose tireless efforts were attributed to the fact that he is a descendent of the *byakkotai*—a military unit composed of teenage samurai from Aizu (now part of the Fukushima Prefecture), who fought in the Boshin War. Fujiwara and Sakurai conclude this talk by observing that, because of these traditional Japanese virtues, Japan was well-qualified to be a model nation for the world in the twenty-first century.

Michael Hoffman (2011) is one foreign commentator who raised alarm at this display of 'extreme nationalism' in a popular national publication (*Shūkan Post* is one of the most popular weekly magazines in Japan), where he argued that conservative right-wing 'fringe thinking', thought to have been 'buried in the rubble of World War II', 'is becoming mainstream'. However, not all foreign commentators viewed this surge in nationalism as a negative outcome. For example, Benedict Anderson (2012, p. 206) stated in an interview that although nationalism had a negative side (especially when exploited by right-wing politicians), it also had a beneficial side for post-disaster Japan because it created a feeling of responsibility, which encouraged Japanese people to help each other and respect laws and societal rules. According to Anderson (2012, p. 207), nationalism had replaced religion as the main source of hope for the future in today's world and the hope for creating a better Japan for future generations was what drove the support that Japanese people gave each other in the aftermath of the earthquake.

A Disaster 'Made in Japan'

Meanwhile, many citizens expressed their discomfort with such an outward display of nationalism and patriotism because they were more concerned with the man-made aspect of the disaster—nuclear radiation. New platforms of expression on the internet allowed strong criticism against the Tokyo Electric Power Company (TEPCO) and the government's response to the disaster to be voiced by citizens from all walks of life. These commentaries often criticised the entire Japanese system, starting with the practices and attitudes that were deemed to be responsible for the unresolved situation at the nuclear power plant in Fukushima, which culminated in protests against the use of nuclear energy in the country. In the words of Murata Mitsuhei, former Japanese ambassador to Switzerland: 'I call it the sickness of Japan. First, we hide, then we postpone and then we assume no responsibility' (in Willacy, 2012, n.p.).[8] This perceived tendency for Japanese authorities to hide information and act as though nothing was happening has often been described as *impei shugi* (hide-ism; a tendency to hide; e.g. Yanagida, 2013, pp. 86–93) and *koto nakare shugi* (preferring peace at any price; e.g. Shiono & Andō, 2012, p. 324). Also on people's lips were perceived Japanese characteristics, such as a tendency to *sakiokuri* (postpone) or *tanaage* (pigeonhole), often referring to the unwillingness of Japanese authorities to prepare for potential disasters, which is thought to have caused the Fukushima incidents ('Genpatsu taisaku', 2014; Tsunehira, 2011). These characteristics can be summed up with the term *genshiryoku mura* (nuclear power village), which is used to describe the way the nuclear industry behaves similarly to a traditional Japanese *mura* (village) society and that is characterised by strong hierarchy and groupthink tendencies (Iida, Satō & Kōno, 2011). Pseudonymous whistle-blower Wakasugi Retsu's controversial 2013 novel *Genpatsu howaitoauto* [Nuclear whiteout], which explores the possibility of a terrorist attack on nuclear power plants in Japan, is an allegorical exploration of the power relationships within this 'nuclear power village'.[9]

However, the blame was not solely placed on this 'nuclear power village'. Energy is a resource that is used by the whole population, which meant that the emotional impact of the tragic disaster evolved into a sense of collective guilt for some citizens, in a manner reminiscent of the post-war period.[10] As Chairman of the Fukushima Nuclear Accident Independent Investigation Commission, Kurokawa Kiyoshi (2012) described it:

---

8   In *Owaranai genpatsu jiko to 'Nihon byō'*, Yanagida Kunio (2013, p. 4) also refers to *Nihon byō* [sickness of Japan], which is a failure of social systems such as the government and businesses to protect human life. Yanagida also refers to Japan as *musekinin shakai* [an irresponsible society] (p. 98).
9   This kind of imagination of terrorist attacks on Japanese nuclear power plants (also explored by other Japanese authors such as Higashino Keigo in the past) has impacted real-life Japanese Government policy following the disaster. For example, nuclear power plants are now required to be fully protected against terrorist attacks, such as a plane crash.
10 Higashikuni Naruhiko, a former prince turned prime minister in 1945, famously proclaimed the motto '*ichioku sō zange*' [collective repentance (of a hundred million people)] to avoid attributing war responsibility to the Emperor.

> What must be admitted—very painfully—is that this was a disaster 'Made in Japan'. Its fundamental causes are to be found in the ingrained conventions of Japanese culture: our reflexive obedience; our reluctance to question authority; our devotion to 'sticking with the program'; our groupism; and our insularity. Had other Japanese been in the shoes of those who bear responsibility for this accident, the results may well have been the same … The consequences of negligence at Fukushima stand out as catastrophic, but the mindset that supported it can be found across Japan. In recognizing that fact, each of us should reflect on our responsibility as individuals in a democratic society (p. 9).

There is a sense that the whole population was guilty of turning a blind eye to the obvious faults of the convenient 'safety myth' of nuclear energy and that all citizens must now become more active in political matters to protect future generations. This leftist movement is driven, at least in some part, by the general distrust towards mainstream information regarding radiation levels and safety,[11] which has encouraged the formation of online groups, including the National Network of Parents to Protect Children from Radiation and the Food Business Safety Network. The state is perceived to be playing down the issue to avoid widespread panic, which has caused some of its citizens to be exposed to dangerous levels of radiation. These fears, which reached hysteric levels on many occasions—one of the most notable examples being the dangerous consumption of gargling solution containing iodine being encouraged on the internet—coupled with the relative ease of participation in the movement through the internet and in mass street protests, have caused this new left-wing movement to rapidly grow. In summary, those who were concerned with the state's handling of the incidents at Fukushima expressed a bleak outlook for the country's future, in the hopes that this would improve transparency and accountability in the nuclear power industry as well as citizen interest and involvement in energy policy.

---

11 As Fukuda (2012, p. 117) contended, there were many problems with the official information regarding nuclear radiation levels. Not only were the government press releases highly technical and difficult for most citizens to understand, there were also differences in information disclosed by TEPCO and various governmental organisations. This discrepancy, combined with the fact that data such as the System for Prediction of Environmental Emergency Dose Information was not made widely available to citizens, were among the causes for this distrust of the authorities.

Japan as (Still) Number One

While the anti-nuclear camp focused on the ills of Japanese society, the pro-nuclear camp continued to paint Japan's future as a technological superpower and denied the breakdown of the safety myth, which was observed by the left-wing camp. This was supported by foreign news stories such as Anne Applebaum's (2011) 'If the Japanese can't build a safe reactor, who can?' in the *Washington Post*, which claimed that the 'technological brilliance and extraordinary competence of the Japanese are on full display', or the coverage of the extensive impact the car part factory closures in northern Japan had on the rest of the world (Boudette & Bennett, 2011; White, 2011)—Japanese technology still mattered. For example, economist Ikeda Nobuo (2012) claimed that it is in fact the 'danger myth' of nuclear power that collapsed after Fukushima because no harmful radiation was produced as a result of the partial meltdown. Tamogami Toshio (2013), a former Chief of Staff of Japan's air self-defence force from Fukushima, who is known for his nationalistic political stance, commented that the nuclear incident effectively proved that Japanese nuclear power plants are safe, even during a magnitude-9 earthquake. He emphasised that no one had died from a radiation accident caused by an operating nuclear power plant in the 50 years of Japanese nuclear power, despite the fear that nuclear power is dangerous. Similarly, physicist Takada Jun (2011) argued in his award-winning essay that 'the country that stands on the vanguard of radiologic technologies in the fields of energy and medical care is becoming a laughing stock around the world' in reference to growing anti-nuclear sentiments in Japan and that what Japan should be doing is to 'take the lead in developing the world's safest nuclear energy technologies'. Takada also gave as evidence the fact that the Onagawa nuclear power plant, which was the closest plant to the epicentre, survived the tsunami. This kind of discourse has also been observed overseas. For example, it was reported in the *Sankei News* (20 April 2012) that Lady Barbara Judge, Chairperson Emeritus of the UK Atomic Energy Authority, praised Japan's technological prowess by commenting that, in the UK, even those in the anti-nuclear camp commend Japan on its nuclear technology.

Because of their belief in the safety of nuclear power, the right-wing camp expressed their concern for the reputational damage (*fūhyō higai*) inflicted by some left-wing activists, who were exaggerating the dangers of radiation in the disaster-hit areas in their argument against nuclear energy and contributing to the prejudice against people and produce from these areas as well as Japan's national brand. An example was the *manga Oishinbo* by Kariya Tetsu and Hanasaki Akira (2013), which depicted the protagonist suffering from a nose bleed after visiting the Fukushima Dai'ichi nuclear power plant.[12] *Oishinbo* was criticised by various authorities, including the Ministry of the Environment and Prime Minister Abe, for spreading 'baseless rumours' (Shushō, 2014).

Another issue that received widespread attention was the rejection of ceremonial wood from Rikuzentakata, Iwate, for the annual bonfire festival in Kyoto, due to radiation fears. In an unfortunate series of events, the initial plan to burn wood from trees killed by the tsunami was cancelled due to complaints from Kyoto City residents, even though no radioactive materials were detected.[13] However, as the news came under the national spotlight, Kyoto City and the organisers of the festival received criticism for perpetuating reputational damage and for being disrespectful to the disaster victims, who wrote their wishes and prayers on the wood. Kyoto City (2011) eventually decided to obtain a new batch of wood (the first batch was burned at a Bon Festival in Rikuzentakata), only to find that the surface of the wood contained a level of caesium higher than what was allowed for internal consumption and decided against burning it. What began as an innocent attempt by the organisers to support the disaster-hit areas came to be an incident that symbolised the lack of *kizuna* beyond the borders of the Tōhoku region, as well as the radiation hysteria in Japan in the months following the disaster. Authorities have been active in their attempts to reverse this negative image. For example, the Fukushima Prefecture created television advertisements featuring members of the popular pop band TOKIO promoting Fukushima produce such as peaches and rice,[14] and Prime Minister Abe (2013) famously portrayed Tokyo as 'one of the safest cities in the world' at the 2020 Olympics Host City Elections and claimed that the situation at Fukushima was 'under control'.

---

12   It is important to note that *Oishinbo* also portrayed rice farmers suffering from reputational damage (despite their rice testing negative for radiation) in Episode 110, which came just before the 'nose bleed' episode (Kariya & Hanasaki, 2013, p. 17).
13   Reported in *MSN Sankei News*, 26 November 2012.
14   There is also the catchphrase *Tabete ōen* (Support by eating), which is used by Food Action Nippon (syokuryo.jp/tabete_ouen/) as well as the Ministry of Agriculture, Forestry and Fisheries (www.maff.go.jp/j/shokusan/eat/index.html).

At the most extreme end of the pro-nuclear movement are the radical right-wing organisations that belong to the *Kōdō suru hoshu* [Conservatives that act] movement and the *netto uyoku* [internet right-wing],[15] who label any opposition to their views as *han'nichi* [anti-Japanese], *hikokumin* [unpatriotic] or even *baikokudo* [traitor]. The activities of this radical right-wing movement are characterised by negative propaganda rather than positive patriotism. Since the anti-nuclear left, referred to most commonly as *sayoku* (written in *katakana* instead of *kanji* to denote foreignness), is considered to be anti-Japanese, they are grouped together with their other un-Japanese enemies—Korean and Chinese people, which also includes *zainichi*, who are Korean citizens residing in Japan. Although the radical right-wing have directed their hatred towards Korean and Chinese people since before 3.11, their actions became more visible after the disaster, with demonstrations in 2013 gathering hundreds of protesters (Hayashi, 2013).[16] The active organisations of extreme right-wing politics such as *Zaitokukai* (the association of citizens against the special privileges of the *zainichi*) and *Genpatsu no hi wo kesasenai demo kōshin* (the demonstration march against extinguishing the flame of nuclear power plants) took their xenophobia and hate speech to the streets, along with their pro-nuclear ideology. Conversely, *netto uyoku* spread their hate speech against those they call *shina jin* (Chinese—derogatory), *chōsen jin* (Korean—derogatory) and *tokua* (short for *tokutei ajia*, which means 'certain countries in Asia', namely South Korea, North Korea and China) online. The *netto uyoku* also typically associate Koreans and Chinese as well as the participants in environmentalist left-wing politics with the centre-left Democratic Party of Japan (DPJ).[17] An example of this is their use of derogatory Korean-sounding nicknames such as *Minsutō* (for *Minshutō*, the DPJ) and *Kangansu* (for former prime minister Kan Naoto). Also observed in the aftermath of the 1923 Great Kantō earthquake and the 1995 Hanshin earthquake, this xenophobia and exclusion of foreign people (especially those from other Asian countries) seems to be an unfortunate trend associated with post-disaster Japanese nationalism. However, in post-3.11

---

15 The *netto uyoku* are differentiated by their anonymous nature to traditional right-wing activists, who drive big black sound trucks on the streets to yell out propaganda to passers-by (*gaisen uyoku*). For a detailed analysis of the *netto-uyoku*'s activities on *2-channeru*, see Sakamoto (2011).

16 However, these protests have also been met by a counter-protest by those who believe radical right-wing groups are 'the shame of this country' (Kendall, 2013).

17 The DPJ was in office between 2009 and 2012, which made history by breaking the Liberal Democratic Party's long-term dominant hold of political power in Japan. The association of the new environmentalist left-wing movement with the DPJ is an oversimplified perception held by the *netto uyoku*. Many environmentalists were critical of the decisions the DPJ made with regards to the Fukushima incidents and voted against the DPJ in the 2012 elections.

discourse, perhaps due to the fact that domestic social issues, such as the living conditions of foreign residents are under stricter foreign scrutiny than in 1923 or 1995, this kind of radical right-wing movement has received both official and unofficial criticism for being un-Japanese. Prime Minister Abe commented that this kind of racist hate speech was 'truly regrettable' and that 'the Japanese respect harmony and should not be people who exclude others … The Japanese way of thinking is to behave politely and to be generous and modest at any time' ('Abe Criticizes Increase in Hate Speech', 2013). Similarly, right-wing journalist Sakurai Yoshiko (2016) observed that those who participated in hate speech against Korean people were lacking in pride as Japanese citizens as well as the kindness, compassion and tolerance typical of Japanese people.

Interestingly, some commentators who are associated with conservative ideology have expressed their anti-nuclear views following 3.11, which complicated the ideological landscape.[18] An example is pro-royal family commentator Takeda Tsuneyasu, who published his *Kore ga ketsuron! Nihonjin to genpatsu* [This is the conclusion! The Japanese and nuclear power] in 2012.[19] Takeda (2012, pp. 203–205) argued that Japan, a country created by Gods according to the *kuni-umi* (birth of the country) myth, should not be using nuclear power because it is a presence that impinges the realm of the Gods. Further, Takeda (2012) claimed that conservatives should not support nuclear power because it 'causes the Emperor anxiety' (pp. 208–210). Another famous example is *manga* artist Kobayashi Yoshinori, who published his *Gōmanizumu sengen special: Datsu genpatsu ron* [Special manifesto of arrogant-ism: on anti-nuclear politics] in August 2012.[20] Kobayashi has been well known for expressing his conservative politics in his *Gōmanizumu sengen* [Manifesto of arrogant-ism] series since he wrote his *Shin gōmanizumu sengen special: Sensō ron* [Special manifesto of neo-arrogant-ism: on war], in which he praised Japan's activities during WWII. Kobayashi's (2012, p. 88) claim regarding nuclear power is that, as a patriot, he cannot accept the use of nuclear power, which pollutes his beloved homeland that many died to protect during the war. In a line of reasoning not too distant to that of Takeda, he observed that conservatives (*hoshu*) should protect

---

18 The book *Migi kara no datsu genpatsu* [The anti-nuclear right-wing] (2012) by Harigai Daisuke summarises the ideologies of the *Migi kara kangaeru datsu genpatsu* network [The anti-nuclear right-wing network], which is a citizen group that takes this ideology onto the streets of Tokyo.
19 This was a revised version, of *Genpatsu wa naze Nihon ni fusawashiku nai noka* [Why nuclear power is not suitable for Japan], which was published in June 2011.
20 For an in-depth analysis of this work, see Sakamoto (2016).

the Japanese national character (*kunigara*) and evoked 'the origins of Japanese spirituality'—respect and fear for nature, which humans cannot completely control (Kobayashi, 2012, p. 119). In an interesting twist, Kobayashi is not against the use of nuclear *weapons*, which, in his view, are necessary for autonomy and peace in Japan (p. 129).[21]

Even within the right-wing camp, the discourse is thus divided in terms of what is considered most valuable for Japan's future: a traditional form of coexistence with nature that protects its beauty, or economic and technological success that allows Japan to continue being a world superpower. How have other Japanese intellectuals responded to this conflict? The next part of the chapter outlines how Japanese authors have portrayed their visions for future Japan.

Remembering Hiroshima and Nagasaki

In Japan, authors are as influential as politicians and other intellectuals in their role of helping the general public come to terms with traumatic events. As Gebhardt (2014) argued in her paper on 3.11 literature:

> in a confusing and worrying situation, statements by writers are expected to serve as a cultural corrective ... these texts might help to capture in words that which has happened to order and clarify thoughts, suppress feelings of panic and instil in people some kind of hope for the future (p. 22).

However, following 3.11, Japanese fiction and non-fiction authors have generally expanded on criticisms of Japanese society voiced by left-wing environmentalists, rather than focusing on 'suppress[ing] feelings of panic'. Authors have also expressed a more nuanced view of Japan's future, compared to other public intellectuals.

---

21   Kobayashi (2011) outlined his pro–nuclear armament view further in the last chapter of his *Gōmanizumu sengen special: Kokubōron* [Special manifesto of arrogant-ism: on national defense], *Genpatsu to kokubō* [Nuclear power plants and national defense] and *Gōsen dōjō: genpatsu wa yabai, kakuheiki wa anzen* [The school of arrogant-ism: nuclear power is dangerous, nuclear weapons are safe] (2012). Former Minister of Defence Ishiba Shigeru is an example of a politician who supported nuclear power precisely because of the technology's potential to be used for the manufacturing of nuclear weapons. Ishiba stated in an interview with *News Post Seven* (5 October 2011) that having the potential to create nuclear weapons in a short amount of time would have a deterrent effect, should Japan come close to having a war.

Ogino Anna (2011), an Akutagawa prize–winning author, made positive and negative observations of post-disaster Japan in *Daishinsai: yoku to jingi* [The great earthquake: greed and honour]. Ogino (2011, pp. 55–56, 59) criticised the Japanese-style top-down organisation that she observed at the evacuation shelter, giving examples of supplies not being distributed efficiently (or sometimes, not at all) because official procedures could not be bypassed and dead bodies that were not removed as quickly as they could have been. Ogino (2011, pp. 237–240) explained these unfortunate events using her view of the Japanese national character: twenty-first-century Japanese are people who have stopped thinking or taking responsibility, living happily in a system that encourages obedience. She concluded that the Japanese tendency to be calm in the face of such disasters also has a negative side—this calmness comes from a blind, unquestioning trust towards authority. According to Ogino (2011, pp. 237–238), Japanese people do not take pride in their citizenship and are happy to obey as long as the economic conditions in their country are favourable to them. However, Ogino (2011, p. 201) also saw some hope for the future in the behaviour of certain individuals who took matters into their own hands in this time of emergency. For example, a high school principal decided to allow evacuees to find shelter at his school, even though his school was not a formally designated evacuation shelter. It is this kind of active, individual response that Ogino (2011, p. 240) saw as a force that moved Japan forward from the immediate aftermath of the disaster.

While Ogino believed that the Japanese, especially in the disaster-hit areas, needed to become more active citizens for reconstruction to occur, other authors questioned whether the Japanese can even be active participants in political discourse. For example, some have pointed out the tendency for the Japanese to jump to conclusions with regards to political affiliations, especially when it came to left-wing ideologies. Muroi Yuzuki (2013), author and Takahashi Gen'ichirō's ex-wife, condemned Japanese society in the 5 July 2013 issue of *Shūkan Asahi* for labelling any concerns about radiation levels as 'left-wing' and argued that not all Japanese citizens are cleanly divided between right-wing and left-wing politics. As *manga* artist and researcher Takekuma Kentarō (2011, p. 152) contended, in post-war Japan, being pro-nuclear has traditionally been associated with conservative politics, whereas being anti-nuclear is being a political dissident and a communist or an anarchist. Murakami Haruki

(2011) expressed a similar view, albeit in a more indirect way: 'The label of "unrealistic dreamer" has been slapped on anyone who expresses reservations about nuclear power' (n.p.).

This left-wing movement was also perceived to have become too extremist by some authors. Yōrō Takeshi, author of the best-seller *Baka no kabe* [The wall of fools], was one of the intellectuals who argued that the tendency to be polarised between extreme views is typical of the Japanese, quoted in a 2011 talk with Genyū Sōkyu, Akutagawa prize–winning author and Buddhist monk from Fukushima, which was published in *Voice*. He claimed that this stems from the fact that Japanese people are less interested in facts compared to Anglo-Saxon people, who wait for objective and scientific data to become available before reaching their conclusions. This leads to a situation in which participants in political debates choose their stance on a more emotional basis. In the same article, Genyū Sōkyu observed that since no scientific conclusion had been drawn on the health effects of low-level radiation, it was necessary for the Japanese to accept that they simply 'don't know'. He even labelled post-3.11 anti-nuclear activism as being 'violent'. Conversely, Yōrō suggested that Japanese political structures encourage this kind of polarisation—residents in the areas surrounding nuclear power plants were able to receive the most amount of compensation when the votes 'for' constructing a nuclear power plant only exceed the votes 'against' by a small margin.

Odajima Takashi, an author and columnist, also raised alarm over this issue. Odajima (2012) drew parallels between the discourse on Fukushima and the discourse surrounding the Nanjing massacre, pointing out that in both cases, the two opposing forces refused to listen to each other, which caused discussion to become meaningless and further increased tensions. Additionally, this kind of attitude causes the topic to become shunned by the average citizen and only discussed by fanatics who fabricate facts to further their arguments. Like Yōrō, Odajima (2012) claims that this leads to a 'typically Japanese' lack of discussion of the truth of the matter, which becomes 'massacred'. Odajima referred to a *Yūkan Fuji* article from nine days prior (14 March 2012) by ex-journalist Uesugi Takashi, which was widely criticised for claiming that 'the cities of Fukushima and Kōriyama are uninhabitable' (the two cities have an estimated population size of

287,365 and 332,176, respectively, as at 1 June 2019).[22] Uesugi's reasoning for this statement was that two journalists from the *Wall Street Journal* made this claim. However, it was later discovered that these journalists never made these comments and an erratum was published on *Yūkan Fuji* on 22 March.[23] Odajima (2012) argued that such fabrications of 'facts' directly hinder efforts to have a meaningful discussion on nuclear power.

The topic that has stirred up the most critical responses from Japanese authors is undoubtedly that of nuclear power. For example, Murakami Haruki, Ōe Kenzaburō and Karatani Kōjin—perhaps the three most internationally recognised public figures from the Japanese literary world—have all expressed their opposition to nuclear power in the wake of the disaster. These three men have been vocal on this issue on the global stage, which has had an important influence on Japan's post-3.11 image. Murakami Haruki famously commented on the disaster in his speech, 'Speaking as an Unrealistic Dreamer', delivered when he received the 23rd Premi Internacional Catalunya in Barcelona in 2011. In this speech, Murakami (2011) expressed hopes for Japan's reconstruction by linking the ability of the Japanese to deal with the frequent natural disasters to the idea of *mujō*—'a resigned worldview' and a perspective that 'all things must pass away'.[24] Murakami (2011) explained that this idea of *mujō* comes from the view that humans are simply renting space on this planet called Earth: 'It's not as if the earth came up and asked us, "Please come live here"'. This view, which has its roots in Buddhism, 'has been seared deeply into the Japanese spirit, forming a national mindset that has continued on almost without change since ancient times' (Murakami, 2011) and allows the Japanese people to rebuild their homes and carry on living after natural disasters. However, Murakami claimed that nuclear power does not belong in such a worldview because it is part of an intangible moral decay, a mindset of efficiency and convenience that 'cannot be so easily repaired'. This led to the author's conclusion that Japan should not possess nuclear power. Murakami (2011) strongly criticised the Japanese Government and the electricity companies that promoted nuclear power

---

22 Data taken from official city council statistics: www.city.fukushima.fukushima.jp/jouhouka-seisaku/shise/opendate/suikeijinnkou/h31suikeijinkou.html; www.city.koriyama.lg.jp/soshikinogoannai/seisakukaihatsubu/seisakukaihatsuka/gomu/2215.html.
23 The full details of the incident can be found here: togetter.com/li/276770.
24 Quotes are taken from the English translation, available at: japanfocus.org/-Murakami-Haruki/3571.

in the interest of profitability and claimed that 'the citizens of Japan will become really angry' this time, even though 'the Japanese are a people who tend not to get angry easily'.

At the same time, like Ogino and many other commentators, Murakami (2011) urged all citizens to accept responsibility—'when it comes to rebuilding damaged morals and ethical standards, the responsibility falls on all our shoulders'. Because Japanese people have 'a positive mind, a respect for things that have passed away and a quiet determination to go on living with vigor in this fragile world filled with dangers' as evidenced by the idea of *mujō*, their task as Japanese citizens should have been to accept 'collective responsibility for the many victims who perished at Hiroshima and Nagasaki' by '[shouting] "no" to the atom'. Murakami (2011) thus included opposition to nuclear power as part of what it means to be Japanese. Further, Murakami outlined his vision for Japan as not only an anti-nuclear nation, but a world leader in non-nuclear energy sources. If Japan could '[combine] all our technological expertise, [mass] all our wisdom and know-how and [invest] all our social capital to develop effective energy sources to replace nuclear power', it would be 'a tremendous opportunity for us truly to contribute, as Japanese, to the world' (Murakami, 2011). In an interview with Austrian journalist Judith Brandner, Murakami commented that the 'strong and earnest' nature of the Japanese people makes them particularly suitable for this monumental task:

> Once national goals are set, everyone tries their best to achieve them. Once something is decided, everyone follows. If it is decided that nuclear power will be phased out, everyone will definitely work together to achieve this and happily reduce their energy consumption. It's just that there is no one to make these decisions (in Kirishima, 2013, p. 32; trans. by author).

Murakami displays as much faith in Japanese national characteristics and technological prowess as those in the pro-nuclear camp, even though the disaster represents 'the collapse of a myth, the belief in the power of technology that has been a source of pride to the Japanese for so many years'. The only difference is that Murakami focused on using this Japanese technological advantage for the development of alternative green technologies,[25] whereas the pro-nuclear camp focused on developing a safer and greener way to produce nuclear energy, namely through the reprocessing of radioactive waste and the attainment of commercial nuclear fusion technology.

In a 2011 essay published in *The New Yorker* titled 'History Repeats: Japan and Nuclear Power', Ōe Kenzaburō also placed Fukushima on a continuum from Hiroshima and Nagasaki as well as the hydrogen bomb testing at Bikini Atoll—three events that have come to represent the dangers of nuclear technology in recent Japanese history. Ōe (2011) described the use of nuclear power in Japan as 'the worst possible betrayal of the memory of Hiroshima's victims' and expressed his hopes that Fukushima 'will allow the Japanese to reconnect with the victims of Hiroshima and Nagasaki, to recognize the danger of nuclear power and to put an end to the illusion of the efficacy of deterrence that is advocated by nuclear powers'. Referring to Japan's three non-nuclear principles—'don't possess, manufacture, or introduce into Japanese territory nuclear weapons'—Ōe suggested that both nuclear power and nuclear weapons do not belong in Japan. Although nuclear power and nuclear weapons are produced using different processes, authors such as Murakami and Ōe feel that Japan should embrace its identity as a completely nuclear-free nation and allow the legacy of Hiroshima and Nagasaki to endure.

Karatani Kōjin (2011) was of a similar view to Murakami and Ōe, in observing that 'the crisis at the Fukushima nuclear power plant cannot help but call forth memories of Hiroshima and Nagasaki' in his article on the US left-wing *CounterPunch* magazine on 24 March 2011. He suggested that the use of nuclear power in Japan was a result of 'criminal deception on the part of industry and government'. However, Karatani (2011) also took the concept slightly further than Murakami and Ōe, urging Japan to undergo a 'rebirth' by abandoning capitalist economic development altogether—'it is only then that people will, for the first time, truly be able to live'. This comes from a perspective held by Japanese citizens since before the disaster, that 'acknowledges the reality and continuing prospect of low growth and that calls for the formation of a new economy and civil society'. This is similar to the observation made by political scientist

---

25 This kind of discourse painting Japan's new future as a world leader in green technologies is also observed outside the literary world. Examples include former US Vice President Walter F. Mondale (2012, p. 121) and US environmental analyst Lester R. Brown (2012, p. 167), who were both featured in the same Kyodo News publication.

Mikuriya Takashi (2011, p. 22), that the disaster will allow Japanese people to finally accept the 'slow life' (a Japanese term used in the same way as the 'slow movement' in English) philosophy, where importance is placed on whether citizens can live comfortably within Japan rather than the country's position relative to the rest of the world. For Takashi (2011, p. 23), this also meant a society that embraces the rapid ageing of Japan's population and respects the experiences and wisdom of the elderly, rather than viewing their existence as a problem. The argument for degrowth has even spread to the political world, proposed by former Minister of Economy, Trade and Industry Edano Yukio as part of his 'Edanomics' policy (Satō & Kawaguchi, 2012) and is an important part of the analysis presented in Chapters 2 and 3.

The End of 'Cool Japan'?

The aforementioned three authors observed that the disaster revealed outdated post-war values in Japanese society, such as an obsession with economic growth fuelled by nuclear power and that this post-disaster period was a good opportunity to rethink these values. To borrow from Mikuriya Takashi's (2011) book title, the 'post-war' period has ended and the 'post-disaster' period has begun. For Takashi (2011, p. 7), the disaster represented a shared national experience comparable to Japan's defeat in WWII, which finally marked the beginning of a break from the post-war, post–economic miracle model. However, this post-war society, with its long period of uninterrupted peace and prosperity, gave birth to some of the most important cultural expressions in modern Japan—popular culture, namely that of *manga*, *anime* and *otaku* (here I am using the term *otaku* as a convenient way to refer to consumers of *manga* and *anime*; however, the term is much more complex in meaning, as examined in Chapter 5). Just nine days after the earthquake, academic and *otaku* researcher Morikawa Kaichirō (2011a, 2011b) tweeted that since '*otaku* culture had been built on the foundation of the stable yet suffocating everydayness' of Japanese society,[26] the crisis of 3.11 may 'cause cracks to form in this foundation'. He gave the simple example of the ubiquitous 24-hour convenience stores, which had been a symbol of this everlasting

---

26 The idea of the 'endless everyday' was proposed by sociologist Miyadai Shinji in his 1995 book *Owari naki nichijō wo ikiro* [Living in 'the endless everyday']. Miyadai (1995) argued that it was this boredom that led to the rise of the Aum Shinrikyō cult in Japan.

'everydayness' and argued that such symbolism was likely to change following the experience of inconvenience during the disaster, which extended to rolling blackouts in the Kantō region.[27] Since Morikawa's tweets, several *otaku* culture experts have expanded on the view that 3.11 represented a rupture from the everydayness of the post-war period, which may cause a fundamental shift in future Japanese cultural expressions.

Azuma Hiroki, known for his philosophical work on *otaku* culture, is an example of an author and a public intellectual whose recent work embodies this concern. Since 3.11, Azuma has published controversial works and philosophical essays as the editor of his *Shisō chizu beta* magazine, hosted debates on the Japanese video sharing website *Niconico* as part of the activities of his publishing company, *Genron*, and been the creator and proponent of the idea of turning the Fukushima Daiichi nuclear power plant into a 'dark tourism' destination. Referring to the tweets by Morikawa, Azuma (2011c) suggested that this sudden break in the everydayness caused by the disaster was likely to become a turning point for the culture of 'Moe' and 'Cool Japan'.[28] Azuma (2012, p. 44) observed that the 1985 animation *Megazōn tsū surī* [Megazone 23] captured the essence of the foundation of pre-3.11 Japanese popular culture—the setting of this cult film is a simulated reality modelled on 1980s Tokyo, 'when people were most happy'. Pre-3.11 mainstream Japanese popular culture had been focused on preserving this happiness, whether imagined or real, by avoiding the question of what it is to be Japanese in this day and age—what should be done about nuclear power, Okinawa, or the issue of intergenerational inequity, just to name a few examples. In the immediate aftermath of the disaster, Azuma (2012, pp. 43–45) viewed his role as helping to create a new mindset to create a new country, by assisting his readers to think about these issues.

Takekuma Kentarō (2011, p. 154) also predicted a shift in *otaku* culture in his article titled 'The day the "endless everyday" ended'. In Kentarō's (2011) view, pre-3.11 *otaku* was characterised by a cynical attitude to life and a reliance on apocalyptic fantasies to deal with the suffocating boredom of prosperous and seemingly endless 'everyday' (p. 155). Since the events of 3.11 exceeded this *otaku* imagination by their sheer scale

---

27 The rolling blackout (*keikaku teiden*) were a measure adopted by TEPCO from 14 March 2011, when electricity delivery was intentionally stopped for three-hour periods in selected regions (TEPCO, 2011).
28 'Cool Japan' is a slogan used by the Japanese Government to promote the country as a cultural superpower.

and proximity, he believed that it was likely that future works with apocalyptic themes would not be able to compete with this reality. Kentarō (2011, p. 151) provided the example of his experience walking through the streets of Shinjuku on the day of the earthquake, when the ordinary and everyday scenery of the city co-existed with the extraordinary sight of the paralysis of transport systems and people spending the night on the streets. He claimed that this looked eerily similar to a scene from the 1993 anime film *Mobile Police PATLABOR 2*, in which men and women in business attire commute to work by walking past tanks parked on the street, in a city on full alert in preparation for a terrorist attack. He suggested that one of the preoccupations of the director of the film, Oshii Mamoru, was to portray the fear caused by our trusted everyday falling apart. Now that this has happened in reality, these apocalyptic portrayals may not appeal as much, or evoke as much fear in the Japanese audience, as they previously did.

The pendulum could also swing in the opposite direction for some, in which such apocalyptic portrayals remind them of the horrors of 3.11 and contribute to issues such as PTSD. Due to this, these apocalyptic works may be considered inappropriate and inconsiderate towards disaster victims (*fukinshin*; imprudent). Many pre-3.11 film, *anime* and *manga* works had their releases postponed or cancelled due to the disaster.[29] This also presented an issue for popular culture responses to subsequent disasters in Japan, such as the Kumamoto Earthquake in 2016. Following the Kumamoto Earthquake, there were many internet users (the so-called *fukinshinchū*, or '*fukinshin* maniacs') who patrolled social media platforms for any mention of *anime* viewing (among other forms of consumption of entertainment) to label these activities as *fukinshin* during a time when many were still suffering. It has become increasingly difficult to publicly portray or consume the apocalyptic scenes typical of *sekaikei* anime and manga, such as *Neon Genesis Evangelion*, which formed the foundations of 'Cool Japan'.[30]

---

29 Some examples of major films that had their releases postponed include Feng Xioagang's 2010 *Aftershock*, Alister Grierson's 2011 *Sanctum* and Lucy Walker's 2010 *Countdown to Zero*.
30 *Sekaikei* fiction consists of stories in which the romantic relationship between male protagonists and heroines are directly related to the fate of the entire world, usually a global crisis or an apocalypse (Azuma, 2007, p. 96). However, *Sekaikei* is not dead: *Kimi no na wa* [Your Name], a 2016 *anime* film explored in Chapter 4, is a post-3.11 example of an extremely popular *sekaikei* work.

Is *otaku* culture really so fragile that it can be destroyed by a seismic movement? And if so, should we make an effort to artificially preserve it? Art critic Sawaragi Noi claimed that the 'post-war' period was nothing more than a period of absence of major earthquakes, which allowed the safe development of *otaku* culture as well as Japan's economic growth up to 1995 (Kurose, Sawaragi & Azuma, 2012, pp. 351–352). If Sawaragi's theory is true, then it follows that *otaku* culture is in danger of extinction. The future of *otaku* culture seems bleak—even contemporary artist Murakami Takashi (2012, pp. 86, 88), whose lifework has been based around 'communicat[ing] to foreigners the sensibility of the Japanese *otaku*', believes that 'the age of *otaku* has ended'.[31] However, contrary to his own comments, Murakami's recent work shows new hope: *The 500 Arhats* (2012), which was exhibited in Doha, Qatar, seemed to be Takashi's artistic statement that Japan was still capable of producing and exporting unique cultural products. As if to mark the beginning of a new cultural era, Takashi's work focuses on a grand fusion between East and West—a departure from his traditional theme of post-war Japan–US relations and its influence on *otaku* culture (Takashi, 2012, p. 355). Whether post-3.11 *otaku* expression will be able to grow out of the formula of 'creating something new out of imported American culture', an active effort will be required if the prosperous and peaceful mindset of the *otaku* is to be preserved. In Takashi's (2012, p. 98) words, *amae* [dependence][32] can no longer be tolerated—*otaku* must also move beyond the traditional idea of amateurs offering art for free over the internet and begin aggressively marketing their work as professional art to survive.

If the *otaku* is seen to be incapable of nurturing their culture in the face of global competition and crises, the same may apply to the Japanese Government. It was only after American author Douglas McGray spelled out the potential of the country's soft power in 2002 that the Japanese Government began officially promoting Japanese popular culture exports such as 'idol' music, *manga* and *anime*, under the 'Cool Japan' policy. This recent increased visibility of Japanese popular culture on the global stage, whether caused by government policy or not, may be partly responsible for the enormous amount of donations and support that

---

31   English references are taken from John Person's translation at the end of *Shisō chizu beta*, vol. 3.
32   *Amae* is a term known for its difficulty of translating into English, which was explored extensively in Doi Takeo's (1971) *Amae no kōzō* [The Anatomy of Dependence]. It was described by Doi (1971) as a uniquely Japanese desire to be liked by others, so that you can depend on them; much like the behaviour of children towards their parents.

poured into Japan from overseas following the earthquake. However, it is not certain what kind of long-term effects the disaster will have on this national brand. As Ian Condry and Yuiko Fujita (2011, p. 2) ask in their introduction to the 'Cool Japan' special issue of the *International Journal of Japanese Sociology*: 'Does the idea of "Cool Japan" have a place in a post-3.11 world? ... In the wake of the "triple disaster," could it be that Japan would go from *kakkoii* (cool) to *yabai* (dangerous)?' Although *otaku* culture is alive and well following 3.11, it is noteworthy that so many well-known authors and *otaku* critics felt that the disaster would introduce a fundamental shift in these cultural expressions.

From the image of a Japan uniting its social and technological forces in the face of a disaster to rise again as a world superpower, to a Japanese system failing to cope with an un-Japanese technology or even a nation being punished for its capitalist sins, Japanese intellectuals and authors have portrayed post-3.11 Japan in various and often contradictory ways. Regardless of these contradictions, one thing is clear: disasters continue to be catalysts that stimulate debates on Japan. The Japanese viewed Fukushima as an opportunity to change or to reinforce and revisit values that were thought to be taken for granted in everyday life.

2
SUSTAINABLE JAPAN

One way in which Japanese authors presented a vision for Japan's recovery was to portray a Japan that stepped down from its position as a global economic and technological superpower to embrace a more traditional relationship with nature, in line with the 'slow growth' movement proposed by intellectuals such as Mikuriya Takashi and Karatani Kōjin. While the movement has not gained mainstream support in Japan, literary texts that present this kind of vision for Japan's future have been some of the most popular responses to the disaster. This chapter focuses on three such texts: *Shi no tsubute* [Pebbles of Poetry] by Wagō Ryōichi (2011), *Kamisama 2011* [God Bless You, 2011] by Kawakami Hiromi (2011) and *Ano hi kara no manga* [Manga Since that Day] by Shiriagari Kotobuki (2011).[1] Rather than simply repeating mainstream ideas from non-literary discourse (such as those from the previous chapter) in a different format, these works either add new dimensions to the debate on Japan's post-3.11 future or convey these ideas in a more accessible way that takes advantage of the power of fiction.

The idea of using disasters as a catalyst for the rethinking of human behaviour dates back to the premodern period prior to 1600 CE, when most Japanese believed that 'natural disasters were the result of imbalances in the five elements of nature caused by social impurities directly linked to human behaviour' (Weisenfeld, 2011, p. 14) and that an underground catfish (*namazu*) acted as a divine messenger, shaking the land on its back

---

1   Another example is Takahashi Mutsuo's poetry, which is explored extensively in Angles (2017), which also examines *Shi no tsubute*.

when it was angered (p. 25). This belief was prevalent in Japan as recently as the early 1920s, when many literary intellectuals referred to the 1923 Great Kantō Earthquake as a form of 'divine retribution'.

What is particularly interesting in the 3.11 case is that, although the Tōhoku region bore the brunt of the damage in the case of 3.11, it was the materialism and modernity of the country that was blamed for this 'divine retribution'. However, this was not the case in the aftermath of the 1995 Hanshin earthquake, when it was the opportunism, materialism and capitalistic tendencies of the disaster-hit Hanshinkan region that was blamed. In particular, this moral wake-up call of the triple disaster is addressed to those who had forgotten their traditional Japanese values and were living a comfortable life in Tokyo at the expense of the innocent disaster victims (the nuclear power plants in Fukushima supplied electricity to Tokyo). Although few today would believe in the existence of a divine catfish, the literary responses analysed in this chapter reveal a continuing desire of the Japanese to seek a moral lesson as a way of coming to terms with disasters.

Alternative Visions of *Kizuna* by Wagō Ryōichi and Kawakami Hiromi

Shi no tsubute by Wagō Ryōichi (2011a) and *Kamisama 2011* by Kawakami Hiromi (2011) are two very early literary responses to the disaster. These two works, albeit very different in genre and style, share an exploration and questioning of the concept of *kizuna* [bonds] that was popularised following 3.11, using traditional Japanese values. Chapter 1 outlined some of the weaknesses of the concept of *kizuna*, as argued by Japanese public intellectuals and authors. Although they did not deny the importance of helping each other in the aftermath of the disaster, the authors examined in this chapter contend that what Japan may need the most to move forward is a different vision of *kizuna*—one that encourages bonds with nature and future generations. Wagō Ryōichi and Kawakami Hiromi are two authors who, by using their writing to offer alternative views of *kizuna* and of 3.11, found strong support among those who were dissatisfied with the official representations of the disaster and sought an alternative.

Wagō Ryōichi is a poet from Fukushima who grew up in the prefecture and now works as a Japanese teacher at a local high school, which complements his career in contemporary poetry. Wagō already had an established career as a poet prior to 3.11, having received the Chūya Nakahara prize for his debut poetry collection, *AFTER* (1998), and the 47th Bansui Prize for his fourth poetry collection, *Chikyū Zunō Shihen* [Earth brain psalms] (2006). Himself a victim of the earthquake, Wagō decided to remain in Fukushima and to continue transmitting his first-hand views to the rest of Japan through his poetry. He most notably achieved this through his use of Twitter—a tool that allowed him to keep publishing his words in a time of emergency, when he did not even have a landline phone connection (Wagō & Kamata, 2011, p. 59). Wagō conducted numerous impromptu poetry sessions on Twitter for a real-time audience using the handle @wago2828.[2] These works have now been published in book format in the trilogy *Shi no tsubute* [Pebbles of poetry], *Shi no mokurei* [Silent prayer of poetry] and *Shi no kaikō* [Encounters with poetry].[3]

Remaining in deserted Fukushima after sending his family off to Yamagata, Wagō was under no illusion that *kizuna* between Japanese citizens was magically strengthened as a result of the earthquake. He reminisces that, at the time, he felt a profound sense of loneliness sitting alone in his room with the realisation that society does not necessarily protect all its members (Wagō, 2011c, p. 130). One of Wagō's central themes at the start of *Shi no tsubute* is precisely the lack of cooperation and understanding between Tōhoku and Tokyo, or the rest of Japan. Wagō (2011a) started tweeting on 16 March 2011, just five days after the earthquake and some of his first words express this concern:

> I hear that no supplies have reached Minami Sōma, the city where I used to live. They say that's because no one wants to go into the city. Please save Minami Sōma (p. 11).[4]

He also observed that people in Fukushima were 'taught to wash their hair, hands and face after going outdoors' (Wagō, 2011a, p. 11) as a way of reducing radiation exposure, despite the serious lack of water in

---

2   Thanks to the ideographic writing system, it is possible to say a lot more in a tweet (which has a 140-character limit) in Japanese than in English.
3   For more information about *Shi no tsubute* and an excerpt translated by Jeffrey Angles, see Wagō (2011b). For an in-depth analysis of Wagō's use of Twitter, see Odagiri (2014).
4   Translated by Jeffrey Angles. All further translations from *Shi no tsubute* are my own and the page numbers are from the print version.

Fukushima at the time. There is silent anger in his words: 'We do not have the water to do so' (Wagō, 2011a, p. 11).[5] This railing against injustice is intensified by the fact that the electricity generated in Fukushima has supplied Tokyo for many decades.

However, Wagō's criticism and initial anger seem to become increasingly tempered as time goes by. He began to appreciate the bonds he forms with the ever-growing number of his followers on Twitter (of which there were only a dozen to begin with). He even mentions the word *kizuna* to refer to his 10-day bond with his readers in a tweet on 25 March (p. 129). At this stage, Wagō seems to feel that, despite the lack of government support and differences in attitude between Tōhoku and the rest of Japan, there was a certain *kizuna* that still existed in the country at the grassroots level. He was encouraged by the feedback from his readers, which helped him 'find himself' again and calm down the angry tone of his writing (Wagō & Kamata, 2011, p. 60).

Through this renewed understanding of the positive powers of *kizuna*, Wagō proceeds to outline his own vision for Japan's future, which contains two elements: *kizuna* between humans and nature and *kizuna* between the current and future generations of Japanese people. The *kizuna* between humans and nature is evoked by the animal metaphors that occur throughout the work. Wagō (2011a) used the vibrations created by galloping horses as a metaphor for the earthquake and described those affected by the disaster as 'sad riders' (p. 22). His choice of the horse is symbolic because Minami-sōma hosts the famous Soma Wild Horse Chase (Sōma-Nomaoi Festival).[6] Many horses in the region were abandoned after 3.11 and were trapped without food or water. Therefore, horses symbolise the innocent sacrifice of the Tōhoku people. Further, horses are represented as divine figures that are 'trying to ascend to the sky' (p. 106). In the Tōhoku region, the horse-god *oshira-sama* is revered as a guardian of the home. The horses in the text are described as angry and in despair (p. 68), which may be a reference to the horses having turned into a kind of vindictive god (*tatarigami*), due to our selfish exploitation

---

5   The tone of the Japanese is difficult to capture in English. The original sentence is: 私たちには、それを洗う水などないのです。
6   Furukawa Hideo (2011), who wrote *Umatachi yo, soredemo hikari wa muku de* [Horses, horses, in the end the light remains pure: a tale that begins with Fukushima] in July 2011, also uses horses as a way of defamiliarising the disaster. Furukawa does this by relating Japanese history through the eyes of these horses in the disaster-hit areas and showing how, by abandoning these horses, the Japanese people severed a long lineage of these animals who played a crucial role in the formation of their country.

of nature and nuclear power. Wagō initially adopts a confrontational tone towards the horses: 'When I start writing, an aftershock. Fine, I'll just write on your back' he writes on 19 March 2011 (p. 48). Eventually, Wagō politely asks for forgiveness from the horses and says that he is willing to be alone in Fukushima if need be, as though offering himself as a human sacrifice to appease the angry animals.

The other animal that appears frequently in the work is the cat, which he uses as a metaphor for nuclear energy:

> Humans felt safe, having domesticated the uncontrollable cats. They loved their best friends, embracing their fluffy safety myth. Every human being on Earth entrusted their obedient slaves with their body and soul. Many billions of cats. Hairs standing on end. Hostility. Revealed (p. 141).

These cats are also metaphors for the radioactive particles that have been 'set free' by the nuclear meltdowns and are now roaming around Fukushima (p. 141). As with the horse metaphor, Wagō implies that humans are at fault for causing this 'cat revolt'. Humans cuddle up to the cats when they need them and then 'abandon them with scorn when things go bad' (p. 213). Wagō seems to imply that all these 'animals' can be tamed, but to do so, a trusting relationship must be maintained between the two parties (p. 208). Whether horse riders or cat owners, Wagō asks his fellow human beings to 'stroke the mane of the horses, tied up in the darkness' (p. 227). This can be interpreted as a call for the Japanese to return to the respectful relationship with nature that they had in pre-industrial times—a form of *kizuna* that seems to have been entirely left out in post-3.11 discourse, which was centred on bonds between humans. Wagō's animal metaphors subvert the official discourse of *kizuna* by bringing to mind the bonds between humans and nature that were neglected before and after 3.11.

Wagō also places emphasis on the *kizuna* that he feels between himself and future generations of Japanese people. He suggests that we view the current generation as a *renketsuten* (link) in history rather than as an endpoint (p. 49), which implies a responsibility for providing the best circumstances possible for future generations. Further, he believes that the way to achieve this kind of *kizuna* is through the power of words (p. 210). To connect with these future generations, Wagō explores new means of expression through his poetry. Wagō usually writes in abstract contemporary verse, but the language used in his Twitter poetry is plain and unadorned. Wagō claims that, pre-3.11, he had been against the idea of poetry being written horizontally, using a word processor and that he had never used direct expressions such as 'sadness', 'dream' or 'life' in his poetry. In this sense, *Shi no tsubute* represents a 180-degree turn in his stance towards poetry (Wagō, 2011d, p. 247). In a public talk with Azuma Hiroki on 28 May 2011, Wagō said he felt as though he needed words that could be delivered immediately and directly to his readers to represent the disaster in real time, like a documentary (Wagō & Azuma, 2011, p. 187).[7] He also acknowledged that this involved the use of language that was more informative than literary. In Wagō's own words, 'the metaphor has died' in the face of the sheer scale and immediacy of the disaster (p. 64). Wagō's goal in his post-3.11 writing has been to engage with reality more directly than his traditional poetry (p. 187) and to engage with a wider readership. As the myth that nuclear power is absolutely safe (*zettai anzen shinwa*) came crumbling down, Wagō also found himself abandoning his 'absolute rules' and challenging the limits of poetry (Fukuma & Wagō, 2011, p. 18) to rebuild his poetry from the debris, pebble by pebble.

Wagō's work ends with a verbal duel with a devil, who tells him that his words are powerless and that they cannot bring about any physical change or bring back the dead. However, Wagō uses his poetry to fight and insists that he will keep writing and thinking about the disaster. He imagines himself being on a boat, paddling towards his goal of 'living this new poetry' (p. 261). Wagō continues to live his poetry by publishing it on Twitter and making his voice heard and thereby opens up possibilities for bringing his words closer to reality. By living his poetry, Wagō also believes he helps the souls of the dead to live on. The book version ends with his afterword, in which he finds a single walnut from the dead tree in his room, which he calls his 'pebble of poetry' (p. 263). Through his poetry, Wagō is reminded of his *kizuna* with his deceased grandmother, whose voice reminds his angry childhood self to be kind to others. His poetry creates *kizuna* where it is otherwise difficult to create, with the deceased and with the yet-to-be-born, in the ineffable devastation of the tsunami and fears of invisible radiation. Wagō acts as an example for post-3.11 Japan to explore ways of imaginatively using language, without being overly

---

7   The video version of this talk is available at: 'Nico nama shisō chizu 01 Wagō Ryōichi × Azuma Hiroki' [Niconico live thought map 01 Wagō Ryōichi and Azuma Hiroki] (30 May 2011), *Niconico*. Available from: www.nicovideo.jp/watch/sm14599601.

concerned with the various rules and conventions of communications. This creative use of language facilitates a rekindling of connections to nature and the creation of *kizuna* with past and future generations.

Kamisama 2011 by Kawakami Hiromi (2011) also builds on the mainstream notion of Japanese *kizuna* by exploring the ideas of *kizuna* between humans and nature and between generations. Kawakami Hiromi is an Akutagawa prize–winning novelist, known for her signature style of mixing fantasy and reality in her writing. Kawakami's *Kamisama 2011* [God Bless You, 2011], is a rewriting of *Kamisama* (1994)—her first published literary work. Short and like a fairy tale in its composition, *Kamisama* is a story about *watashi* (I), who is assumed to be a young woman, who goes on a walk with a friendly talking bear.[8] The 2011 version has the same plot as the original, except for the fact that the events take place in a world post-3.11, probably near the Fukushima power plant, where one has to measure one's own radiation exposure every day and where there are no longer any children. The disaster of 3.11 is never referred to explicitly in the work, but indirectly as *ano koto* (that thing). Despite the plot of the story being the same, the 2011 version *feels* completely different, because 'that thing' has permeated every aspect of life.

Through a seemingly innocent juxtaposition of these two versions, Kawakami demonstrates the devastating effects of 3.11, in which everything that was normal in the past has changed beyond repair. The juxtaposition serves to highlight the fact that the abnormalities of life post-3.11 make us appreciate these normal moments that were perhaps overlooked prior to the earthquake. The 2011 version also demonstrates that we can no longer read the original version in the same way—and, by extension, we can no longer read or write any piece of literature in the same way. Kawakami achieves this effect in her work by inserting words such as 'plutonium', 'caesium' and 'sV' (sieverts) that would perhaps not otherwise have appeared in her fantastical writing.[9]

It is significant that Kawakami chose to rewrite this short story at this particular moment. Even in the original version, the bear in the story seems to represent the kind of real *kizuna* associated with traditional Japanese values and customs. When the bear moves to the same building

---

8 Although the bear is referred to with male pronouns here, the gender of the bear is not stated in the novel.
9 All English translations for *Kamisama*, *Kamisama 2011* and the postscript are works of Ted Goossen and Shibata Motoyuki, taken from *March was Made of Yarn*.

as *watashi*, he goes to greet all his neighbours on the same floor of his building (and to the three remaining households post-3.11 in *Kamisama 2011*) with some *soba* noodles and 10 postcards. *Watashi* seems to consider this unnecessary, which is a reflection of the erosion of these traditional bonding customs in Japanese society. Further, the bear appears to be moved by the fact that *watashi* is a distant relative of someone who helped him a lot in the past (or during the post-3.11 evacuation process in *Kamisama 2011*) and uses the old-fashioned word *enishi* (fate) to describe the situation. These gestures and words lead *watashi* to consider the bear to be old-fashioned and she reasons that the bear's non-human status is to blame for this—the bear needs to be overly considerate to others to be accepted in human society. The fact that the bear's traditionally Japanese actions appear odd and old-fashioned shows how much Japanese society has changed and how little *kizuna* there remains in Japanese society. Later on, when the bear offers to sing a lullaby to *watashi* before her nap, *watashi* refuses, saying she can fall asleep without it (p. 13). This prompts a disappointed expression on the bear's face, probably because the lullaby was intended less as a pragmatic tool to help *watashi* fall asleep than as a moment of bonding between them. He feels slightly offended that his offer was refused. *Watashi* seems unable to even recognise these signs of *kizuna*, let alone to strengthen her bonds with others.

In *Kamisama 2011*, the nuclear meltdowns in Fukushima are shown to have exacerbated this lack of *kizuna* between humans. Although the bear is punched and kicked by a little child in *Kamisama*, this violence is portrayed partly as a childlike and innocent act. However, in *Kamisama 2011*, where there are no longer any children, two men in protective gear ('Long Gloves' and 'Sunglasses') simply come up to the bear and *watashi* and pull on the bear's fur while talking about its resistance to radiation. Although there is less physical violence involved, the way the man in the sunglasses refuses to look the bear straight in the eye and talks about the bear as if he is not even there makes the encounter much more hostile. Conversely, the bear remains considerate and polite in *Kamisama 2011*, hiding his true feelings from *watashi* by saying, 'I guess they meant well' (p. 30). However, he sounds much less certain than in the original version, in which he says 'young people don't mean any harm, you know' (p. 10).

The fact that this messenger of *kizuna* takes the form of a bear is significant. The bear may not literally be a creature of another species, but rather a metaphor for those who are discriminated against in Japanese society for looking different. The bear, who eats pâté and radishes with a baguette for lunch, whereas *watashi* eats an *umeboshi* (pickled plum) rice ball, is a foreign figure to some extent, although bears are often seen around humans in Fukushima. This bear seems to belong neither in bear society nor in human society. In *Sōjō no chūshoku* [The luncheon on the grass], a story that appears in the original *Kamisama* collection of short stories as a sequel to *Kamisama*, the bear eventually feels ostracised in a human society that lacks *kizuna* and goes back to live with his fellow bears. Tragically, Kawakami seems to suggest that there is no longer a place for real *kizuna* in modern Japan. Whether one views the bear as an animal or as a metaphorical figure, it is clear that the novel is making a comment on Japanese society. In a society in which strong community ties have been lost, people have much to learn about *kizuna* from these outsiders, whom Kawakami refers to as 'symbols of minorities' (Kawakami & Numano, 2012).

Kawakami also implies that an Earth without bears or nature is not a sustainable place for humans to live. As Kawakami points out in the afterword to her book, Japanese people traditionally believed in a divine presence or spirit in all existing objects and living beings (*yaoyorozu no kami*), including mountains, rivers, rain and animals, as well as wells and even toilets (p. 39). Evoking this respectful *kizuna* that humans had with nature, Kawakami asks what the God of Uranium would think of our exploitation of this natural resource (p. 43). Kawakami is suggesting here that we have made a kind of vindictive god (*tatarigami*) out of the God of Uranium and that Japanese people have forgotten their general sense of reverence for those elements of nature that make their current lifestyles possible. She also warns her readers of the dangers of playing God. The nuclear reactions that happened over billions of years have reduced radioactivity to a level that finally ensures that human beings can inhabit the planet. Kawakami points out the irony that humans are risking turning Earth into an uninhabitable planet again by playing with nuclear power.

Conventional Japanese literature focuses on the portrayal of the self, or *watashi* (as typified by the 'I novel' genre, known as *watakushi shōsetsu* or *shishōsetsu*). Although the boundaries of the genre are subject to debate, 'I novels' are generally written from the point of view of the author, whether in the form of a first-person or third-person narrator and have strong autobiographical tendencies.[10] Kawakami's works

---

10   For an in-depth exploration of the genre, see Fowler (1992).

portray a different worldview, in which *watashi* is but a tiny existence in a world that will continue to revolve without these individuals. *Watashi* is not completely insignificant—Kawakami believes that each person's perspective still matters (Kawakami & Numano, 2012). In Kawakami's worldview, although humans have a contribution to make, they must realise that they are not as significant as they think. Such a view leads to better *kizuna* with nature. *Kamisama 2011* warns humans who act as though they are rulers of the vast playground of planet Earth that they are children, who still have much to fear from nature. Unlike the traditional Japanese association of earthquakes with an angry catfish, which aims to convey a similar message using scare tactics, Kawakami's story evokes feelings of shame, with particular pertinence in contemporary Japan.

Like Wagō, Kawakami also evokes the *kizuna* that exists (or that needs to be strengthened) between Japanese people and future generations. Novelist Takahashi Gen'ichirō (2011a) includes a chapter in his post-3.11 novel *Koisuru genpatsu* [A nuclear reactor in love], called *Shinsai bungaku ron* [An essay on earthquake literature], in which he reviews some of the literary texts he believes to be relevant to 3.11. Although it is by no means clear whether this chapter reflects Takahashi's opinion, since it is part of a novel and not an essay, his analysis of Kawakami's text is worth mentioning. The Kawakami work discussed by Takahashi is an imaginary text, built on both versions (*Kamisama* and *Kamisama 2011*). Takahashi's version is *Kamisama (2011)*, which is a new and merged text that adds parentheses to Kawakami's *Kamisama* and *Kamisama 2011* to indicate parts that have been added or deleted. Takahashi focuses his analysis on the aforementioned confrontation scenes, in which the child punches and kicks the bear in the original version and the two men, who were accompanying the child in the original version, simply pull the bear's fur and talk about him as if he is not there, in the post-3.11 version. Takahashi claims that superimposing the two texts in this manner creates an effect of the children talking behind the men as if they are ghosts (p. 210). Although the ghost-like presence of children could be interpreted as the spirits of the young victims of the earthquake and tsunami, Takahashi prefers to consider them as being the future victims of radiation poisoning—children who will be killed by radiation or who will never be brought into this world due to fears about the effects of radiation (p. 211). For Takahashi, *Kamisama (2011)* is Kawakami's display of commitment towards future generations as a member of current society, in line with Kawakami's humble and respectful attitude towards the world.

Kawakami's vision of community also involves *kizuna* and offers reconciliation with those who were directly involved in the nuclear meltdowns. Kawakami prefers to refer to nuclear incidents as 'that thing' (*ano koto*) to avoid placing the full blame on those who operated the power plant (e.g. by calling them *genpatsu jiko* or nuclear accidents). She shows that the incident was not created solely at the nuclear power plants in Fukushima, but rather there was a large network of people who contributed to it, including politicians, workers and consumers. This displays Kawakami's willingness to accept some of the blame as a member of society who used electricity derived from nuclear power without questioning its safety. In this vision, all Japanese citizens who used electricity were in some way involved in the disaster and bear some responsibility for future consequences. Kawakami does not use quotation marks for *watashi*'s dialogue, as though she is intending to merge the reader's consciousness with *watashi*'s. The whole story reads as though it is a daydream. Kawakami guides her readers to accept what has already happened and move forward, living in harmony with nature, so that their homeland can be passed onto future generations without further damage.

Wagō and Kawakami challenge and then expand on the narrative of *kizuna*, which has been repeated in mainstream media following 3.11. Rather than denying or questioning the existence of this *kizuna* in Japanese society, Wagō and Kawakami present visions of *kizuna* that they believe to be more relevant to the physical and emotional reconstruction of the disaster-hit areas, at times referring back to traditional Japanese worldviews. Most notably, both authors emphasise the importance of *kizuna* with nature as well as with future generations as part of their new vision for Japan, even though these elements were not included in the popular notion of *kizuna* that was used by the mainstream media and the general public.

Traditional Living in *Ano hi kara no manga* by Shiriagari Kotobuki

Manga artist Shiriagari Kotobuki's post-3.11 work is similar to those of Kawakami and Wagō in that he also places emphasis on a more sustainable future for Japan. In terms of style, Shiriagari's *manga* was an approachable, yet no less serious, form of social engagement, which was appreciated by many in the months following the disaster. Shiriagari's work *Umibe no mura* [Seaside village] in the May 2011 issue of *Comic Beam* broke the post-3.11 *jishuku*—self-restraint or self-censorship, to borrow Jacqueline Berndt's term (2013, p. 72)—silence in the *manga* industry (responding to the *fukinshin* criticism outlined in the section 'The End of "Cool Japan"?' in Chapter 1), which saw publishers refrain from carrying works related to disasters or nuclear power as a sign of respect towards the disaster victims and their families. Most notably, the chapter *Genshiryokyu mafia* [Nuclear-power mafia] in *Hakuryū-LEGEND* [White dragon-LEGEND] by Tennōji Dai and Watanabe Michio, the first instalment of which was published in February 2011, was discontinued because it coincidentally portrayed the death of a subcontract worker in a nuclear power plant (Berndt, 2013, p. 75). Despite these circumstances, partly fuelled by a necessity to keep writing for his serialised *yonkoma* (four-frame) *manga* on the national daily, *Asahi Shimbun* (under the title *Chikyū Bōeike no hitobito* [The Earth Defenders]), Shiriagari continued to publish at his usual pace following 3.11. For example, the *yonkoma* was published as usual on Saturday 12 March 2011; on Monday 14 March, Shiriagari made his first reference to 3.11. Many other *manga* artists followed suit in their portrayal of the earthquake following Shiriagari's courageous publications.[11]

Ano hi kara no manga [Manga since that day] is a publication containing a collection of works by Shiriagari, all written in the few months following 3.11. The publication belongs to the *Beam Comix* series published by Enterbrain, with many works first published in the monthly *manga* magazine *Comic Beam*, from the same publisher. The selection of texts is varied because the publication traces Shiriagari's writings in chronological order, starting from the *yonkoma* from *Chikyū Bōeike no hitobito* on the back of the front cover, which was published on 14 March 2011, to the wordless comic *Sora to mizu* [Sky and water], published in the August 2011 issue of *Comic Beam*. Some of the works, such as *Chikyū Bōeike* are drawn in Shiriagari's characteristic humorous 'gag' *manga* style,[12] drawn in a deliberately childish and rough way, whereas others, such as *Sora to*

---

11 See Berndt (2013, p. 72) for an overview of non-fiction *manga* works published after 3.11, including documentary-style *manga*, essay *manga* and educational *manga*.

12 The *gyagu* or 'gag' *manga* form usually involves humorous *manga* made up of one or four frames, which appear 'in Japanese newspapers as well as manga magazines and anthologies' (Bryce & Davis, 2010, pp. 40–41), typically drawn using a simplistic style. Further, 'humor in manga encompasses an astonishing range of styles or expressions such as satire, gaglike punch lines, surrealistic absurdities, parody, comedy, caricature and outright nonsense' (p. 40) and 'gag' *manga* is just one of them. Mary Knighton (2014) explored Shiriagari's 'gag' *manga* works from *Ano hi kara no manga* in detail.

mizu and *Umibe no mura* [The village by the sea] (May 2011) are more experimental. The publication was met with considerable critical and popular success, reprinted over six times within a year of being published and awarded one of the 15th Media Arts Excellency Awards from Japan's Agency for Cultural Affairs in February 2012. Shiriagari also received one of the 2014 Medals of Honour with Purple Ribbon from the Emperor for his recent work.

Because these texts are in chronological order, the publication provides a rare insight into the development of public sentiment surrounding the earthquake. In Shiriagari's (2011b) own words, 'scientists can produce numbers and politicians can produce policies, so I thought about what manga artists could do and decided that I could portray *kūki* (air or atmosphere, here mood)'. Shiriagari explains that although he does not know for sure what the scientific data surrounding 3.11 represents, he thought he would be able to add feelings and *kūki* to these representations by using his imagination and felt that this was part of his role as an artist. The text is similar to the aforementioned works by Wagō and Kawakami in that it attempts to represent what was not portrayed by facts or the mainstream media in response to the disaster. For Berndt (2013), *Ano hi kara no manga* invited readers 'to contemplate and communicate on what kind of life to lead and what fundamental changes to accept', rather than telling them what to do or think (p. 74). Since before 3.11, Shiriagari's style (especially in his *yonkoma*) has been to 'drop the ball in the middle of the debate' (2004, p. 16), exposing flaws in both sides rather than adopting a particular view. This is perhaps why his *manga* became so popular following the disaster. Shiriagari does not spell out the tragedy or devastation of the disaster, preferring instead to use his words and images for portrayals of hope and humorous stabs at society. Shiriagari observes that mainstream popular Japanese *manga* depict universal feelings in stories that develop at high speeds, which grip readers around the world by giving them an adrenaline rush (J. A. C. Project, 2006, p. 72), which is a similar form of entertainment to an attraction at an amusement park (Shiriagari, 2011c, p. 23). Shiriagari's own work is quite different to this mainstream form of *manga*, which is commonly appreciated in the West and provokes thought by being more ambiguous.

Shiriagari's stance with regard to post-3.11 expression has been to maintain his socially engaged gag style in the face of the disaster and continue writing, rather than letting this unprecedented situation influence his form. As Knighton (2014) contended, despite the name of Shiriagari's publication, 'Manga since that day', what really changed 'since that day' was not so much his style but rather 'the serious attention his manga garnered when he dared to take the crisis as subject matter for humor and commentary so soon after 3.11'. Shiriagari is no stranger to the portrayal of disaster and death since before 3.11: his *Jakaranda* [Jacaranda], published in June 2005 by Seirin Kōgeisha, is a 300-page story of a colossal tree that starts growing in the middle of Tokyo, crushing buildings and killing people in its way. He also humorously explored the topic of death extensively in works such as *Hinshi no essayist* [The dying essayist] and *O-i memento mori* [Hey, memento mori], as well as in his best-known work, *Mayonaka no Yaji-san Kita-san* [Yaji and Kita: The Midnight Pilgrims], which has also been turned into a film. Further, his 1986 *manga Gerogero pūsuka* (a new edition of this was published post-3.11) responded to the Chernobyl disaster by portraying a world in which only the elderly and children up to 14 years of age could survive.

In *Ano hi kara no manga*, Shiriagari suggests that there may be a solution to the problems that Japan is facing in the Japanese fondness for nature and modest ways of life. *Umibe no mura* is one of the works portraying Shiriagari's vision for Japan's future—50 years after 3.11, humans have abandoned nuclear energy and fossil fuels, relying on solar panels for electricity. There is no longer any air-conditioning in homes or street lights in the cities and being able to watch television is a rare event, dependent on the functioning of the solar panels. Although the grandfather of the family finds it difficult to adapt to this new way of life, both men and women of the next generation are more accepting of the change and their children are brought up to believe that this way of life is normal. Although they have heard of nuclear power plants, these children can only imagine what life would have been like for their parents when they were younger because this modest way of life is the only one they know. The youngest child of the family, who is the first in the family to have developed wings (this phenomenon is suggested to be part of the evolutionary process), is symbolically named 'Mirai', or 'Hope'. The story does indeed end with hope—the construction of a renewable energy power plant in the village is announced, which is likely to improve the quality of life in the community. The last page, composed of a single panel portraying a starry sky, follows the granddaughter's words of encouragement to her grandfather that these changes may bring back the material wealth that he longed for, to which he replies, his face covered in tears, 'But back in our days, we didn't have such beautiful starry skies' (pp. 33–34).

Shiriagari (2011b) explains this work as being made possible by the power of cultural expression, which allows for the lack of material wealth to be considered as something beautiful. He describes this tendency to find beauty in modest ways of living by giving as examples the Japanese concepts of *hakanai* (fleeting), *mujō* (derived from the Buddhist concept of impermanence and the aesthetic of transience) and *aware* (or *mono no aware,* meaning empathy and sadness, which comes from an awareness of impermanence). The parents' generation in *Umibe no mura* have obtained happiness by gaining awareness of this transient nature of material wealth and striving instead for spiritual wealth: 'Many things were lost … and we decided to try a different path … We decided to choose everlasting happiness instead of living conveniently, under the constant fear of losing our material wealth' (p. 26). Although the family's wooden house appears run-down, with laundry hanging outside and filled with retro objects, such as the low *chabudai* dining table with *zabuton* floor cushions, there is a sense of strong community ties (*kizuna* in post-3.11 language) and a carefree way of life reminiscent of the Shōwa 30s (the mid-1950s). These core years of the Shōwa period, which are often subjects of nostalgic depictions in Japanese popular culture, typically represent stress-free happiness and hope for the future in the Japanese consciousness.[13] The two-page image of evolved, winged children flying over the remains of the nuclear power plant, covered in windmills, which was also published in the *Magnitude ZERO* collection of illustrations, symbolises the spiritual freedom obtained by future generations as a result of the earlier generations giving up their material wealth (pp. 28–29).[14]

However, Shiriagari (2011d) claims that *Umibe no mura* does not represent his ideal future, but rather just one version of multiple possible futures that he arrived at through a process of elimination. Shiriagari started on the work around 20 March and this rather bleak portrayal of Japan's future was Shiriagari's attempt to portray hope at a time when he was observing uncertainty everywhere. Shiriagari is not suggesting that humankind should abandon modern technology. Instead, he offers a comforting portrayal of the resilience of the Japanese people and their fondness for a more primitive way of life, which would allow them to survive and get by in the worst-case scenario. In this way, Shiriagari fully

---

13 For an exploration of the 'Showa Retro Boom' phenomenon in Japan, see Thompson (2011).
14 Since Shiriagari's publication, this idea of 'living with less' has taken off, both in Japan and the rest of the world, with the minimalist movement as well as the huge success of Marie Kondo's books on decluttering.

harnesses the power of literary imagination. The ability to portray imagined alternative futures, regardless of whether they are likely to happen, is part of what distinguishes literature from other more factual media.

Shiriagari (2011c, p. 20) observed that people stopped being affected by trivial matters following the disaster and 'raised their faces up', looking towards the future of the world surrounding them. Despite the tragedy of the earthquake, he observed a positive trend in 'people getting interested in matters which they previously considered to be unrelated to them, such as the situation in the Tōhoku region or even visions of how the world will look like in the far future' (Shiriagari, 2011c, p. 20). Imaginative *manga* works depicting this post-3.11 *kūki* in Japan, such as those by Shiriagari, are valuable resources for gaining insight into the future visions of the Japanese. In the words of Berndt (2013), 'being a site of imaginary worlds rather than direct depictions of social reality, manga may be expected to make important contributions' (p. 78) in picturing an alternative future post-3.11.

Wagō, Kawakami and Shiriagari all portray the issue of moral debasement in contemporary Japanese society due to technological advances and convey a sense that the disaster occurred as a wake-up call to alert the Japanese to their ethical degradation. This took the form of portrayals of the erosion of traditional values and community ties, as symbolised by the out-of-placeness of Kawakami's bear, the degradation of the relationship between Japanese people and nature as depicted in Wagō's work and the old man who hangs on to his capitalist values and greed in Shiriagari's *Umibe no mura*. Current Japanese society is contrasted with traditional Japanese society, which is portrayed as being ideal and altruistic, characterised by a respectful, Shintoistic and harmonious relationship between nature and humans. Traditional Japanese values, which are romanticised and idealised, are used as a way of reclaiming Japanese identity in the face of the perceived breakdown of Japan's status as a technological superpower. In this way, this group of 3.11 literature shares many of the concerns that have been explored in other environmental texts. In post-Chernobyl literature, which is a prime example of environmental literature, the warning against environmental degradation was a means of recovering Ukrainian cultural identity and traditional values under industrialising Soviet rule (Sukhenko, 2014, p. 128). Ukraine is an interesting case study because it has 'its own unique cultural traditions and perspectives regarding the natural world, rooted in pre-Christian beliefs and rituals' (Sukhenko, 2014, p. 114), which are similar to Shintō. A comparison between these post-3.11 texts and post-Chernobyl literature is likely to be a fruitful object for future study.

3
OPPRESSIVE JAPAN

One of the main criticisms of Japanese authorities and the media following the triple disaster was that there was a lack of freedom of press, information and expression—to raise concerns for radiation levels, or to make any comments that are perceived to dampen the spirit of *kizuna* and reconstruction. In Chapter 1, I discussed how certain commentators argued that *kizuna* led to excessive groupism and suppressed dissent, which drew attention away from the negative consequences of the disaster. I also discussed how negative opinions and depictions of the disaster were often labelled as causing *fūhyō higai* (reputational damage) for the residents and farmers of Fukushima, as observed in the case of the 'nose bleed' in the *manga Oishinbo*.

Several critical developments that followed the triple disaster were instrumental in drawing further attention to the issue of freedom of speech in Japan. First of all, the 2013 *Act on the Protection of Specially Designated Secrets*, also known as the 'State secrets bill', was designed to protect information relating to national defence. This event caused much debate due to the perceived ambiguity as to what constitutes a secret or punishable offence under this law. Protesters against the Act gathered in November and December 2013, twice filling to the brim the 3,000-seat-capacity Hibiya Outdoor Theatre in Tokyo. This concern was also reflected in the 2016 World Press Freedom Index by Reporters Without Borders, which ranked Japan 72nd out of 180 countries (ranked 11 lower compared to 2015 and 61 lower compared to 2010), below Asian neighbours, such as Hong Kong and South Korea, who were ranked 69th and 70th, respectively.

Shortly after the World Press Freedom Index results were released, the issue of freedom of speech received much media attention again when David Kaye, a UN special rapporteur on the right to freedom of opinion and expression, visited Japan in April 2016. Kaye reported in his preliminary observation that while there was a high level of freedom of expression and speech, there were issues in terms of the freedom and independence of press, in both print and broadcast media. Specifically, he drew attention to the issue of self-imposed censorship:

> Numerous journalists, many agreeing to meet with me only on condition of anonymity to protect their livelihoods, highlighted the pressure to avoid sensitive areas of public interest. Many claimed to have been sidelined or silenced following indirect pressure from leading politicians.[1]

There is a growing sentiment in Japan that while there is no official government censorship, freedom of information and press was compromised in post-disaster media reporting. This sentiment is conveyed in a growing number of dystopian texts by authors such as Tawada Yōko, Henmi Yō and Yoshimura Man'ichi, which are set in a future Japan, in which these freedoms have been further compromised. Conversely, Takahashi Gen'ichirō chose to tackle these issues more directly by composing his novel out of the very language that is shunned in Japanese society. In this chapter, I analyse how these texts portray and imagine different discursive environments in Japan's future.

Dystopian Responses by Tawada Yōko, Henmi Yō and Yoshimura Man'ichi

Many Japanese-language responses to 3.11 situate Japanese society in a post-nuclear disaster apocalyptic dystopian future, in which high levels of radiation have become the norm and a totalitarian government is in place. A selection of these works will be outlined briefly here because they yield more or less similar results in terms of images for Japan's potential future—although there are differing degrees of negativity and hope across the works, they point to right-wing tendencies and ineptitudes of the (future) Japanese Government and their tendency to

---

1   Full text available at: www.ohchr.org/EN/NewsEvents/Pages/DisplayNews.aspx?NewsID=19842.

hide information.² Transnational author Tawada Yōko (2012), who writes in both Japanese and German, perceptively led this group of responses by publishing *Fushi no shima* [*The island of eternal life*] in the collection *Soredemo sangatsu wa mata* [*March was made of yarn*].³ According to the limited information the Japanese protagonist and narrator of the story could obtain in Germany, Tawada's dystopian Japan is closed to the rest of the world in a new form of *sakoku*⁴ and run by a private corporation by the name of 'Z Group', whose identity is hidden behind black masks. In this story, radiation from Fukushima has had the strange effect of making centenarians immortal, while children are weak and dying from radiation disease. Despite this tragedy, Japanese citizens manage to find entertainment in the form of *go* and *shōgi* board games and 'with no television, there is nothing to do during the long evenings but read, yet as the lights go out at sundown, storytellers have appeared to recite the stories of old comic books or animated films to the accompaniment of guitars or lutes', in a 'weird return to life in the Edo Period' (p. 11). This idea of Japan, the former technological and economic giant, taking a step back and coming to terms with living within its means is similar to Mikuriya Takashi's proposal of the slow life philosophy explored in the previous chapter.

Tawada developed this dystopian theme fully in her novella *Kentōshi* [*The Emissary* (US); *The Last Children of Tokyo* (UK)], published in a collection of the same name in 2014 (which also contains *The Island of Eternal Life*).⁵ Instead of a Japanese citizen living in Germany, *The Emissary* is written from the perspective of Yoshirō, who is a strong and immortal 107-year-old man who devotes his energies to looking after his weak seven-year-old great-grandson Mumei. Mumei (whose name literally means 'no name' because his parents were not there to name him following his birth) is so weak that he struggles to walk more than a few metres, to get dressed without assistance and even to eat solid food. Yoshirō and Mumei live in temporary housing on the Western fringes

---

2   There are many other dystopian works I have not covered here, such as *Baraka* by Kirino Natsuo (2016), *Hangenki wo iwatte* [Celebrating the half-life (of caesium)] by Tsushima Yūko (2016) and *Beddosaido mādā kēsu* [Bedside murder case] by Satō Yūya (2013).
3   The title evokes 'Fukushima' as well as '*Fuku no shima*', which is an appellation used for advertising campaigns in the region, such as '*Fuku ga mankai, fuku no shima*' [Happiness in full bloom, the island of happiness] (fukucam.jp/).
4   The term *sakoku* refers to the policy of national isolation in Tokugawa Japan, in which foreigners were not allowed to enter the country and Japanese were not allowed to leave.
5   The English translation of *Kentōshi* by Margaret Mitsutani (2018), *The Emissary*, was the winner of the inaugural National Book Awards for Translated Literature.

of Tokyo because the city centre has become uninhabitable. Areas such as Okinawa and northern Japan are said to be prospering by producing valuable crops such as fruit and rice. While the exact cause of this is never mentioned explicitly, it is hinted that the setting is a future Japan, where a much worse version of Fukushima has occurred (other than Yoshirō's immortality, there are also references to contaminated produce and mutated giant dandelions), as described in *The Island of Eternal Life*.

However, Tawada's dystopian imagination of Japan's future is not characterised by an Orwellian display of surveillance and political oppression. Instead, what gives her novella an eerie, dystopian feel is an extreme lack of clarity surrounding the exact nature of the system: how it came about, who is ruling the country and what would happen if you break the unspoken law. In Tawada's dystopia, citizens refrain from doing anything that might upset the privatised government because they live in fear, even though they do not know what it is exactly that they fear. For example, foreign languages and cultures are not completely banned, but because there is an invisible consensus that it is not desirable, citizens refrain from doing anything that could be interpreted as being foreign. In a manner reminiscent of wartime in 1940s Japan, native words are preferred to foreign imported terms: *tsunagi* instead of *ōbāōru* (overalls) and *kawaya* instead of *toire* (toilet). Because they are no longer used, foreign terms are associated with the older generation and children are made fun for using the English 'mama' instead of *okāsan*. The baker that Yoshirō frequents was an abstract painter in a previous life, but decided to take up baking instead for his personal safety because his paintings would often be interpreted to be depicting foreign scenery. Yoshiro buries a half-finished draft of a novel that he wrote (also titled *Kentōshi*) at the 'cemetery of things' rubbish dump because he feels that he included too many foreign place names in it. This future Japan is eerily frightening because it is a self-perpetuating dystopia, which is powered by invisible consensus, rather than set laws. Although a legal system exists, the laws keep changing all the time. Tawada (2014b) explained this in an interview with literary scholar Robert Campbell:

> If a dictatorship is born in Japan (and I fear that this may happen), I don't think it would be in a simple form where there is a clear government and those who criticize the regime get sent to prison. We've seen dictatorships like that everywhere and they still exist. Instead, I imagine it to be a scary time where a shapeless, sticky

and dark fear would spread and no one does what they should be doing, as human beings, because they restrain themselves saying: 'I'm not going to do that because I'm scared'.

Tawada provides a future vision for what would happen if the current self-restraint (*jishuku*) of expression is taken to an extreme.

Another factor that makes this dystopia eerily recognisable to post-3.11 Japanese readers is that citizens have accepted and adapted to this way of life, which is presented as being tolerable. Satire is allowed on newspapers, which also publish letters from Japanese citizens living abroad. One letter claims that 'it is more profitable and also safer to continue being pirates with my foreign comrades than to return to Japan' (p. 110), making Yoshirō laugh out loud. This small freedom gives a false sense of illusion that 'life is not so bad', despite travel being restricted domestically and banned internationally and information being heavily controlled (helped by the fact that the internet is no longer used). However, there are also some arguably positive aspects to the system, including that wealth has become unimportant and that the country is no longer excessively centralised around Tokyo. Tawada's dystopian Japan is not without hope, which is presented towards the end as Mumei is selected as a messenger to travel to India, in the hopes that the data on his health will help others to find a cure for his condition. *Kentōshi* is more forward- and outward-looking than *Fushi no shima* in that the solution is presented in the form of increased intercultural communication and cooperation.

Conversely, *Aoi hana* [The blue flower] by Henmi Yō (2013) and *Borādo byō* [The bollard disease] by Yoshimura Man'ichi (2014a) present a bleaker view of Japan's future as a totalitarian dystopia, in which government control is maintained through the means of terror, propaganda or drugs that prevent people from thinking. *Aoi hana* is the monologue of a man, an internal refugee who is fleeing earthquakes and foreign bombs (Henmi, 2013, p. 12) following the death of all his family members. The man walks along the ruins filled with radioactive corpses in search of *poranon*, a happy-drug that brings to mind the methamphetamine *hiropon*, which was widely popular following WWII and famously used on *kamikaze* soldiers. Despite this reference to the war, the setting of the novel is clearly designed to defamiliarise post-Fukushima Japan. In a way that brings to mind the post-3.11 official attempt to unite citizens in the name of *kizuna*, television advertisements consist of pro-war messages by the Advertising Council Japan (p. 36) and a song that 'makes everyone feel the sense of fulfilment that comes with caring for and helping others and the happiness that comes with not resisting' and those who dislike the song are 'suspected of antisocial personality disorders and a tendency towards unpatriotism and watched carefully by their organizations and society' (p. 119).

Death and totalitarian control are also prevalent in *Borādo byō*, which tells the story of a town called Umizuka, from the perspective of a young girl called Kyōko. In Umizuka, residents are brainwashed to stay united in their allegiance to their 'clean and safe town' by singing the 'Umizuka song' and participating in community activities. In reality, radiation sickness is everywhere and the disfigured children continue dying,[6] but the town's residents must keep their myth alive through the fervent propaganda of *musubiai* (coming together), which is reminiscent of *kizuna*. Those who are suspected of having the slightest amount of doubt in Umizuka's greatness or *musubiai*, such as Kyōko and her family, are reported and taken away by mysterious 'men in suits'. Yoshimura's dystopia is characterised by an eerie facelessness, in which the exact nature of the town's government is unclear, but residents must watch their every move and utterance to ensure that they do not do anything that makes them stick out from the majority. For example, Kyōko's mother throws away the meat and vegetables she buys (she needs to buy them to keep up appearances in public) and feeds her daughter imported canned foods and instant noodles, which she believes are safer. However, when they are at a community lunch with other townspeople, where they are served local produce, Kyōko's mother tells her that she must eat everything. Umizuka's eeriness is amplified by the fact that the story is narrated by Kyōko, who as a child does not fully understand her situation. Kyōko is constantly scolded by her mother for what seem like insignificant acts for both her and the reader, such as staring too much at a flower or a baby's mouth. It becomes clear by the end of the novel that the flower and the baby's mouth were both disfigured by radiation and that staring at these was not acceptable because it meant that she noticed that they looked different. The implication is that the successfully brainwashed townspeople do not even see the world because they become blind to the reality around them.

---

6   Although Yoshimura (2014a) only refers to the sickness as 'poison', there are various clues in the novel that point to radiation being the cause, such as Kyōko's pet rabbit having no front legs (p. 162). Yoshimura (2014b) claims that a non-3.11 reading is possible and that the cause could be a poisonous gas or a virus.

The dystopian works that I have outlined above each have in common an eeriness that comes from a lack of clarity surrounding the government and the diseases affecting citizens, which is a metaphor for the insidious and invisible nature of radiation. These works are convincing in their dystopian portrayals of the country because they build on the fear of the invisible that many Japanese felt post-3.11, as well as real-life restrictions on freedom of speech during the war. In both *Aoi hana* and *Borādo byō*, mindlessly conforming to mainstream ideology by taking drugs or singing propaganda songs is the only way of being normal and surviving in this future Japanese society. This provides a powerful critique of the culture of *shikō teishi* (the suspension of thought) and avoiding unpleasant discussion, which is believed to have become apparent in post-3.11 Japan.[7] This critique is carried out even more directly and controversially in Takahashi Gen'ichirō's *Koisuru genpatsu*, which I explore below.

Conformity versus Pornography: Takahashi Gen'ichirō's *Koisuru genpatsu*

If the dystopian responses to 3.11 portray a future Japan in which minority opinions and critical thinking are quickly suppressed by social consensus, Takahashi Gen'ichirō's (2011a) post-3.11 novel, *Koisuru genpatsu* [A nuclear reactor in love], demonstrates how this may be overcome to allow for greater freedom of expression. Similar to the dystopian responses, Takahashi portrays the atmosphere of conformity and social pressure, which he believed was pervasive in post-3.11 critical discourse. He demonstrates that this is created by a mix of Japanese blind trust for authority, legitimate-sounding rhetoric used by the authorities and the existence of many taboo topics that are never properly discussed. However, Takahashi's novel is also a kind of social experiment, which confronts readers by bombarding them with language that would be considered to be inappropriate by many in Japan, especially following

---

7   *Shikō teishi* has been a keyword in Japanese critical discourse since around 2010, appearing in book titles such as *Shikō teishi shakai: 'junshu' ni mushibamareru Nihonjin* [The 'thought suspension society': a people being ruined by obedience] by Gōhara Nobuo (2009) and *Taima Hisuteri: shikō teishi ni naru Nihonjin* [The cannabis hysteria: the Japanese who cannot think] by Takeda Kunihiko (2009). There was also some interest raised following the results of the World Values Survey 2010–2014, which demonstrated that 73.8 per cent of Japanese answered that they believe newspaper and magazine reporting to be reliable and 69.7 per cent answered that television reporting was reliable, compared to 22.8 per cent and 23.2 per cent respectively in the US (Maita, 2015).

such a devastating disaster. Instead of simply showing the process by which consensus is formed, Takahashi demonstrates by example that such consensus can be broken by a strong presence of inappropriate and incorrect language. If read in this way, Takahashi's novel has the effect of blurring the line between correct and incorrect, which seems to have become more rigid post-3.11 and shows hope for greater freedom of expression in future Japan.

Since before the disaster, Japan has often been described both domestically and overseas as a society with groupthink tendencies, in which individual opinions are not valued. Decisions are said to be made on the basis of *kūki* (air) and those who do not follow the consensus are described as *kūki ga yomenai* (unable to read the air; '*KY*' for short), which is synonymous with lacking social skills in Japanese society.[8] It is a cliché of Nihonjinron that, to survive in the closed *mura shakai* (village society), the Japanese must adhere to the majority group at all costs, as 'the nail that sticks out gets hammered' (*deru kui wa utareru*) and might even be subjected to *mura hachibu* (ostracism/excommunication from the group) (Christopher, 1984, p. 53; Reischauer, 1977, pp. 135, 141). As outlined in Chapter 1, the disaster was perceived to have reinforced this cultural threat to freedom of expression. Due to the polarisation in opinions on questions such as nuclear power, Fukushima essentially created two 'villages' that the Japanese must choose between. Intellectuals such as Odajima Takashi (2012) argued that a very small selection of opinions received public attention in Japan and that when there were two opposing forces, they refused to listen to each other, which created tension rather than discussion. Takahashi (2012a, p. 129) also viewed post-3.11 Japanese society as an environment that was dangerously polarised, especially between pro-nuclear and anti-nuclear camps and has actively commented on this on his Twitter account @takagengen, as well as other media.[9] According to Takahashi (2012a, p. 130), members of Japanese society have been forced to make a choice between these two stances, to determine which one is *tadashii* (correct),

---

8   For example, Kōkami Shōji (2009) explored this in detail in his Nihonjinron work *Kūki to seken* [The 'air' and society].
9   A selection of his comments on Twitter have been published in a book, *'Ano hi' kara boku ga kangaeteiru 'tadashisa' ni tsuite* [What I've been thinking about 'correctness' since 'that day'] (2012), from which these quotes are taken. Takahashi (2012) has also published the short story collection *Sayonara, Kurisutofā Robin* [Goodbye, Christopher Robin] and the essay collections *Hijōji no kotoba: shinsai no ato de* [Words in crisis: after the earthquake] (2012) and *Bokura no minshushugi nandaze* [This is our democracy] (2015) and has appeared at various public talks.

to be a rightful citizen—an intellectual atmosphere that stymies healthy debate and creativity. *Koisuru genpatsu* is a more literary and imaginative expression of these concerns, explored through the lens of language.

Keeping with his metafictional stance, Takahashi has always played with the idea of a central and stable plot or storyline in a novel, which is true to some extent for *Koisuru genpatsu*. Takahashi's works typically attempt to provoke thought, rather than to tell a coherent story. Although ostensibly about a group of men who attempt to create a charity adult video for the victims of 3.11,[10] the story mostly happens in a complex web of tangents and no actual filming occurs in the novel. As the protagonist, Ishikawa asks, 'How much progress have we made in the story? Are we nearing the end, or have we entered a dead-end? I have no idea. Has it even started? I often get this feeling, actually' (p. 230).[11] Some of the most important scenes in the novel occur in these tangents, such as the story of the war veteran president of the adult video production company where the protagonist works as a cameraman. The president was on the battleship Yamato when it sunk on 7 April 1945. Floating on the water, the president has a comic and poignant conversation with his friend Katahira, who is a 20-year-old virgin, about what they imagine vaginas to look like. Katahira dies shortly after and the president decides that if he makes it home alive, he will dedicate his life to thinking about sex—the only thing that matters. Another tangent occurs when the 55-year-old pornography actress, Yoshiko, gives a lesson to Saori, who is in her fourth year of primary school, on how to protect herself from the sexual advances of men. Yoshiko, who was raped by her primary school teacher, has some unconventional views on education—she believes that schooling should consist entirely of practical lessons on sex and death, which take priority over book-learning. Each of these tangents have a story of their own to tell, whether they are individual histories or snippets of social criticism and the charity adult video that Ishikawa is making is what binds these stories together, rather than being the story that Takahashi wants to tell.

Takahashi makes his reader question whether *Koisuru genpatsu* is even a novel, just like it is unclear whether the adult videos in the novel are indeed adult videos, with their lengthy historical scenes and singing.

---

10   The tagline for the book is: '大震災チャリティーAVを作ろうと奮闘する男たちの愛と冒険と魂の物語' [A group of men give their all in making a charity adult video for the Great Earthquake … A story of love, soul and adventure].
11   All translations of Takahashi's writing are my own.

As part of his attempt to avoid any kind of expression that can be considered to be normal, conventional or mainstream, Takahashi also challenges his readers to go beyond genre conventions. For example, the obi strip around the cover of the book asks, 'Do you accept this novel?' and Takahashi repeatedly attempts to break the fourth wall by conversing with his readers throughout the novel, addressing them as *anta*, which is an affectionate second person address (p. 29). He also employs his signature self-reflexive style in the narrative, making Ishikawa correct and ridicule himself—playing the role of both *boke* and *tsukkomi* in Japanese comedy:[12] 'Suddenly, on the screen, Mr Monkey (*osaru-san*) appears. Well, it's really just a monkey (*saru*), but today I just feel like calling him "Mr Monkey"' (p. 11). Perhaps the most striking metafictional technique employed is that the adult video in the novel, and consequently the novel itself, is partly narrated in musical style, which eliminates any remaining possibility of suspension of disbelief. Characters suddenly burst into song during the dialogue, in a manner reminiscent of Dennis Potter's 1986 BBC television series *The Singing Detective*, or the literary works of Thomas Pynchon. The song selection is a combination of foreign pop songs with some Japanese popular songs.

Takahashi's career as an author has revolved around the issue of the lack of freedom in both literary and political expression in Japan. Following his involvement in the radical student movement of the late 1960s and his eventual arrest and aphasia, Takahashi became sensitive to the ways in which the Japanese language was used to define and suppress political minorities.[13] In particular, the aggressive use of the terms *bōryoku* (violence) and *bōryokudan* (violent groups) by the mainstream media to characterise the student movement led Takahashi to fear the Japanese language itself, including how it is used as a source of violence.[14] In his previous novels, Takahashi wrote against this kind of aggressive political

---

12   In *manzai* stand-up comedy, there is usually a comedian who acts as *boke* and another who acts as *tsukkomi*. The *boke*'s role is to make silly and funny remarks, which the *tsukkomi* corrects, causing the audience to laugh.
13   Although through a different medium, there can be some parallels drawn between Takahashi's works and the non-fiction and documentary work of Mori Tatsuya, whose Aum Shinrikyō documentary *A* is critically acclaimed outside of Japan.
14   Takahashi (Yoshimoto & Takahashi, 2005, p. 304) gives the example of the response of the Chancellor of Tokyo University following the death of a far-left revolutionary group member in the 1967 Haneda Incident: 'minshu shugi no na no moto de bōryoku wa ikenai' [violence is wrong in a democracy]. Takahashi (1998, p. 225) used the term 'fear' to describe his relationship with language. See Yamada (2011) for an in-depth exploration of other events that shaped Takahashi's literary project.

language that attempts to define and oppress, by exploring the boundaries of the Japanese language beyond a one-to-one correspondence between its signs and meaning. As Yamada (2011) claims, referring to Takahashi's first two novels, *Sayōnara, gyangutachi* and *Jon Renon tai kaseijin* [John Lennon v. The Martians], these are 'metafictions, or fictions that self-consciously underscore the conventions of signification' (p. 5). In his earlier works, Takahashi achieved this by 'invit[ing] readers to experience and even collaborate in the unbounding of meaning in the interpretation process' (Yamada, 2011, p. 18). This can be observed in the titles of his novels, which frustrate our desire to assign a single and stable meaning to them: *Yūga de kanshō teki na Nippon yakyū* [Japanese Baseball: Elegant and Sentimental] and *Jon Renon tai kaseijin* [John Lennon v. The Martians], for example, and similarly, *Koisuru genpatsu* [A nuclear reactor in love].[15] In this sense, *Koisuru genpatsu* continues many themes from his previous works: exploring new possibilities for unassertive language that encourages multiple interpretations and testing the limits of the Japanese language, while being aware that he is still using the language that he is criticising.

Published in November 2011, just eight months after 3.11, *Koisuru genpatsu* can be differentiated from Takahashi's previous works in that it responds in real-time to the aggressive language that proliferates in post-3.11 Japan on both left- and right-wing sides of the political spectrum. In addition, he addresses the issue of correctness—when a certain political discourse gains majority support in a group in Japan, it also becomes correct, which then silences all other minority views. The novel paradoxically highlights this politicalness and correctness of mainstream expression in post-3.11 Japan by exploring minority views and the realms of language with the least aggression, which is deliberately unassertive, inappropriate and, at times, nonsensical.

Takahashi's criticism of the post-3.11 Japanese discursive environment focuses on the social pressure to conform to what is right and what is done by the majority—to donate money to charities, to refrain from frivolous activities and entertainment in the spirit of *jishuku* (voluntary self-restraint or mourning) and to conserve electricity (*setsuden*). For example, many graduation ceremonies around Japan were cancelled

---

15 One could interpret this title as a reference to the single-mindedness of those at the opposite extremes of the nuclear power debate (as in the saying *koi wa mōmoku* [love is blind]), or simply the heatedness of the debate, being equated to the excitement of love. However, the title still thwarts our attempts to ascribe meaning to it, by making the subject of this love the nuclear reactor.

following the earthquake because it was considered to be inappropriate to hold celebratory events in such circumstances. Takahashi, who lectures at the Meiji Gakuin University, planned on delivering a speech to those students who decided to turn up on campus anyway. Although Takahashi was unable to deliver the speech, he made it available on Twitter. In this speech, Takahashi (2012a, p. 33) tells his students that it is okay not to conform to what is 'right', if they do not feel that that is genuinely what they want to do. The opening sequence of the charity adult video in *Koisuru genpatsu* contains slogans such as 'hang in there, Japan', 'Japan is one' and 'we are all Japanese' (p. 16)—slogans that bear a strong resemblance to those used in 3.11 campaigns. To this, Ishikawa has the following reaction:

> To be honest, I'm a bit sick of it all. The repetition of words like 'Japan' and 'Japanese' is starting to sound rather pushy … No, it's not right to say things like that. If everyone likes it, there is no reason to protest. They can do as they like. But I really wish they would give it a rest with the slogans (p. 16).

Here, Ishikawa seems to be speaking for all Japanese people, who are feeling overwhelmed by the slogans and social pressures in post-3.11 society. Through Ishikawa's words, Takahashi reveals a part of post-3.11 society that does not appear in official discourse—those who feel uncomfortable with these slogans but are unable to speak out against them due to the pressure to conform.[16]

However, Takahashi is not condemning the act of charity itself; he is simply criticising people who donate money as a result of social pressure. Takahashi is suggesting that charity has become an automatic reflex for Japanese people, which prevents them from reflecting on what is needed in the disaster-hit areas. Ishikawa claims that he cannot understand anything except for adult videos, so he should 'stay quiet' and donate without asking questions—'after all, as long as you pay a bit of money, no one will complain, right?' (p. 196). What Ishikawa does not understand, at this stage of the novel, is that everyone can contribute in their own way and this is not necessarily by giving money: the president and the

---

16   These slogans are reminiscent of other periods of crises in Japan, as Takahashi (2012a) points out: 'The same thing happened during the wars of the Meiji period, when the wars started in the Shōwa period and also when that ended and Japan turned into a democracy. Just like what is happening now, using pretty words, people fervently insisted on conforming to what is "right", while denouncing all that is "inappropriate", "unpatriotic" or "reactionary"' (p. 33).

chairperson, who are originally from Tōhoku, go home to help their families, whereas Ishikawa's colleagues Yama-chan and Kameda go to volunteer in Iwate and start an outdoor childcare centre in Fukushima, respectively. Takahashi's message is that Japanese people should think on their feet and help people in creative ways when they feel the need to do so, not just always mindlessly donating for the correct good cause to which everyone else donates.

Takahashi begins his novel with a quote from an imaginary book, *Intānetto jō no meigen shū* [A collection of quotes from the internet]: 'I dedicate this book to all those who passed away … No, saying that would be too shallow'. He follows this with 'a letter from a reader', which reads 'this is extremely inappropriate. I hope there will be punishment for those involved'. Takahashi's response to this typically Japanese, 'legitimate' opinion is expressed through the protagonist of the novel, Ishikawa, who appears and speaks directly to the readers (*anta*) in the casual first-person *ore*, instead of the more formal *watashi*, in a more colloquial tone (also represented by the more curvy, playful font):[17]

> It goes without saying that this is a work of complete fiction. Even if some parts of it resemble reality, that's just a coincidence. If you even entertain the idea that there may be a slight chance of something written in this book happening in real life, you're barking mad. How can such a crazy world exist? Go see a psychiatrist! Right now! That's the only piece of advice I can give you. See you later.

These three pages clearly display that Takahashi is aware that his writing may be viewed as inappropriate in the post-3.11 context and he does so deliberately. Ishikawa's retort retains elements of the same violence inherent in the language that criticises him, such as labelling his readers as 'barking mad'. However, because his language is more illegitimate, this violence is easier to observe for his readers than in the legitimate-sounding rhetoric of mainstream discourse.

Takahashi makes it clear that he is deliberately avoiding conventional Japanese forms of mourning disaster victims because he believes that those words do not carry any substance. Later, Ishikawa questions: 'I am sensitive to my own pain, but maybe I am insensitive to the pain of others

---

17 It is assumed that the speaker is the protagonist as the pronoun *ore* is used, which is the pronoun Ishikawa uses throughout the rest of the novel.

… Is it possible at all to understand other people's pain, though?' (p. 127). Takahashi suggests that since it is not possible to understand the suffering of others, it is insincere to pretend to understand. Takahashi does not pretend to be able to understand or that a legitimately written dedication in his book would do anything to let their souls rest in peace. From the beginning of the novel, Takahashi calls for his Japanese readers to base their evaluation of information on its content, rather than its source or its appearance of legitimacy.

Takahashi favours pornography as a way to talk illegitimately because it does not follow the moral and aesthetic codes of mainstream discourse and can have the power to bring socially formed preconceptions to light. Pornography is a device he previously used in his 1999 novel *Adaruto* [Adult], which focuses almost exclusively on non-mainstream pornography, such as those featuring old women or scatological elements, in a way that makes his readers question what exactly is normal and what is an unusual fetish. However, as Takahashi (1998, p. 118) contended, 'normal pornography' that attempts to follow the rules and 'ideologies' of pornography has the potential to be didactic and to play a part in dictating how sex should be done 'correctly'. This is why Takahashi seems to feel an affinity for the unconventional pornography of Japanese directors, such as Baksheesh Yamashita and Company Matsuo, who actively challenged conventions in the pornography genre by including 'bizarre things no one has ever seen before and unimaginable kinds of people doing all sorts of things', which forced viewers to leave behind their societally conditioned conceptions of love and sex (p. 119). For example, Ishikawa describes the video of 72-year-old pornography film star Yone as something that is as 'frightening as the leakage of contaminated water from Fukushima' and reports that, when confronted with this 'frightening' image, many viewers chose to close their eyes to avoid looking at it (pp. 128–132). As Takahashi (2012b) explains, 'we become lost for words when confronted with nude old women, because, unlike young girls, society doesn't have the words to describe what they look like. I want my readers to become lost for words in my novel'—old women do not usually figure in socially formed preconceptions about sex. Takahashi's use of unconventional pornography in his works relates closely to his political concerns that mainstream discourse defines 'the correct way to think about love and sex' and that unconventional pornography has the power to destroy these preconceptions, just like literature.

Although the authorities and the government clouded their post-3.11 arguments in legitimate and authoritative sounding rhetoric, using keywords such as *kizuna, jishuku* and *tabete ōen* (support the disaster-hit areas by eating their produce), Takahashi implies that the problem is compounded because Japanese people blindly trust official-sounding discourse without questioning its content. While the Japanese loyalty to and respect for their rulers has been a subject of wonder in the West since WWII, Japanese intellectuals have recently criticised this tendency as *shikō teishi* (suspension of thought), which is characterised by a kind of laziness when it comes to critical thinking with regards to official discourse. In his novel, Takahashi uses language that is as far removed as possible from legitimate-sounding political rhetoric to create obstacles to this Japanese style of unquestioning obedience. Readers are prevented from trusting anything in the book because characters in *Koisuru genpatsu* lack confidence and express themselves in colloquial speech (even heads of state including former prime minister Kan Naoto) and hardly a page passes without some form of sexual slang. This illegitimate effect is amplified by the fact that disaster and death are considered serious issues that must be discussed using legitimate language.

Another example of Takahashi's criticism of legitimate-sounding rhetoric is a chapter entitled *Shinsai bungaku ron* [An essay on earthquake literature], inserted towards the end of the book, which appears to be a discussion on the role of 3.11 literature. In stark contrast to the rest of the novel, the content of this chapter is much more serious and written in normal language. As Ishino (2013, p. 31) observed, this chapter is the only part of the novel that is logical and coherent, which may cause readers to conclude that this chapter represents the crux of what Takahashi wanted to say in his novel. Because they feel so relieved to finally read something that they can understand after being bombarded by Takahashi's absurd writing, most readers would not stop to question whether its content were reliable (p. 31). However, this chapter is also a work of fiction, which discusses imaginary works with the names of artists and authors written in *katakana*, like the other characters in the novel. The eight-hour version of *Nausicaä of the Valley of the Wind*, as well as *Kamisama (2011)*, which are discussed in the chapter, are both fictional works, despite being based on their real versions (by Miyazaki Hayao and Kawakami Hiromi respectively). Although the chapter deals with some of the concerns that Takahashi explores during the rest of the novel, its content cannot be taken at face value. Takahashi frustrates readers' attempts to find any easy explanation of the novel. Takahashi suggests that reality does not have easy explanations and that Japanese people must learn to take all discourse surrounding the disaster with a grain of salt and to be suspicious of language that appears to be legitimate and authoritative, whether it be his own essay or any other commentary on the disaster.

In *Koisuru genpatsu*, Takahashi reveals that many taboos remain in Japanese society by using pornography as a direct metaphor for them. The words of the 55-year-old pornography film star Yoshiko highlight this similarity: 'the problem is that no one wants to talk about it ... So you never gain an understanding of what it is' and the real reason why people do not talk about it is because 'it's hidden away, so you can't see it' (p. 160). *Koisuru genpatsu* is Takahashi's attempt to encourage debates on delicate matters in Japanese society—sex, money, death and, perhaps most importantly, nuclear power. Pornography is a highly appropriate metaphor for nuclear power in that they are both essential parts of the everyday lives of Japanese people, yet are hidden away from the public eye. Pornography is also rigged—it is a *yaochō*, a 'put-up job', in which everyone knows what will happen at the end, despite any unwillingness feigned by the participants (p. 10). In a similar way, Japanese nuclear politics is also rigged because it is governed by political and financial interests. Through his metaphor of pornography, Takahashi suggests that what needs to change in Japanese society is not the taboo or sexual perversion, but the lack of discussion about these subjects, which make it seem as though they are not happening. Takahashi shows that the hesitation and shock the reader feels when reading his novel plays an important role in perpetuating these taboos.[18]

Takahashi's boundary-testing demonstrates that taboos can be overcome when there is enough discussion on the subject—readers eventually get used to the sexual explicitness and inappropriateness of the novel and begin to question why it is a taboo at all. The novel demonstrates that the act of talking about a taboo, in any shape or form, can make it more acceptable, even in Japan. However, it is also true that debates surrounding the taboo subject of nuclear power would not have occurred in Japan in

---

18 An example of this is the reaction of Waseda University to this book. Takahashi revealed on Twitter that the university banned the use of *Koisuru genpatsu* as part of the title of a talk he was going to give on campus in October because they considered the expression to be inappropriate (this is further evidence to Odajima's claim that nuclear power is becoming an issue that no one wants to be involved with in Japan). The combination was probably considered problematic in that it carried the risk of making it appear as though he was making a pro-nuclear statement and being inconsiderate to the disaster victims and that Waseda University supports this.

the first place were it not for the Fukushima disasters. Sadly, it seems that the power of speech is insufficient, in many cases, to instil enough of a sense of urgency in the general population to *start* such debates. This is why Ishikawa decides not to use his alien assistant's supernatural powers to go back in time and make it so that 3.11 never happened at the end of the novel—not only would this be turning away from reality, but it would also reverse an invaluable opportunity to begin the debate on taboo topics in Japan, including nuclear power. To borrow the words of the chairperson of the adult video production company, Japan has been 'shaking' for decades, without anyone realising it (p. 94) and 3.11 simply brought to light all the existing problems of Japanese society. The best we can do is not to pretend that it never happened, but to face the issues squarely and to keep speaking about them.

Post-3.11 critical discourse has been characterised by the use of easily discernible markers to identify and label 'enemies'. In *Koisuru genpatsu*, this is illustrated through the example of two words: *hōshanō* (radioactivity) and *hōshasei busshitsu* (radioactive material). Although it is technically incorrect, the term *hōshanō* is often used to refer to radioactive materials in Japan in expressions such as *hōshanō more* (leakage of radioactivity), especially in the media because the term is easier to say. However, following 3.11, the correct usage of these terms has been an indicator of the depth of the speaker's knowledge of nuclear power, which has led to nit-picking. Takahashi seems to feel that this is an issue of minor importance relative to the urgency of healthy debates surrounding the future of nuclear power in Japan. As Ishikawa puts it, 'Why do I have to worry about such things? People tell me I shouldn't get it wrong. Why? I don't understand at all' (p. 180).

Another example is the discussion of two cover songs: the Korean versions of Itsuwa Mayumi's song *Koibito yo* ([Oh, lover], probably referring to Rhee Hwa Sook's version) and *Yuki ga furu* [Tombe la neige] by Salvatore Adamo. In Japan, Korean copying of Japanese culture is often derogatorily referred to as *pakuri* (stealing). However, Ishikawa reveals that the Korean singers sung these songs with such pride that he was moved to the point of tears, claiming that 'it really doesn't matter whether a song is *honmono* (real) or *pakuri*' (p. 44). What is important here is Takahashi's choice of *Yuki ga furu* as his example—written by Salvatore Adamo, an artist born in Sicily and raised in Belgium, who was known for performing all over the world in numerous languages. Although the song is well known in Japan, it was originally written in French and sung by Adamo in many languages, including Korean. Takahashi most likely deliberately included this example to further blur the line between real and fake or right and wrong. By referring to these examples, Takahashi suggests that whether one's language is correct or not (both in the sense of word selection and the choice of the language itself) is unrelated to the value of what is expressed.

On the very last page, Takahashi once again brings up the issue of what constitutes an adult video, and by extension a novel, with what appears to be a conversation between Ishikawa and the president:

> What do you think?
> Suggestion dismissed.
> Why?
> Because that's not porn! (p. 276)

With this conversation, Takahashi paradoxically demonstrates that even such labels of genre are unimportant and unnecessary in the interests of free expression. If not a novel, Takahashi's novel could be called a performance, much like the actions of the *Yubisashi otoko* [pointing man], who gained fame for filming himself pointing his finger at the LiveCam at the Fukushima Daiichi Power plant. The back cover of the novel references this video with an image of Takahashi pointing at his readers. In Takahashi's (2012a, p. 283) own words, the 'pointing man' is saying, 'You're all pointing at others and attacking them, but why don't you try point that finger to yourself for once?' Takahashi's finger-pointing performance is a powerful criticism of the tendency to hide away from real debates in post-3.11 Japan.[19] Takahashi's question, 'do you accept this novel?' becomes a question aimed at Japanese society as a whole when read in this light. Takahashi encourages Japanese people to go beyond narrow-minded labels such as left-wing or right-wing and to pay more attention to the content. Although Takahashi admits that he is powerless as an individual, he displays hope in the collective power of Japanese society. As he argues, 'there is no freedom of expression in Japan because Japanese people do not want it' (p. 73); that is, he believes that it is possible for Japan to break out of the stifling cloud of conformity if the Japanese people decide to work together. Takahashi attempts to aid this

---

19 In this way, Takahashi's work shares much in common with the music and performances of the anti-nuclear protestors in Tokyo following 3.11; see Brown (2018) and Manabe (2016).

process by stirring up controversy for controversy's sake, in the hopes that he will be able to desensitise Japanese society to unconventional opinions and expressions and to encourage healthy debates.

The dystopian works explored in the first half of this chapter are different in nature to Takahashi's novel. In the dystopian works, minority opinions are suppressed, whereas they are celebrated in Takahashi's work. However, if dystopian literature is considered to provide negative examples of what society should *not* aim for, we can also say that the authors in this chapter express hope for a more democratic future Japan, in which minority opinions can be easily expressed and heard.

4
HETEROGENOUS JAPAN

As mentioned in Chapter 1, Azuma Hiroki (2011a, p. 12) observed in September 2011 that 3.11 served to reveal the lack of solidarity in Japanese society. The disaster highlighted that, contrary to the popular Nihonjinron belief of Japan being a homogenous nation, significant economic and cultural differences existed between the disaster-hit areas and Tokyo. To give one oft-cited example, just as the disaster-hit areas began their long journey to recovery, television programs in Tokyo were already discussing what would happen if a disaster of such a scale were to occur in the nation's capital, which emphasised the Tokyo-centric nature of public discourse in Japan.[1]

Jake Adelstein, an American *Yomiuri Shimbun* journalist and author of *Tokyo Vice* (a chronicle of Adelstein's experiences in crime reporting in the city), highlighted this lack of solidarity in his work *Muenbotoke* (Adelstein, 2011a), which was first published in *Shambhala Sun* and rewritten for *2:46—Aftershocks: Stories from the Japan Earthquake. 2:46* is a publication that contains essays, artworks and photographs by Japanese and non-Japanese authors, created within a week of the disaster through collaboration on Twitter. Among this collection of mostly non-fictional accounts of the disaster (by names such as William Gibson and Barry Eisler), Adelstein's (2011a) *Muenbotoke* is unique in its fictional and indirect approach. The story is about a middle-aged couple who commit double suicide and become *muenbotoke* (the dead who do not have any living relatives to look after their graves). Symbolically, the surname

---

1   In April 2017, Reconstruction Minister Imamura Masahiro resigned after commenting that the earthquake 'was okay because it happened over there, in Tōhoku' ('Imamura Fukkōshō jinin', 2017).

of the couple is Akutagawa, which evokes Akutagawa Ryūnosuke who famously committed suicide due to a 'vague anxiety about his future'. However, unlike Akutagawa Ryūnosuke, Mr Akutagawa's anxiety for his future is much more tangible: he had been recently laid off from his job as a temporary employee at a construction company and was simply too poor to carry on living.

Adelstein's account of the story is interspersed with the story of the self-sacrifice and imagined death of the nuclear power plant staff at Fukushima, which is in italics and written in a more journalistic and impersonal tone. This interspersing vividly portrays the paradox in Japanese society: that there appears to be cohesion and cooperation in the society as a whole, but on closer inspection, many individuals are excluded from this society. It is suggested that this self-sacrifice, going hand in hand with extreme isolation of certain individuals, are difficult for foreigners like Adelstein to comprehend. Adelstein (2011a) incredulously asks, 'Many of the staff at the nuclear power plant stayed on the job long after radiation levels had risen past even the laxest of safety standards, to prevent a full meltdown. Why?' (p. 56). He explains that 'they are willing to give their lives to save the lives of thousands of other people, people they know, people they don't know and people they will never meet' (p. 57), which evokes the notion of the Japanese group mentality, or *kizuna* (see Chapter 1), in the post-3.11 context.

However, members of Japanese society can also be cold towards people they know and people they have met—such as social outcasts like Mr and Mrs Akutagawa, 62 and 59 years old respectively, who were found dead in their apartment in Totsuka, Shinjuku. The use of Totsuka as a setting highlights the juxtaposition between the couple's real-life plight and Japan's perceived image as an altruistic group community. Totsuka is known as *fukushi no machi* [the welfare town], due to the presence of many non-government organisations, such as Amnesty International, Médecins Sans Frontières and Peace Boat. Mr Akutagawa 'was practically invisible' (p. 57), except to the debt collectors who regularly threatened and harassed him. The few people that know something about him do not seem to be moved or surprised by his death at all, behaving as though it was inevitable. As Adelstein (2011a) argues, 'it's amazing to me that people can live in an apartment complex right next to each other for years and not know each other at all' (p. 57). Although Adelstein (2011a) admits that 'a lot of Japanese people hate to ask others for help' (pp. 57–59), the statement leaves the readers questioning who the socially isolated couple could have possibly talked to, rather than finding reassurance in the possibility of help available on demand. Just like 'the unseen radiation they were exposed to has probably already killed [the nuclear power plant staff]' (p. 57), the Akutagawas had already 'been dead for a long time' (p. 57). Having no family, the Akutagawas do not receive any care even when they are truly and officially dead—the police only care about whether Mr Akutagawa killed his wife with her consent, so they can fill in the necessary paperwork, in case he needs to be prosecuted post-mortem. Only Adelstein goes to the effort of visiting the grave, from which they have 'probably been evicted or displaced by the ashes of other *muenbotoke*' (p. 59) by the time of writing because no one would have paid for the upkeep fees—in Adelstein's (2011a) words, 'even the dead can only rent in Tokyo' (p. 60).

Interestingly, Adelstein (2011a) does not ask his readers to pray for the Akutagawas, but ends the story with the last component of the Fukushima narrative in italics:

> *May their memories last longer than the accident that took their lives. Because remembering them is all we can do for them now and for all those who lost their lives. And in that act of remembering, hopefully we will lead better lives and remember to care for all living things. We owe the dead that much* (p. 59).

By concluding his narrative with this praise for the (imagined) heroes of the disaster, Adelstein brings our attention to the lack of such a discourse for the thousands who silently passed away like Mr and Mrs Akutagawa, without any recognition for their contribution to society. Adelstein's story is a reminder for the Japanese, especially in the cities, to remember these sacrifices that make their modern lifestyle possible, as well as a challenge to the discourse of *kizuna* and national unity, which was prevalent at the time of his writing. Similarly, the three authors that I explore below paint post-3.11 Japan as a heterogenous space (at least temporarily), despite the common perception of the country as being highly homogenous.

Tradition versus Modernity: Richard Collasse and Shinkai Makoto

As I mentioned above, a way in which the Japanese 'homogeneity myth' was questioned in the cultural response to the disaster was to highlight the major economic and cultural differences that exist between the nation's capital and countryside. Albeit very different in style, the 2016 blockbuster film *Kimi no na wa* [Your Name] by Shinkai Makoto and the French novel *L'océan dans la rizière* [The ocean in the rice paddy] by Richard Collasse both deal with a 'culture shock' that occurs as a result of these two sides of Japan being brought together after a disaster. While Shinkai presents a vision of post-disaster Japan in which homogeneity is restored, Collasse paints this heterogeneity as a positive and essential part of a reconstructed future Japan.

The universe of *Kimi no na wa* is split into two storylines that eventually merge. One of them is situated in Itomachi, which is a sleepy fictional town with a population of 1,500 in the Prefecture of Gifu, where Mitsuha, a girl born into a family of Shintō shrine maidens, wishes to escape her world of rituals and offerings. The other storyline, three years later, is inhabited by Taki, who is a privileged high school boy in Tokyo, with all the luxuries associated with living in the capital, including stylish cafe food, cinemas and Italian restaurants with chandeliers. The disaster that occurs in the film is an allusion to 3.11. Although in Itomachi the disaster is caused by a meteor fall, it is eerily reminiscent of 3.11 in its sudden and devastating nature. In Tōhoku, the giant tsunami waves started reaching residential areas half an hour after the earthquake, similar to how the beautiful meteor unexpectedly splits into two and starts falling onto the village, giving residents little time to escape. The recurring nature of this fictional disaster (it recurs every 1,200 years) is also reminiscent of the fact that the Tōhoku tsunami brought attention to the large tsunamis that previously occurred in the region, including in 869, 1611 and 1933.

In *Kimi no na wa*, the economic and cultural gap between Tokyo and the disaster-hit rural area is highlighted by means of strong juxtapositions. In the animated film version, this difference is manifested in the visual contrast between the beautiful scenery of the Hida mountains and the bustling technological cityscape of Tokyo. For example, in the Itomori scenes, the train station is mostly empty (the local train only passes by once every two hours), whereas in Tokyo trains are shown to arrive and depart continuously in every direction. Most importantly, the difference in the lives of these two characters is underscored by the repeated representation of surprise as the characters experience each other's lives through frequent body swaps. In the book version, Taki repeatedly describes Mitsuha's universe as being similar to that of a folkloric tale (*mukashi banashi*), while Mitsuha feels as though the conversations of Taki's schoolmates are taken straight out of 'celebrity posts on Facebook'.

The portrayal of Mitsuha's life in Itomori is not just a portrayal of difference, but also an extremely exoticised portrayal—in this mountainous land, shrine maidens such as Mitsuha and her sister continue to perform divine dances in traditional costume, craft intricate *kumihimo* ropes by hand and produce sake by chewing rice and mixing it with their virginal saliva in their mouths. This exotic appeal of Itomori is perhaps best demonstrated by the sudden boom in real-life 'pilgrimage' or *seichi junrei* to the Gifu Prefecture, a phenomenon in which fans travel to find sites that may have inspired certain scenes in animated films. The exoticised and, to some extent, eroticised gaze of the city dwellers towards these sacred, virginal sites is also apparent in the merchandising related to the film, such as the local sake, Hōrai, which was made available for purchase in the 'saliva sake' bottles from the film. The film led some Japanese to rediscover parts of traditional Japanese culture, much like the 'discover Japan' or the 'exotic Japan' tourism campaigns by the Japanese National Railways in the 1970s and 1980s,[2] and reminded them that many parts of Japan are still rural, even if they are not quite as exotic as the film portrays.

In the film, these gaps are shown to be overcome by young love (or, at least, the strong will to not forget each other), as well as the bond of *musubi* (knot)—a key concept that is repeated many times in both the film and the novel and is highly reminiscent of *kizuna*. The concept is introduced in a key scene where Taki (in Mitsuha's body) goes to visit the shrine god's body in the mountains to make an offering of Mitsuha's saliva sake, with her grandmother Hitoha and younger sister Yotsuha. During their journey, Hitoha explains the many meanings of *musubi*:

> The linking of threads is *musubi*. The linking of people is *musubi*. The passing of time is *musubi*. It's all the same. *Musubi* is *kamisama*, the gods and their power. The *kumihimo* ropes that we make

---

2   The 'discover Japan' campaign is explored in detail in Marilyn Ivy's (1995) *Discourse of the Vanishing*, which is discussed in more detail in the next section.

are also the work of *kamisama* and represents the flow of time itself. Gathering together to form shapes, twisting and tangling, sometimes going back, getting cut off and then linking up again. That is *kumihimo*. That is time. That is *musubi*.

With this awareness that time is not necessarily linear, Taki later succeeds in going back in time by drinking Mitsuha's sake and saves Mitsuha and the town from the disaster, despite the various challenges posed by the extremely fragmented nature of his memory of his time in Itomori.

Although it is tempting to view this as a simplistic tale of human bonds that are facilitated by the *kamisama*, overcoming differences and even disasters, it is important to remember that the final encounter between Mitsuha and Taki occurs as a result of a series of miraculous events, as well as strong romantic sentiments. While presenting a strong message of hope for these two main characters in the film, Shinkai does not clearly show how this translates to hope in real-life, post-disaster Japan. In particular, the bonds, or *musubi*, become much less important once the objective of the two characters has been achieved. In short, the ancient *musubi* traditions of the fictional town of Itomori, from the dances to the rope-making and the sake-making, which are so carefully passed down from generation to generation, function solely as a device for saving Mitsuha and thus lose much of their meaning once disaster has been averted by a successful evacuation of the town's residents.

The ending of the film takes place in Tokyo and indicates that all the main characters from Itomori end up moving to Tokyo after narrowly escaping the disaster, despite the fact that there are many bigger towns and cities around Gifu Prefecture, such as the city of Gifu, Nagoya or Kyoto. In this strangely Tokyo-centric ending, the film shows that Mitsuha and her friends, Tessie and Sayaka, have survived the disaster, but no information is given regarding what remains of Itomori or how its cultural traditions are being preserved. If anything, the disaster is presented as a liberating force that allowed these characters to escape the small town and its customs. For example, it is revealed in *Kimi no na wa: Another Side Earthbound* (2016), which is a prequel to the film written by Shinkai's collaborator, Kanoh Arata, that Tessie wanted to move out of Itomori after high school, but thought that he would be unable to do so due to his personal circumstances—his father owned a local building business that he was expected to inherit. Blood links are still considered to be of utmost importance when it comes to inheriting family businesses in the community and it would cause confusion and inconvenience to the company's employees if he does not stay to continue on the business. Tessie describes these customs as the *shigarami* (a term that expresses these human ties in a negative way, unlike *musubi*) that keeps him tied to the small town. The disaster cuts these chains that bound him and is implicitly presented as a positive event that allowed these young characters to develop their potential in the nation's capital, away from restrictive small-town customs.

Overall, while Shinkai presents a kind of rural Other in the traditions of the fictional town of Itomori, the film also contributes to the 'homogenous Japan' myth in that this is presented as an anomalous case that needs to be corrected by means of integration into mainstream Japanese culture. Shinkai ultimately presents a future Japan in which heterogeneity has been erased and happiness is found in the homogeneity of urbanised Japan. In Shinkai's fictional universe, rural heterogeneity only remains as a source of nostalgia for 'old Japan', which is consumed for entertainment but is no longer part of contemporary Japanese identity.

L'océan dans la rizière [The ocean in the rice paddy] by Richard Collasse (2012a), author and CEO of the Japanese subsidiary of the French brand Chanel, is also a story of a young man from Tokyo who saves a youth from the disaster-hit areas, although Collasse manages to portray the countryside around Fukushima in a much more positive light than Shinkai does. *L'océan*, which has been translated into Japanese as *Nami: Sōsuke, 17sai no ano hi kara no monogatari* [The wave: the story of Sosuke since that day when he was 17] (2012), tells the story of Sakai Sosuke, a 17-year-old boy who lives in a traditional household in a fishing village, until the tsunami comes and takes away almost all his known family members and loved ones, friends and belongings. Although the story's main characters are fictional, more than a few scenes and peripheral anecdotes are based on true testimonies given by survivors of the disaster. For example, Sosuke and his friends are part of a student jazz band in Kesennuma, the 'Swinging Dolphins', which exists in real life (although it is called the 'Swing Dolphins') and his sister's character is based on the young woman who was employed by the council of Minamisanriku and was tragically swept away while issuing an evacuation warning on the radio.

Through his experience of working as a volunteer in the region, giving makeovers and massages to female disaster victims in temporary housing and shelters, Collasse felt that Japan had split into two: those who are going on with their everyday lives in Tokyo and those who are still in a difficult living situation in the disaster-hit areas (2012b). Further, Collasse expressed his discomfort with the issue of municipalities across Japan rejecting the plea to incinerate and bury debris from the disaster-hit areas (as it was perceived to be radioactive, even when it was scientifically proven to not be), observing that 'it's sad that a foreigner like me has to point out that the Japanese are no longer helping each other' (2012b).

To portray this gap between the disaster-hit areas and the rest of Japan, Collasse also split his novel into two, between the story of Sosuke and his traditional background and his 23-year-old uncle Eita, an *otaku*, *freeter* and semi-*hikikomori*[3] from Tokyo, who spends most of his days locked up in a room in his parents' house. Eita, who arrives in Kesennuma with his Ray Ban sunglasses and Harley Davidson bike, is the epitome of the materialistic and spoiled Tokyo youth. However, Eita is also Collasse, or the French reader in general, who is reading about the experiences of the victims in their comfortable armchairs. Collasse confesses, 'In a way Eita represents me. Seeing the devastation in Tohoku made me realize how blessed a life I was living' (Kunisue and Hirata, 2013, n.p.). In many ways, this division also plays on the stereotype of Japan as the country where old Japanese traditions coexist with new Western influences: Collasse demonstrates that while this stereotype is true to some extent, these two sides of Japan are so separated geographically and culturally that it can produce a culture shock between them when they meet.

Although there is an initial culture shock when Eita and Sosuke meet, with Sosuke maintaining a strong demarcation between 'you' (the people from outside of the disaster-hit areas) and 'us' (people strongly affected by the disaster), the two young men eventually become as close as real brothers and work together towards reconstruction, in what is perhaps Collasse's expression of hope for the young generation. Unlike Taki, Eita is not a hero who came to save Tōhoku. His motivation is much more banal—curiosity, as well as the fact that he was ordered by his father to go. Unlike *Kimi no na wa*, in which all characters end up in the capital, in *L'océan dans la rizière*, Eita discovers his *raison d'être* in Kesennuma

---

3 The term *freeter* refers to Japanese youths who are not in full-time employment. *Hikikomori* refers to Japanese youths who cut themselves off entirely from society.

and decides not to return to Tokyo. Tōhoku is a location of healing, both for Eita and Sosuke. Eita remarks that it was 'not the ideal solution' to catapult Sosuke into the urban jungle of Tokyo so he can build a new life, as his father had intended (p. 283). For Eita as well, who was 'sinking deeper and deeper into a bottomless pit' (p. 329) in his life as a *hikikomori* in Tokyo, Kesennuma represents a land of new opportunity, where he will take up his new responsibility as young Sosuke's caregiver and 'reconstruct himself' (p. 319). In contrast to the exoticised portrayal of rural Japan in *Kimi no na wa*, Collasse portrays a more reciprocal relationship between the capital and Tōhoku, in which Tokyo is helped by Tōhoku just as much as it helps Tōhoku.

Towards a Tōhoku Identity: Gretel Ehrlich's *Facing the Wave*

Based on Gretel Ehrlich's (2013a) journeys to the Fukushima, Miyagi and Iwate prefectures, *Facing the Wave: A Journey in the Wake of the Tsunami* takes these regional differences one step further, towards a future vision of a strong and unique Tōhoku identity. To explain this, it is necessary to establish the history of how the region has been constructed in the Japanese popular imagination. The history of the Tōhoku region is marked by struggles with Japan's central government. After a string of defeats in various civil wars, Tōhoku was eventually forced into replacing their successful mix of hunting, gathering and farming with rice farming (for which the land was not suited). This provided the capital with food and kept the region dependent on the resulting income, which caused extended periods of famine in times of cold weather. In the early twentieth century, Tōhoku-born scholar Yanagita Kunio attempted to bring a positive image to his homeland, which had become associated with poverty and backwardness. As a producer of rice, Tōhoku was reconstructed as the core of Japan's homogenous rice-eating culture, where Japan's *genfūkei* or old Japan could be found (the term *genfūkei* usually refers to scenes from childhood memories, but is also often used in this meaning of 'scenery that evokes collective nostalgia', regardless of whether you actually spent your childhood there). This can be observed in Yanagita's (1940) *Yukiguni no haru* [Spring in snow country], in which he refers to Japan as *mizuho no kuni* (a country abundant with rice). Tōhoku was symbolically pushed towards the centre and away from its Other roots (which includes Ainu influences) by Yanagita and his ideas remain influential in Tōhoku's image construction. One can observe the continued influence of Yanagita's scholarship in the work of Umehara Takeshi (1994), who also argued in his *Nihon no shinsō—Jōmon/Ezo bunka wo saguru* [The depths of Japan: exploring the Jōmon Ezo culture] that pre-industrial Tōhoku culture was at the heart of Japanese identity, although he focused on the prehistoric *Jōmon* (cord-marked, referring to the pottery style characteristic of the period) culture that was developed in the region, instead of rice farming.

However, Tōhoku is still not completely free from Othering representations vis-à-vis central Japan. For example, Marilyn Ivy (1995) analysed the twenty-first-century exoticisation and commercialisation of certain Tōhoku destinations such as Tōno and Osorezan, which were marketed as being so different from the rest of Japan that the average Japanese must discover them as tourists, as in the 'Discover Japan' campaign of the Japanese National Railways. Today, Tōhoku occupies a complex position in the Japanese consciousness, in which Yanagita's legacy as well as the Nihonjinron myth of the Japanese *tan'itsu minzoku* (homogenous people) coexists with this Othering, exoticising force.

The question of Tōhoku's place in Japan has been brought to the fore following the Fukushima disasters, which highlighted the fact that the capital lives on power supplied by its surrounding regional areas. Akasaka Norio (2014), a member of the government's Reconstruction Design Council in Response to the Great East Japan Earthquake, controversially declared on *Asahi Shimbun* that Tōhoku remains Japan's internal colony. Akasaka's (2014) argument was that the underlying power structure between the region and the central government has not changed. The Tōhoku region now supplies nuclear power, machinery parts (produced by low-waged labour) and rice to central Japan, instead of the 'soldiers, prostitutes and rice' of the pre-WWII period.

Ehrlich's work is important because it addresses both this ingrained image of Tōhoku as an exotic Other, as well as its more recent assimilation into the hegemony, through portrayals of various residents in the disaster-hit areas and their journey of recovery following the tsunami. Ehrlich constructs a unique and positive image of Tōhoku culture, complicating the one-dimensional negative image of an irradiated zone now universally evoked by the toponyms of 'Fukushima' and 'Tōhoku', or 'Northern Japan'. Ehrlich's Tōhoku differs to the rest of Japan in their resilient fishermen, a unique and respectful relationship with the dead and a culture of coexisting with different groups.

Facing the Wave portrays a distinct difference in culture between the fishermen and the rice farmers of the areas Ehrlich visits. Fishermen are demonstrated to be full of survival know-how, courageously riding out to the sea towards the tsunami to save their expensive boats. Fishermen are also shown to be working independently to restore their lifestyles as soon as possible, such as the man in North Miyako Bay who survived to tell his tale: 'There was a big hole in the hull. Now I've fixed it. The government is busy. There's no use waiting for them' (p. 79). By December 2011, fisherman Hirayama and his son were selling their catches of saury and had 'already rebuilt their tool and storage shed and [were] making buoys for clam season' (p. 178) in the lively Miyako harbour. The presence of these strong fishermen in the book, who identified themselves as 'men of the sea', living 'according to our instincts and needs' (p. 80), directly challenges the myth of a rice-based Tōhoku, constructing it as a place that is Other to central Japan. The areas that Ehrlich visits are also shown to have a rich cultural heritage based on fishing, such as the *hamauta* of the last geisha of Kamaishi, a song that 'always brought fish into the nets' (p. 82). Residents of the small outer island Ehrlich visits in Matsushima Bay, where the main industry is fishing, are portrayed to be carrying on with their festivals and celebrations despite the disaster damage.

Conversely, Tōhoku farmers, who depend on their land, are shown to be more vulnerable and dependent on government support. For example, Kazuyoshi, who is the uncle of Masumi, a woman Ehrlich stays with, loses everything and is forced to take up a short-term government job involving debris cleaning. Masumi's great uncle Satoru also has difficulty recovering due to his attachment to the land—his happiness depends on whether the government will let him rebuild the house that he grew up in, where his family grew their own rice, vegetables and flowers. Satoru attempts to plant a vegetable patch at his temporary home while he waits for permission, but this is also destroyed shortly by a typhoon and his 'hope darkens, as if hope itself was tenebrific, the cause of night' (p. 166). Although we are told in the epilogue that Satoru was able to rebuild his house and start living there, no one in the book returns to rice farming within the timeframe of the book. As Kazuyoshi explains, 'all our machines and everything was covered in four feet of mud' and 'no matter how deeply we dug in the old rice field, we still found debris' (p. 151).

This contrast is particularly interesting in light of the aforementioned debate surrounding Tōhoku as being the rice capital of Japan. Akasaka (2009), who believes that Tōhoku derives much of its culture from the times before rice-growing was forcefully instituted in the region, has torn Yanagita's thesis apart even further following the disaster (2014) by claiming that it is better to not replant rice in the rice-farming communities that were inundated by the tsunami. According to his research, these rice fields were located on land that was reclaimed from the sea in a process called '*kasaage*' in the Edo period, when the population was rapidly growing and are naturally at high risk of tsunami damage. Now that Tōhoku's population is ageing and shrinking, it does not make sense for these saltwater-inundated areas to continue producing rice, in Akasaka's view. Although Ehrlich does not go as far as to object to the idea of rice farmers going back to their pre-disaster lifestyles, her work does contest the notion of Tōhoku people being not much more than rice producers for the capital and hints that rice farming may become less important in the region's future.

Another way in which Ehrlich explores the unique traditions of Tōhoku is through her portrayal of how the living relate to the dead—a specialty of Yanagita's, as demonstrated by his *Tōno monogatari* [Legends of Tono], an anthology of folk legends from Tōno, in Iwate Prefecture. Ehrlich explains that the dead 'continue to be a "living" presence in the household' even after death: 'They are demigods, guarding the house and instructing young and old in matters of moral rectitude' (p. 141). There are also many ways of interacting with the dead in Tōhoku. Even the Western-educated Masumi pays Jin the 'apprentice shaman' to take a ghost off her and follows with enthusiasm the latest earthquake predictions of an Iwate blogger whom she calls a *kamisama* and *uranaishi* (fortune-teller). The Tōhoku region is also known for their *itako*, who are 'blind mediums who communicate with the dead' (p. 121), whom Ehrlich spent many weeks talking to when she was in Japan 23 years earlier.

These kinds of superstitious beliefs are still widespread in the Tōhoku region. As Marie Mutsuki Mockett (2015, p. 27) remarked in her post-3.11 memoir:

> It may seem odd to a Westerner to learn that Tōhoku is awash with ghosts; we associate ghosts with superstition and Japan has the image of being a highly modernized country. But the soul of Japan is still very much connected to her twelve-hundred-year-old history and within that belief system, ghosts are a powerful and meaningful presence.

Ghost sightings were the subject of a 2013 *NHK Special* program entitled *Naki hito tono 'saikai'* ['Encounters' with those who passed], which was a rare involvement for a TV channel known for its objective and factual reporting.[4] Ehrlich's serious treatment of ghosts echoes this recent acceptance of the supernatural as a form of healing in mainstream Japanese media, but also presents this omnipresence of the dead as being an important part of Tōhoku's culture. Ehrlich (2013a, p. 46) remains open-minded and respectful throughout her journey towards this idea of the dead coexisting with the living, asking herself whether the dead are 'also alive' if 'the cosmos is constantly splitting into a multiverse in which quantum objects are broken and unbroken at the same time'.[5] When walking through the former site of Kannonji, 'the temple behind Ookawa Elementary School that was washed away', she comments that 'no boundaries exist' in this space (between the dead and the alive) and attempts to imagine herself interacting with the ghosts there, giving them 'a pair of legs to walk on' (p. 137). Ehrlich seems to be following in the footsteps of Lafcadio Hearn, whose work she mentions in her bibliography:[6] while not being a complete believer of these ghosts, Hearn (1897) admits in his *Living God* (which, coincidentally, introduced the term *tsunami* to the West) that he finds himself 'for a moment forced into the attitude of respect towards possibilities' (p. 4).

Ehrlich portrays this coexistence between the living and the dead in a positive light and questions the negative, fearful relationship that some Tōhoku residents have with their ghosts. Ehrlich explains that 'even after Buddhism merged with Shinto, old Shinto beliefs', according to which 'death is an unseemly corruption; ghosts are ubiquitous and to be feared … prevail in Tohoku to this day' (p. 16). Masumi's mother, Kazuko, packs garlic and salt in her lunches and places salt on her garden shrine 'to scare the bad spirits away' (p. 12). When Ehrlich visits the 'river where the dead were pulled by grieving relatives out of the mud' in Ishinomaki, Masumi becomes scared after feeling a ghost on her back, throwing salt in the air

---

4   See Parry (2014) for detailed summary of ghost sightings in post-3.11 Tōhoku, and Kudō (2016) for the reporting of 'ghost customers' by taxi drivers in Ishinomaki.
5   This sentence is particularly interesting because ideas from quantum physics are also explored by Ruth Ozeki, another North America–based writer whose post-3.11 work is analysed in Chapter 5.
6   Lafcadio Hearn, aka Koizumi Yakumo, spent his later life in Japan and wrote extensively on the spiritual traditions in the country. One of the very few sources of information on Japan in the Western world at the time of publication, in the late nineteenth century his writings were greatly influential in the creation of Japanese hetero-images. Following their translation into Japanese, these texts became an important source of self-images for the Japanese.

to scare it away (p. 136). Ehrlich asks: 'Do ghosts need to be scary? … Shouldn't we, instead, try to make them feel at home?' (p. 138). Ehrlich points out the strangeness of the fact that certain ghosts are revered as demigods, whereas others are feared as a form of corruption (*kegare*).[7] However, whether they are liked or disliked, Ehrlich demonstrates that such spiritual beliefs are a part of what makes Tōhoku culture unique.

If Ehrlich's Tōhoku is a place where (at least some of) the dead and the living come together, it is also a place where the living live in collective harmony. As Ehrlich explains.

> Japanese ideas about religion, architecture, theater and literature are based on *wa* and *shunyata*—concepts of plenitude and uncertainty, of togetherness framed by impermanence (p. 12).

This concept of *wa* (togetherness) is like the concept of *kizuna* (see Chapter 1). Although it could be said that *wa* refers to collective harmony, whereas *kizuna* refers to individual bonds, they are both used in very much the same way in discourses on Japan. In Nihonjinron discourse, *wa no kokoro* (spirit of wa), which comes from Confucianism, is often described as being the foundation of the Japanese spirit.[8] The basis for this argument is usually Shōtoku Taishi's 17-article constitution, which sets it out as an ideal. Ehrlich (2013b) describes it as the Shintō idea of 'together living', but it is a concept also influenced by Buddhism and Confucianism, like Shintō itself. This can be observed in the kind of altruistic sharing behaviour mentioned by Ehrlich, such as the young woman who continues her routine gift of farm vegetables after the tsunami, 'apologiz[ing] that she had only one orange to give' (2013a, p. 45) and the fisherman who 'trolled up a bag with 10 million yen inside' and donated it to aid relief (p. 182).[9]

Although Ehrlich repeats the age-old stereotype of Japanese collective harmony portrayed in both the domestic and international media, she shows that the disaster also had the effect of forming unexpected *wa* in Tōhoku. Ehrlich observes that, traditionally, 'to be a hippie in northern Honshu means taking a political stand' (p. 63) and that any deviation from the hegemony is seen to be undesirable for the collective *wa*. Wakao-san,

---

7   This kind of shunning inevitably brings to mind the other fear of unknown 'corruption' in post-3.11 Tōhoku: the prejudice against the 'new *hibakusha*', as Ehrlich calls them (p. 202).
8   An English-language example of this is Robert Whiting's *You Gotta Have Wa* (1990, p. 113).
9   Ehrlich balances this with mentions of looting (pp. 17, 78) and of 'people who are trying to get more than they deserve from the government' (p. 151).

an oceans campaigner for Greenpeace, feels the need to confirm that 'I'm Japanese. Maybe not as much, but yes' (p. 69), showing that activists are indeed on the fringe of the definition of what it is to be Japanese. However, the disaster had the effect of bringing these people together in Tōhoku. For example, members of the Sea Shepherd Conservation Society, who were opposing the capture and killing of Dall's porpoises in the town of Ōtsuchi, turned into volunteers following the tsunami. Ehrlich also observes that 'many of the local fishermen in the Fukushima area now welcome the Greenpeace campaigners—the very people they've been fighting in southern whaling waters' (p. 68). In short, 'the March disaster changed protocol and erased territorial boundaries' (p. 186). This brings the Japanese closer to the true meaning of Shōtoku Taishi's ideal of *wa wo motte tōtoshi to nasu*, which is often interpreted as 'harmony at all cost (by supressing differences, if necessary)', but was originally intended to mean 'harmony despite differences'. In this sense, Ehrlich's Tōhoku *wa* is a broader concept than *kizuna*, which is unlikely to form between people who disagree, but *wa* can refer to a coexistence despite differences in opinion. Ehrlich hints at a continuation of this trend as she documents that a geisha from Tokyo learned the *hamauta* from the 84-year-old Miyagi geisha Ito-san, which was a rare occurrence because geisha acts are 'never passed from one region to another, much less from one province to another' (p. 187). Ito-san, who in many ways represents the longstanding tradition, appears excited about the fact that she saw Caucasian and male geishas in Tokyo, where she went to perform her song. It is suggested that the tsunami will continue to be a catalyst for this acceptance of minority views and lifestyles to spread from Tōhoku to the rest of Japan.

Ehrlich also reveals that the concept of *wa* is no longer synonymous with unquestioning passivity and obedience in Tōhoku, especially when faced with inept authorities. Great uncle Satoru represents this attitude with his words: 'We Japanese tend to be too polite, so the government doesn't do anything … We have to change how the country is ruled' (p. 147). Ehrlich observes how the post-3.11 behaviour of the authorities has had an impact on the Tōhoku people's trust in the government: 'When the government tests, they wave a dosimeter over the top of the fish as they come off the boats, but that doesn't work' (p. 69), reports one fisherman; whereas Jin the shaman observes that the authorities do not hesitate to cover-up the extent of radiation damage because the effects will only be felt when they are long gone. In some cases, the Tōhoku people even wilfully disobeyed the authorities, ignoring the order of the police to leave bodies as they found them (p. 58). Further, this kind of resistance is shown to have influenced the authorities in turn. For example, in the cordoned-off areas, the police had sympathy for the abandoned animals and encouraged the animal rescuers who were there 'illegally' (p. 90). Perhaps most importantly, plant manager of Fukushima Daiichi Masao Yoshida began pumping seawater into the reactor core, against the wishes of the TEPCO officials, in an attempt to cool it down (p. 26). Ehrlich thus portrays Tōhoku as the centre of civic engagement and change, which is driven by the disaster. Despite the stereotype of *gaman* (persevering in the face of adversity, often by putting others before yourself), Ehrlich demonstrates that the Tōhoku people are not the meek and obedient rice farmers that they are portrayed to be today. Her portrayal evokes their warring Emishi ancestors from pre–rice growing times, who refused to be subjugated by the central government for many centuries.

The strength and uniqueness of Ehrlich's work lies in her literary and symbolic reconstruction of Tōhoku as a place, as well as the objective evaluation of traditions allowed by her status as a semi-outsider. Ehrlich's portrayal of post-3.11 Japan is not radically different from the media portrayals of a Japan that is calmly and collectively responding to the disaster, but she situates these characteristics carefully in a Tōhoku context, which, surprisingly, was not a common feature of Japanese-language cultural responses—mainly written by mainstream authors based in Tokyo, many of whom had not even visited the areas affected by the tsunami. Further, Ehrlich paints post-3.11 Tōhoku as a fertile ground for new ideas and collaborations, which also retains the positive aspects of traditional culture. Ehrlich's work, filled with personal stories from the disaster-hit areas, is a powerful antidote for the one-dimensional association of Tōhoku with nuclear disaster in the English-language media.

The traditional lifestyles of the Sanriku fishermen and farmers that were brought to the fore in the aftermath of the earthquake sparked an interest from both Japanese city dwellers and non-Japanese alike in various areas of rural Japan, where 'the core of Japanese identity' is thought to be found. The future visions for rural Japan that I have explored in this chapter ranged from portraying rural Japan as the exoticised Other that must eventually be assimilated into a modern and Westernised Japan, to an attempt to explore the idea of a distinct Tōhoku identity. The two non-Japanese authors (Collasse and Ehrlich) presented a more nuanced and positive view of the region's future as a place of healing and resilience, whereas the Japanese response (*Kimi no na wa*) was to paint its assimilation into Tokyo culture.

5
(STILL) COOL JAPAN

In a desperate attempt to cool down the overheated fuel rods at Fukushima, the Self-Defense Forces (SDF) sent in helicopters to dump seawater down on the power plants from 17 March 2011. The image of tiny-looking jets of water mercilessly getting dispersed in the wind before hitting the buildings elicited despair and even laughter from many Japanese. Yoshida Masao, who was the Fukushima Daiichi plant manager at the time, later described this act as 'meaningless' and 'ineffective', likening the image to 'a cicada peeing'. This failed attempt was followed up by another more successful attempt, in which concrete pumping trucks—nicknamed *kirin* [giraffes] for their long 'necks', which can measure up to 60 metres—were brought in from China and the rest of Japan to pour water directly onto the plant. It seemed as though the image of Japan as a land of technology and 'cool' was crumbling further as these decidedly 'uncool' and low-tech solutions were broadcast around the world.

Japan has long been in possession of its own brand of soft power, which has been especially noticeable following WWII, when Japanese mass entertainment and technology started to be consumed all over the world (spearheaded by *Godzilla* in the 1950s). However, it was only in 2002 that Douglas McGray coined the term 'Gross National Cool' to explain Japan's soft power and the economic value of Japan's cultural exports was recognised by the government. Ironically, the subsequent government recognition and institutionalisation of Japan's cool as the 'Cool Japan Strategy' by the Ministry of Economy, Trade and Industries, only served to make the country less cool. There are also issues of appropriation. For example, with Japanese *manga* and technology having started off as imports from the West (or, at least, heavily influenced by the West), there has always been a certain unease surrounding the promotion of these cultural products as being quintessentially Japanese. Further, Japan is also viewed to be in a technological identity crisis, in which it is unable to effectively market its consumer brands overseas, especially in comparison to its neighbour South Korea, who has had enormous success with both its cultural and technological exports in recent years (e.g. Samsung and K-POP).

Perhaps this context explains the massive box office success of the 2016 film *Shin Godzilla,* which portrays Japan as a country that has 'still got it' and gives hope to a Japanese audience feeling disillusioned by its own government, industries and people. The images contained in these works point to a Japan that is, although no longer number one in the economic sense of the 1970s and 1980s, very much still number one in culture and attitude. Conversely, Ruth Ozeki introduces a more philosophical perspective on what could be cool in post-disaster Japan, which is explored in the second half of this chapter.

Shin Godzilla's Vision for a 'Cool Japan'

Hardcore Godzilla fans awaited the July 2016 release of *Shin Gojira* [*Shin Godzilla*, aka Godzilla Resurgence] with a healthy dose of scepticism. Not much was revealed about the film prior to its release, apart from the fact that it would be a live-action film co-directed by Anno Hideaki, the anime director of *Evangelion* fame (*Evangelion* is a cult anime series of the 1990s) and that it would feature many well-known mainstream actors, including Hasegawa Hiroki, Takenouchi Yutaka and Ishihara Satomi. Although it was expected that *otaku* with an interest in *Evangelion* would go and watch the movie, it was not a hotly anticipated mainstream release. However, as viewers started to emerge from half-empty movie theatres to rave about the film on social media, its popularity exploded to become an 8.2-billion-yen box office success by the end of the year. Part of the reason behind the film's commercial success was that it was designed to be viewed multiple times. The numerous hints and intertextual references that bombarded the audience at super speed made it possible for viewers to discover something new during each viewing. Further, the film could be read as a kind of feel-good movie that represents an alternative reality and future in which the 3.11 disaster is overcome by the collaborative effort of the Japanese. In portraying this feel-good alternative to the 3.11 disaster, it also managed to elevate certain aspects of Japanese culture to cool status and stroke the audience's nationalistic pride.

In many ways, *Shin Godzilla* can be thought of as a return to the 'roots' of the Godzilla series—the original Japanese *Godzilla* of 1954. The main plot of the film is just like for any other Japanese Godzilla film: a giant monster referred to as 'Godzilla' comes to Japan and causes havoc. The twist that is given to the 2016 version is that the only way to destroy the monster seems to be to drop an atomic bomb on Tokyo, which is a scenario that is narrowly averted by the quick thinking of the Japanese team headed by Deputy Chief Cabinet Secretary Yaguchi Randō (played by Hasegawa). There have been many Godzilla films made in Japan over the past 65 years, but the most important point of comparison for *Shin Godzilla* is the original *Godzilla* of 1954 because they both encourage the audience to reflect on real-life nuclear disasters that directly impacted Japan. These two films are also different in nature to most of the Japanese Godzilla films that came in between, which feature other giant monsters that Godzilla fights against and are aimed at a younger audience.

The original *Gojira* [*Godzilla*] (1954) was inspired by the *Daigo Fukuryūmaru* (Lucky Dragon No. 5) incident in March of the same year, in which a group of Japanese tuna fishermen became exposed to nuclear fallout from the US hydrogen bomb testing at Bikini Atoll (the so-called 'Operation Castle'). This incident was met with outrage in Japan, where the memory of Hiroshima and Nagasaki was still fresh. The directors of the film, Honda Ishirō and Tsuburaya Eiji, made a film about a prehistoric creature that gets chased out of its habitat by nuclear bomb testing and goes on a rampage in Tokyo—Godzilla was born. With regards to this first Godzilla, Susan Napier (2006) says the following:

> Many scholars, me included, believe that the initial Godzilla—with his links to nuclear testing and radiation—may in many ways be seen as a displaced version of the atomic bomb. His story and its ultimately happy outcome—Godzilla is vanquished through Japanese science—may, therefore, be read as a form of cultural therapy, allowing the defeated Japanese to work through the trauma of the wartime bombings in the scenes of panic or destruction and, with the film's happy end, giving them a chance to reimagine and rewrite their devastating defeat (p. 10).

While the US nuclear testing was a direct catalyst for the creation of the film, the atomic bomb was equally important as a source of inspiration for the monster.

Just like the first *Godzilla* was a form of cultural therapy that responded to the horrors of the atomic bombings, it is possible to read *Shin Godzilla* as a manifestation of the desire of the Japanese to overcome the 3.11 nuclear disaster. Featuring a monster that is inspired by that of the original film in design, the 2016 version clearly pays homage to this cultural therapy heritage. Set in late 2016, *Shin Godzilla* strongly references the triple disaster by replicating its four stages in the four Godzilla appearances in Tokyo: the earthquake, the tsunami, the helicopters pouring water on the Fukushima Daiichi power plant and then, finally, the 'giraffe' concrete pump vehicles coming to the rescue. The very first glimpse the audience gets of the 2016 Godzilla is its tail as it emerges from the sea—its long body resembling that of a catfish, which in Japanese folk mythology is said to be a divine messenger that brings about earthquakes. We soon find out that the monster in this film has the ability to rapidly metamorphose in response to various environmental and biological conditions, as the monster grows limbs and manages to walk along the Nomi River in Kamata, Tokyo, causing flooding and forcing residents to be chased by a wave of water in a manner reminiscent of the tsunami. By its third appearance in Tokyo, Godzilla can stand on its two feet, albeit gingerly and appears unfazed by the attacks of the helicopters of the SDF and the US strategic bombers (this SDF attack was highly reminiscent of the 'cicada pee' watering of 2011 in its ineffectiveness and visual composition). Further, by this point we find out that the monster is fuelled by nuclear power and leaves radioactive material and chaos in its wake, much like an angry, walking version of the Fukushima Daiichi power plant. The scenes of people taking pictures and videos of Godzilla on their mobile devices, sharing radiation measurements on social media networks such as Twitter and gathering in evacuation shelters after being instructed to leave the city also evoke the 3.11 disaster, except this time the consequences are borne by the capital instead of north-eastern Japan. As if all this was not enough, Anno's intention to reference the triple disaster is made crystal clear in the way that Godzilla is described as *sōteigai* (beyond expectation) multiple times by one of the ministers (TEPCO used the same term to describe the tsunami height in 2011). In the finale, the monster becomes frozen in the middle of Tokyo thanks to the concrete pump vehicles, much like the unresolved situation in Fukushima.

Ultimately, Godzilla is a beast of a metaphor that represents different things to different people and this is part of its symbolic value. Some scholars have read Godzilla as a symbol of a larger power, such as a kind of divine *kami* figure, an allusion that is 'especially evident in the scenes that herald his arrival', marked by earthquakes and typhoons (Boss, 2006, p. 105). Katō Norihiro (Katō & Fujimura, 2016) believes that the monster serves as 'an empty vessel for the unconscious' for the Japanese, even capable of representing the Emperor (Godzilla's suffering embodying his suffering as a marginal figure). However, it would be fair to say that both the 1954 and 2016 Godzillas have their origins in nuclear disasters and that the 2016 Godzilla would not have been created were it not for the 2011 triple disasters.

However, what I would like to highlight in my analysis of the 2016 *Shin Godzilla* is not what exactly Godzilla itself could represent, but rather the interesting ways in which the film portrayed previously criticised Japanese culture and values as being cool that results in a form of cultural therapy for the horrors of the 2011 triple disasters. This may be one of the reasons why the film could not replicate the huge commercial success it had domestically in overseas markets. Although the total gross box office figure in Japan was US$75.4 million, the US figure was a modest US$1.9 million and negligible in other markets. For comparison purposes, the film *Your Name* of the same year (covered in Chapter 4) grossed US$235.3 million in Japan, US$5 million in the US and a staggering US$83.7 million and US$27.9 million in China and South Korea respectively (*Shin Godzilla* was never released in China on the big screen, but the South Korean number makes a stark comparison).[1] The three main aspects of 'Japan cool' in the film that appealed to the domestic audience (but not to foreign audiences) were Japanese technology, *otaku* and corporate values. Although there is some overlap between these three aspects, I analyse them each below.

'Cool' Technology

The Fukushima incidents were not the first time Japanese technology came under fire in recent years. Since the 2000s, Japanese technology companies have been criticised for being unable to respond to global needs. Japan has become known as a kind of Galapagos, which has evolved

---

1 Numbers for the two movies taken from *Box Office Mojo*: www.boxofficemojo.com/movies/?page=intl&id=shingodzilla.htm; www.boxofficemojo.com/movies/?page=intl&id=yourname.htm (30 October 2018).

in isolation from the rest of the world, producing products that are highly specialised to its local market, yet unwanted overseas. As contemporaries in neighbouring countries such as Samsung, Huawei and Oppo become more and more successful in the global market and de-throne previous Japanese market leaders such as Toshiba and NEC, there has been a growing sense that Japanese companies are no longer having the global impact that they used to.

One of the possible reasons why *Shin Godzilla* made post-3.11 Japanese (but not other) audiences feel good may be because there is a long-running theme of 'Japanese technology saving the world (especially from US technology)' in Japanese Godzilla films, which is perhaps not appreciated as much by non-Japanese viewers. In the original *Godzilla* (1954), American science is shown to have created the monster by conducting nuclear tests in Bikini Atoll and destroying Godzilla's seafloor habitat. Conversely, in the Hollywood *Godzilla* (2014) by Gareth Edwards, the US nuclear tests are shown to have been well-meaning attempts at killing the monster. Japanese science is portrayed to be of a much more responsible variety in the 1954 original. Serizawa decides to take the secret of his 'oxygen destroyer' weapon to his grave by using it to kill both himself and Godzilla to prevent the possibility of this new and destructive technology being used for war. As Anderson (2006) explained:

> At least one Japanese scientist thus proves himself to be more ethically engaged and concerned for others than the implicitly negligent US scientists who unleashed the A-bomb and the H-bomb upon humanity in general and Japan in particular (p. 25).

The 1954 film shows Japanese technology being used to undo the harmful consequences of US nuclear technology.

In *Shin Godzilla* (2016), Anno complicates the origins of the monster by characterising Godzilla as a prehistoric deep-sea creature that consumed some radioactive waste that was illegally dumped into the sea by various countries during the late 1940s and 1950s (including both Japan and the US). This can be read as reflecting the mixed origins of the Fukushima nuclear power plants, some of which were built by the General Electric Company and some of which were built by Toshiba or Hitachi. However, regardless of the origins of the monster, Japanese technology saves its motherland (and potentially the world) in the film. The UN Security Council plans to kill Godzilla by dropping a nuclear bomb on Tokyo (a move driven mainly by the US), but the Japanese Government manages to prevent this.[2] After hypothesising that the monster uses its own blood to cool down its system, the Japanese team manages to feed Godzilla a large amount of blood coagulant to make it perform a kind of reactor scram, causing it to literally freeze in its tracks. The solution is highly symbolic of Japanese technology—it is not new or flashy, but requires high precision and involves a lot of blood, sweat, tears and overtime. The scenes of the blood coagulant being poured into Godzilla's mouth is almost identical to the real-life scenes of the concrete pumping vehicles pouring water on the Fukushima nuclear power plants that aired on television; except in this case the solution single-handedly solves the problem and evokes nationalistic pride (instead of shame) in the Japanese audience.

By the second half of the film, it becomes clear that the battle of Japan v. Godzilla has turned into that of Japanese technology v. US technology. At first, the Japanese SDF deploy AH-64 Apache helicopters to first fire their autocannons, then their 30 mm chain gun rounds, then rockets to no avail. Tanks and self-propelled howitzers follow suit, but Godzilla remains completely unscathed and unfazed. Japanese officials can do nothing but watch in awe or grit their teeth when American forces drop Massive Ordnance Penetrator bombs on the creature from their B-2 stealth bombers, which at least has the effect of injuring Godzilla and angering it. This display of American might is necessary to make the eventual Japanese victory as awe-inspiring as possible.

From the beginning, the film repeatedly makes reference to the issues surrounding US–Japan relations, underscoring this tension. The US is portrayed as self-serving and untrustworthy. For example, when asked whether the US scientists have managed to make any progress on understanding Godzilla, Yaguchi comments that he has been told 'no', but 'that may not be the truth' and that 'it's better not to rely on them now'. Further, it is revealed by Kayoko Ann Patterson, a Japanese-American who is sent as a special envoy from the US president (and whose own internal conflict mirrors the tension between the two countries), that the US had been aware of the existence of Godzilla all along, prior to the incidents. The US remains completely self-interested from the start, dumping nuclear waste into the Pacific Ocean, then not bothering to tell Japan about the monster that is born in its midst and then deciding to drop a B83 nuclear

---

2   The idea of using nuclear weapons to combat Godzilla is not unique to the 2016 version. For example, the US and the Soviet Union attempt to use tactical nuclear weapons in Japan in the 1984 Godzilla film directed by Hashimoto Kōji, but they eventually give up on the idea.

bomb on Tokyo to prevent the 13 per cent chance of Godzilla landing on the West Coast of its country. It becomes clear at this point in the film that to let the US bomb Tokyo under these circumstances would signify for Japan a complete acceptance of this relationship of subjugation and exploitation.

This is the tension at play during the climax of the film, when the countdown towards the nuclear bomb detonation begins and the Japanese team rush to prepare their alternative 'Yaguchi plan' before this happens. At this stage, the American scientists who had joined the team earlier are nowhere to be seen because they have clearly abandoned the mission (relying on the nuclear alternative) and it is up to the remaining Japanese scientists and politicians to gather enough blood coagulant, vehicles and manpower to conduct the Yaguchi plan. While the US attempts to blindly obliterate Godzilla by using a thermonuclear bomb, the Japanese team attempt to try and understand the monster and decipher the hints left by Maki Goro, a former Japanese scientist who was working on Godzilla by request from the US Department of Energy. The US forces treat Godzilla as a kind of vermin that must be eliminated, but the Japanese characters in the film repeatedly refer to its 'God-like', awe-inspiring nature by using terms such as *kami* (God, spirits) or *sen'nin* (a mountain-dwelling immortal sage, which also evokes oft-repeated debates on nuclear power as a kind of 'fire of Prometheus', a technology that is beyond the full understanding of humans). Directors Anno and Higuchi further underscore this divine portrayal by employing a motion capture of *Nō* artist Nomura Mansai's slow movements to give the monster a majestic presence on the screen.

The ability of the Japanese team to understand Godzilla as an unprecedented form of being, instead of just viewing it as an enemy to be bombed and attacked, is symbolised by university professor Hazama Kunio's solution to decode the map left by Maki Goro. The lines on what appeared to be a map of Godzilla's cellular processes represent folding lines and the map can only be read and understood when it is folded into its 3D *origami* shape (*origami* being a piece of Japanese culture that has cutting-edge scientific applications such as nanotechnology and space satellites). This breakthrough led the committee to discover that Godzilla's cells are able to break down any element that it encounters to power itself through nuclear fusion (meaning it can survive in air or water, without eating), but also that there is a type of extremophile bacteria that lives on these cells, which block this reaction to some extent. Through an extremely advanced understanding of biology, the Japanese team manage to produce both the blood coagulant and this extremophile bacteria to be fed to the monster at the same time, to prevent the blood coagulant being broken down by Godzilla's cells. The details of whether the science is sound or not is arguable, but the main message is clear—Japanese science is so sophisticated that scientists can fully understand a creature like Godzilla within a matter of days and even reproduce from scratch the bacteria that is present in its body.

Japan's ethical science eventually wins over the world and many countries agree to lend their supercomputing power to Japan, despite the risk of having their valuable research stolen, and even the US participates in the plan in the end, by contributing high-end drones (these are crucial for the execution of the plan, along with the *shinkansen* bullet trains and the commuter trains that transport many Tokyoites every day—the recognition of which adds another element of pride and enjoyment for the audience). The success of the plan represents a victory of Japan's cool technology over the brute force approach of the US. Japan decides to take the humane approach of coexisting with the frozen Godzilla and brings the world together in the process. As a final blow to the US plan, the very last shot of the film, showing winged human-like creatures frozen mid-evacuation from Godzilla's tail, points to the possibility that the US strategy would have been completely ineffective, aside from the fact that a nuclear bomb would have been detected by Godzilla's radar and shot down in the first place, the monster would have simply metamorphosed during this time into winged humanoids who would have flown away from its tail and wreaked havoc on earth. That is, only Japanese technology was capable of saving the day.

'Ota-cool'

What is interesting about this technology is that it is a bottom-up strategy, devised by the rag-tag ad-hoc committee that Yaguchi Randō gathered, made up of 'Kasumigaseki [an area of Tokyo where government offices are located] misfits who will never by promoted anyway: lone wolves, weirdos, otaku, trouble-makers, outcasts and academic heretics', among others. This creates an environment in which these unique individuals can voice their opinions and ideas freely, and it is this team that ultimately decode the information left by Maki Goro, find out essential information about Godzilla and come up with the plan for freezing it. What these oddballs lack in communication and social skills, they make up for in their highly specialised technical expertise, a characterisation that is often employed to describe the *otaku*. This is significant because the *otaku* were the initial supporters and the target audience of the film (as I mentioned earlier, Anno has a semi-divine reputation among this community as the creator of the *Evangelion* series).

Here I am not using the term *otaku* in a derogatory sense, but in a sense that is closer to *Ota-king*, from Okada Toshio's (2000) definition (Okada is an *otaku* scholar and a well-respected *otaku*): the *otaku* is *not* just 'those who like anime, manga and games', which leads to them being 'anti-social and gloomy people who stay at home all day' (p. 13), but instead positively defined as 'a new type of human, born in the twentieth century, who have an extremely evolved sensitivity to moving images' (p. 14). In Okada's definition (p. 14), *otaku* have 'an evolved sense of vision' developed from hours upon hours of watching different anime frame-by-frame to detect the slightest differences in style between different animation directors and also to gain a deeper understanding of how these directors create their works within their budget limitations. In short, *otaku* are a species of advanced viewers who seek satisfaction in their ability to analyse these subculture works deeper than the average viewer by understanding external factors such as budgets, industry trends and production processes, but also the highly technical aspects of content creation. Although this may result in the 'antisocial and gloomy' image from the rest of society, many *otaku* are very social when it comes to discussing and sharing their findings and quite happy in their belief that their refined eye allows them to enjoy content much more than other non-*otaku* viewers.

The Godzilla team members can also be considered to be *otaku* who have an extremely refined eye when it comes to their respective fields (e.g. molecular structures, computers, trains and weapons), but do not bother with other details of their lives, such as appearance or what others think about them. Most committee members speak like fast-forwarded, expressionless robots, except when they make an exciting discovery regarding Godzilla. It is clear that Anno knew some of his audience members will be of this *otaku* type because of his *Evangelion* past and that he was trying to appeal to this crowd. For example, the extreme amount of information displayed on the screen every second in a similar way to *Evangelion* (e.g. names of people with their titles, names of government committees and the type of bomb, aircraft or train that is being used to attack Godzilla) is clearly not designed to be fully read and comprehended by a casual one-time viewer, but rather for the *otaku*-type viewer to decode during the course of multiple viewings of the film.[3]

What Anno perhaps did not expect so much is that these *otaku* characters would be received so positively by the mainstream audience and not just his hardcore *otaku* fans. This was evidenced by the fact that some of the most popular characters in the film were Ogashira Hiromi and Yasuda Tatsuhiko, the two *otaku*s in the committee played by Ichikawa Mikako and Takahashi Issei, rather than those played by the headliner actors Takenouchi Yutaka and Ishihara Satomi. Ogashira Hiromi's popularity in particular was extraordinary, with numerous fans and professional *manga* artists alike submitting illustrations of the character on Twitter under the #Ogashira Hiromi hashtag.[4] In the film, Ogashira is a socially awkward young woman who wears no makeup and expressionlessly talks to people without looking into their eyes, much like Yasuda—hardly a recipe for a conventional film heroine (unlike the glamorous Kayoko Ann Patterson, played by Ishihara Satomi). It was the tiny hint of a smile she shows at the end, when she realises that the radiation damage left by Godzilla in Tokyo was not as bad as it had previously been believed, that resulted in a huge *gyappu moe* (a term that describes falling in love with anime or manga characters who display seemingly contradictory traits or gaps, such as a handsome and sophisticated-looking man who is very clumsy) sensation—so much so, that 24 different versions of this scene (shot from different angles) were included in the bonus footage of the Blu-ray edition of the film, along with numerous versions of a scene in which Yasuda screams and jumps up and down upon finding out that the monster is radioactive, in another rare display of emotion.

One factor that perhaps made these *otaku* characters more digestible for the mainstream audience was that they were not the so-called *kimo-ota* (disgusting *otaku*) who dress unfashionably and are unfit and ungroomed.

---

3   There are many other parallels drawn between the film and the *Evangelion* series: most noticeably the music, which was created by Sagisu Shirō for both films (one song, 'Decisive Battle', is used in exactly the same way before each battle), as well as the unresolved nature of the ending. Various lines and appellations similar to *Evangelion* are scattered throughout *Shin Godzilla*. For example, an important strategy in *Evangelion* is called *Yashima sakusen* (the Yashima strategy), while the final strategy in *Shin Godzilla* is *Yashiori sakusen* (the Yashiori strategy). *Yashima sakusen* also evokes the 3.11 disaster because some *Evangelion* fans were using the term to describe their efforts to save electricity, while nuclear power plants were closed down in Japan.
4   Some examples of this can be seen on *Togetter*, a Japanese Twitter aggregator website: togetter.com/li/1012670 (30 October 2018).

Even Yasuda, who is arguably the most *otaku* character in the film (being the only character who is explicitly referred to as one), with his twitchy face and unfitted suit, is portrayed as stylish in some ways, with his iPhone, MacBook Air and limited edition 18k gold Apple Watch, whereas all his bureaucrat colleagues type away on their grey Fujitsu and Panasonic laptops. In a memorable escape scene, Yasuda is seen calmly grabbing his MacBook—clearly his only important possession—and walking away while everyone else scrambles to gather their belongings. Likewise, although Yaguchi is a model train *otaku*, who displays his collection proudly in his office (and perhaps also had a hand in coming up with using trains as a weapon in the final battle against Godzilla), he is without doubt a cool character, who is not only extremely capable but also always dressed sharply—even when he 'hasn't showered for days', his shirt looks as white and crisp as ever, his hair without a trace of oil and his face cleanly shaven.

In the past, images of the *otaku* ranged from creepy and dangerous (as exemplified by the paedophile and necrophile '*otaku* murderer' Tsutomu Miyazaki) to unfashionable and socially awkward (as exemplified by the *densha otoko* [train man] whose successful love story became a social phenomenon around 2004/05). In contrast, the *otaku* qualities of the committee members portrayed in *Shin Godzilla* are portrayed and received as being cool, representing a 180-degree turn from these negative images. *Shin Godzilla* accurately reflects the heightened status of *otaku* in Japanese society today, in which *otaku* are now welcomed as valuable tourists and consumers by small Japanese towns and *otaku kei danshi* (*otaku*-type men) are even viewed as the most desirable type of men for marriage by some women, due to their perceived loyal nature.

'Shachi-cool'

This brings us to the third feel-good aspect of the movie, which is that the heroes are not superhuman beings, but rather average Japanese who work as bureaucrats, chemical engineers, plant workers, firefighters, SDF and administrative assistants who bring rice balls to committee members. The implication is that it is through the collective effort of all Japanese citizens that Godzilla, or the 3.11 disaster, would be overcome. There is no one 'hero' in this film—while leadership roles such as the prime minister are important, his task is limited to listening to advice and putting an administrative stamp of approval on their ideas (after asking 'where do I put the stamp?'). At each stage of the fight against Godzilla, the involvement of numerous different departments and people is emphasised, with the camera rapidly cutting between characters every few seconds for most of the film. In one scene in which the team are analysing the decoded results of Maki Goro's map, provided by super computers from all over the world, the results are displayed in the foreground with the committee members gathered round in the background, giving the audience the impression that they are inside the computer that they are looking at. The focus on the screen is rarely on one character, but rather on a group of characters, gathered around the meeting table or a computer.

These characters are not just great team members, they also work incredibly hard. It would not be far-fetched to describe these individuals as a kind of *shachiku* (corporate livestock), which is a term that has become popular in Japan in recent years to describe employees who become so enslaved to their bosses and exploitative companies (often called 'black' companies) that they lose their free will and mindlessly work long hours. In one scene, followed by an aerial shot of the protesters outside of the National Diet building, the staff inside are shown to be exhausted and falling asleep in the most impossible positions on their chairs or their desk as a man collects a large rubbish bag full of empty instant ramen bowls. Morning comes and the delivery of rice balls and tea creates an excuse for a brief break. During this break, Shimura, Yaguchi's right-hand man, reveals that some team members have not gone home or seen their families for many days, despite having permission to do so and are all working on what they can, without even being told what to do. What is perhaps more surprising to a Western audience is that this is talked of as a most noble act that 'really moves' Shimura and leads Yaguchi to conclude that 'this country is not half bad'. Being a good worker is clearly shown to be more important than being a good father, mother, husband or wife during a crisis situation.

As a Godzilla film, *Shin Godzilla* is unique in its complete lack of romance or familial and personal relationships. Of the committee members, only Mori, who acts as a vice-chairperson to Yaguchi, is shown to have family (a photo of his wife and baby is shown on his mobile phone background for a brief second during the aforementioned break) and no one, apart from him, attempts to contact their loved ones despite the emergency. The heroes are shown to be utterly devoted to their jobs to the point of absurdity (one would assume that in real life, there would be at least a few staff members who decide to flee or at least not want to volunteer to work 24/7 under these circumstances) and this is presented as an admirable trait that is necessary to overcome national crises such as a Godzilla attack (or, symbolically, the 3.11 triple disaster). These hardworking men defeat Godzilla by holding meetings, following necessary bureaucratic procedures, stamping documents, bowing to each other and working overtime, instead of going home and looking after their family, just like any good worker.

The film has the effect of making modern-day 'corporate livestock' audiences feel good about their jobs and their lifestyles, in what could be termed 'shachi-cool', in the same vein as 'ota-cool'. This is a clever strategy on Anno's part because many of the audience members who grew up watching the *Evangelion* series in their adolescent years and who became adults in the 'employment ice age' of 1993–2005 are now likely to be part of this unmarried, 'corporate livestock' group. This is in contrast to the age group of their parents and superiors, the so-called *dankai* (baby boomer) generation, for whom the economic situation was ideal throughout their different life stages. In the film, this generation is depicted from the viewpoint of the *shachiku* generation, as mostly inept and narrow-minded individuals, who are unable to adapt to change. At the beginning of the film, following the Aqualine underwater tunnel accident in Tokyo, the prime minister laughs off Yaguchi's idea that the accident may have been caused by a giant underwater creature. This is immediately followed by a shot of Godzilla's tail rising up from the sea, proving the prime minister and his cronies wrong. Many comic relief moments in the film are based around these older characters, such as the prime minister asking, 'What? I decide here? Now!? You didn't tell me about this in advance' when asked to give permission to deploy the SDF against Godzilla (showing that the prime minister does not usually make any real decisions), or the exchange of 'what!? it moves?' and 'of course, it's alive' by his ministers, upon receiving the report that Godzilla is moving towards the Tama River (demonstrating how slow these old men are at 'getting' new concepts). Conveniently, this older generation ends up being killed off in the third Godzilla attack on Tokyo because the helicopter that was carrying them to safety gets hit by the atomic laser beam emitted from the monster's mouth. The extent to which this made the audiences of the film feel good is shown by the loving nickname used by fans online to refer to this incident: *naikaku sōjishoku bī-mu* (Cabinet *en masse* resignation beam).[5]

---

5   Another important reason why Godzilla fans used this nickname instead of referring to the incident was that they were trying to prevent the spread of spoilers to encourage more people to go watch the film. However, the name clearly makes a joke out of the situation.

The film presents a convenient alternative reality to 3.11 for the long-suffering *Evangelion* generation, in which the *rōgai* (a derogatory term used to describe old people who are useless and cause others trouble, without realising it themselves), who usually boss them around and make them do unnecessary tasks, are killed off and the younger generation become the heroes who save Japan. In doing so, it also portrays the *shachiku* as a kind of cool figure—highly competent and hardworking who are simply unable to reach their full potential due to the older generation. This can be seen as a return to the positive concept of the *kigyō senshi* (corporate warriors) of the 1990s, except that the *shachiku* is a much more passive figure, preferring to work in groups rather than to stand out through individual achievements.

This kind of corporate *shachiku* mentality is even carried over to the SDF. For example, when a platoon leader is asked whether they will ask for volunteers to go and attack Godzilla from a helicopter, which is an unprecedented and dangerous mission as the target may behave in an unexpected (*sōteigai*) manner, he simply replies that they will follow their usual rotation because they have all been ready for the worst since they joined the SDF. While this is a tear-jerking moment for the audience, it is doubtful that most members of the SDF, which has never been dispatched to combat, have actually prepared themselves for the possibility of death in combat when they signed up (as evidenced by an earlier attack scene by the Tama River when a nervous Private First Class is heard saying, 'It's still hard to believe we will actually be fighting here'). In this way, this *shachiku* mentality is also highly nationalistic and current in the context of a Japan that is currently debating whether to expand the range of the SDF's activities by changing the Constitution. It may also be important to note here that the film had the full cooperation of the SDF, which the SDF famously only allows for films that portray the forces in a positive way.

The speech delivered to the SDF by Yaguchi further reinforces this romanticisation of self-sacrifice for one's own country:

> During the *yashiori* plan, you may be hit by radiation beams or suffer from acute radiation poisoning. I cannot guarantee that you will make it back alive. However, I am begging you to go! Our nation's power is gathered here today. The SDF is the last bastion of hope for defending this country. I am entrusting you with the future of our country. That is all.

It is possible to read all this as a kind of big 'black joke'—it is clear that the 'real Japan' is not like this at all, the older generation are still alive and will not be suddenly killed off by a single radiation beam, the *shachiku* are more likely to commit suicide or become depressed than to defeat monsters and Japanese technology has not been cool for many decades. Did Anno want the Japanese audience to reflect on how terrible they really are, instead of believing that they would be capable of overcoming such a national crisis? One could say that the old scientists in the film, who said there is nothing that can be said about Godzilla using the current level of science, are absolutely correct—no one can understand such a beast, let alone find a way to beat it in a matter of days. We could even say that the decidedly uncool idea of nuking Tokyo and sacrificing most of the country to save the world from the monster seems like a much more reliable solution, given the circumstances.

Katayama Morihide, a political scientist who also writes widely on music, suggests that one possible reading is to view the second half of the film as a fantasy, which is contrasted against the reality of the first half (Katayama & Yamanaka, 2016). That is, the world does indeed 'end' following Godzilla's rampage in Tokyo and what happens afterwards (the Yashiori plan and its success) is just an ideal scenario of 'what could have been' for the film and also for Fukushima. He points out that the music also underscores this. During the scenes of the catastrophe, the melancholic chorus of the classical-style music in the background evokes a Gregorian *Dies irae* melody, a symbol for the Last Judgement, often used for Requiem Mass. However, after this, from when Yaguchi's team rebuilds in the city of Tachikawa, 40 km west of central Tokyo, the music changes to a mix of upbeat and dramatic melodies from *Evangelion* and *Uchū daisensō* [*Battle in Outer Space*] (1959),⁶ which helps the audience to suspend disbelief when the young government suddenly starts to function and everything falls into place to defeat the monster.

Whether we read the ending as being realistic or not, I argue that it was Anno's intention that the film would be read in many different ways. In the film, Maki Goro leaves the following cryptic words with his notes, before disappearing: 'I did as I pleased. Do whatever you want'. The 2016 collection of essays by *Nikkei Business Online*, which contains the above

---

6   Composer Ifukube Akira, who created the soundtrack for the 1954 *Godzilla*, also created the soundtracks for *Battle in Outer Space*. The two films were both made by the Honda Ishirō and Tsuburaya Eiji duo, who created many other films together for Toho.

Katayama article, is a testament to the fact that many have taken Anno up on this challenge and have developed their own readings. However, for the general Japanese public, I argue that Anno's film played an important role of psychologically healing the nation from post-3.11 frustration and anger, like the original post-war *Godzilla* of 1954 helped to restore faith in the nation. By elevating Japanese technology, *otaku*s and *shachiku*s to cool status, Anno shows that the Japanese are very much capable of dealing with a disaster like Fukushima in the future, so long as the old *rōgai* are removed and the young talents and misfits are able to shine.

Quantum Zen as a Philosophy for the Twenty-First Century in Ruth Ozeki's *A Tale for the Time Being*

The portrayal of Japan as continuing to be relevant in the modern world was not limited to tangible areas such as advanced technologies. The following example that I explore involves the portrayal of Zen Buddhism, meditation practices and the concept of *ikigai* as philosophies that continue to be cool and globally helpful in the twenty-first century. Whether people are conscious of their influence, there is no doubt that Eastern philosophies are frequently relied upon in the West as ways to relieve the tensions of modern corporate life, as well as to find meaning in life, such as yoga and the mindfulness movement. More recently, the concept of *ikigai* (a Japanese version of *raison d'être*) took off outside of Japan with the publication of Héctor García and Francesc Miralles's book, *Ikigai: The Japanese Secret to a Long and Happy Life*, which was also popular in other Western languages such as French and Spanish (first published in Spanish in 2016). *Ikigai* has now become the next lifestyle 'it' word, along with Danish *hygge* or the Swedish *lago* and has inspired numerous other publications.

Ruth Ozeki's 2013 English-language novel, *A Tale for the Time Being*, portrays Japan as a centre of this spiritual cool. An American-Japanese author raised in Connecticut and an ordained Buddhist priest who currently divides her time between the US and Canada, Ozeki is undoubtedly well placed to be a proponent of Zen. Ozeki demonstrates the continued power of Japanese ways of thinking in three main ways: first, by showing the power of Buddhist 'radical interconnectedness' in bridging gaps between people; second, by revealing how Zen can be used to combat contemporary social issues such as suicide; and third, by exploring the concept of *ikigai*, although her teenage protagonist and her grandmother use the term 'superpower' instead. In doing so, Ozeki contributes to the more recent representation of Zen as a philosophy and logical way of thinking that can help modern humans to find their purpose in life, rather than being a religion (as the term 'Buddhism' evokes to most Western readers). Although Ozeki is not the first to introduce Zen Buddhism to the West, it is still not widely regarded as a solution to real-life problems, such as suicide prevention in the Western world. Especially in the US, Zen Buddhism was consumed by most as a stylised, frivolous fad, even when it was at the peak of its popularity, in the late 1950s (Iwamura, 2011, pp. 33–35). Although this may be changing today with newer forms of Buddhism-based practices such as the mindfulness movement, meditation continues to be associated with relaxation in most of the Western world rather than the serious philosophy that Ozeki attempts to describe in her book.

A Tale for the Time Being received wide critical acclaim for its thoughtful combination of the *Bildungsroman* genre and philosophical explorations. The book was shortlisted for the Man Booker Prize and won the Los Angeles Times Book Prize for Fiction and UK Independent Booksellers Award. It has also been translated into French, Spanish, Italian, Portuguese, Russian, Hungarian and Japanese. The plot is deceptively simple: a Japanese-Canadian writer, Ruth (a semiautobiographical character based on Ozeki), picks up a freezer bag containing a diary and other valuable items that seems to have washed ashore on Cortes Island, British Columbia, as a result of the 3.11 tsunami. The diary, which is concealed between the covers of Proust's *A la recherche du temps perdu*, contains the story of a teenage girl, Nao, who spent her childhood in the US—her father worked as an IT professional in Silicon Valley before the dot-com bubble burst. Back in Japan, Nao faces horrific bullying at her school as well as her father's repeated suicide attempts and depression as a result of not being able to provide for his family. Hope is presented towards the end of Nao's story when she receives the care and wisdom of her great-grandmother Jiko, who is a 104-year-old ex-anarchist poet and a Zen Buddhist nun. The novel begins in Nao's voice, as she decides to tell the story of her great-grandmother's life in the diary of Nao's last days on earth, before she commits suicide. Through the act of reading the diary and working through the other clues in the freezer bag, Ruth's life becomes intertwined with Nao's and Ruth becomes more and more obsessed with Nao and her current situation; even though, as her husband Oliver reminds her, the diary was written more than a decade ago and it is probably already too late to save Nao. Did Nao commit suicide? Was she a victim of the tsunami? The reader never finds definite answers to these questions. Instead, the resolution of the book lies in an exploration of Zen Buddhism, quantum physics[7] and the interconnectedness of all things.

Ozeki had written Nao's story prior to 3.11, but had spent many years attempting to find an appropriate reader for the diary; she had even experimented with a nameless, genderless, ageless reader (2013d). However, the events of 3.11 inspired Ozeki to write herself, as well as her husband and her surroundings into the story, which was something she had avoided before as she considered it to be too 'self-conscious' (Ozeki, 2013c). The addition of Ozeki into the novel establishes a link between Nao's pre-3.11 story and 3.11, as well as between the novel and the reality of 3.11. By inserting herself into the novel, Ozeki dissolves the various boundaries between self and other—between herself and her readers, non-Japanese and Japanese, as well as non-victims and victims. This is just one of the ways in which the Buddhist concept of interconnectedness is manifested in the novel. In Ozeki's (2013b) words: 'Two of the most important tenets of Zen Buddhist philosophy are impermanence and no-self. All phenomena are impermanent. As such, nothing has a fixed self or identity, but instead, all things exist in a state of radical interconnectedness'. Ozeki attempts to transcend the self-versus-other binary and show that identity, on both personal and national levels, is constantly in flux, existing in a web of complex interactions.

Having a hybrid identity and being an author, Ozeki's alter ego Ruth is a highly appropriate reader for Nao's story, who bridges the gap between Western readers and the 'Japanese' Nao. At first, Ruth is somewhat tormented by her status as a spectator. Ruth admits to 'feeling vaguely prurient, like an eavesdropper or a peeping tom', although she also points out that novelists in general 'spend a lot of time poking their noses into other people's business' (p. 27). Ruth's genuine concern for Nao's wellbeing eventually overrides this hesitance. When beachcombers hear about Ruth's discovery and come to hunt for washed-up safes and valuables on her island, she gets angry at them, even though she has decided to keep Nao's freezer bag, as her neighbour and friend Muriel

---

7   Quantum physics or quantum mechanics deals with physical phenomena at an atomic and subatomic level, where the laws of classical physics no longer apply.

points out. Being a Japanese-American, Ruth is also able to add footnotes to Nao's story, providing her own insight and explanations where Japanese terminology and concepts are used. This helps Ruth to better understand Nao's story because her Japanese vocabulary was 'out of date', making her resort to internet searches for pop culture references (p. 50). The footnotes are not limited to definitions of Japanese terms and include personal remarks such as '88. Miyagi … Sendai is in Miyagi!' (p. 206) when Ruth realises that Nao is about to go to an area of Japan that was hit hard by the earthquake and tsunami. There are some footnotes that refer to the appendices at the end of the novel, such as '9. For more thoughts on Zen moments, see Appendix A' (p. 20). In some instances, Ruth does not have the answers. For example, she is unable to find the *kanji* for the name of Jiko's temple (p. 247) and her limited knowledge of French means that she incorrectly interprets the line in Monique Serf's song *Le mal de vivre*, 'vaille que vivre', as 'It's brave to live?' (p. 314).[8] Although these footnotes help Ruth, they are also useful for the reader who requires these further explanations, which raises the question of whether it is really Ruth (the character) that wrote them or Ozeki (the author). Strangely, there are also footnotes in Ruth's part of the story (pp. 103, 143), which has the effect of dissolving the boundaries between Ruth and Nao, as well as between Ozeki and the reader (the layering bringing to light the double role of Ozeki as author and reader of her own writing). The numbering of the footnotes is continuous throughout the novel, from the Dōgen and Proust quotes that are provided at the beginning of each of the four parts of the novel to Nao and Ruth's respective stories and also in the appendices.

Radical Interconnectedness

As mentioned earlier, Ozeki demonstrates her idea of 'radical interconnectedness' most noticeably through the relationship between Ruth and Nao. Ruth begins to feel 'oddly protective of Nao and her diary' (p. 212) as she reads through her story, even feeling 'a strong sense of almost karmic connection with the girl and her father' (p. 447). Although she becomes increasingly curious about Nao and searches for clues on the internet, Ruth decides not to rush ahead and 'read at the same rate she'd lived' (p. 537), so that 'she could more closely replicate Nao's experience' (p. 63). Ruth becomes so involved in Nao's story that she begins to

---

8   It should be 'we must live the life we have. We must soldier on', according to Ruth's French neighbour, Benoit (p. 220).

influence it herself. For example, words disappear from the last pages of the diary as Nao finishes recounting past events and catches up to her present, her 'now' (the homonymy is particularly apt here). Ruth makes the words reappear by responding to Nao's cry of help through a dream. In an unexpected surrealist twist to an otherwise very realistic story, it is this dream encounter that reunites Nao with her father, which creates a happy ending for her story. There is a sense that Nao (the author of the diary) is being helped by Ruth (the reader of the diary) just as much as Nao helps Ruth.

Ozeki's Zen 'radical interconnectedness' is presented as being as much a solution for the problems afflicting post-3.11 Japanese society as it is for her post-3.11 novel. Most importantly, the concept is helpful in alleviating the strict demarcation between victim and non-victim that often occurs after a disaster. For example, those who are direct victims of 3.11 have the tendency to distance themselves from non-victims or indirect victims because they feel as though non-victims cannot possibly have a full understanding of their devastation.[9] This results in a situation in which only disaster victims are engaged with disaster-related issues and non-victims feel as though it is somehow wrong to get involved. Ozeki's radical interconnectedness provides an alternative to this, giving non-victims the right to care. Ruth finds that even though 'she received confirmation that the people she knew were safe … she couldn't stop watching' the footage of the tsunami (p. 165), because 'the images pouring in from Japan mesmerized her'. Ruth is a non-victim, who does not personally know anyone involved in the disaster (with the exception of Nao, who may or may not have been a victim), but she still cares deeply about all those affected. Nao's story seems to awaken this sense of interconnectedness in Ruth, reminding her of the impact such events can have on her own life, even if it is not immediately visible. The reader is also led to empathise with the suffering of disaster victims such as Mr Nojima, a sanitation worker who lost his whole family and house in the tsunami, speaking in a video that Ruth is watching. Through the representation of Mr Nojima, a fictional character who represents the real-life experiences of many tsunami victims, Ozeki encourages empathy that extends beyond our immediate circle of family and friends. While watching the tsunami footage, Ruth remarks that 'there was a haphazard quality to the images,

---

9   Wagō Ryoichi, the Fukushima-based poet explored in Chapter 3, expressed this as a feeling on the part of the victims that 'we can feel the pain, but those who are not in pain would not understand', which creates barriers between victims and non-victims (Wagō & Sano, 2012, pp. 202–204).

as if the photographers didn't quite realize what they were filming … not understanding the danger they were in … but always, from the vantage point of the camera, you could see how fast the wave was traveling and how immense it was' (p. 166). Being at a similar 'vantage point' with regards to the disaster, with a knowledge of what might come to hit Nao, Ruth obsesses over her troubles and attempts to retrospectively become involved in her story, even though she knows it is probably too late.

Ozeki further highlights this interconnectedness by tightly weaving together various elements in the plot. Like the gyres that connect the Japanese ocean to Cortes Island in British Colombia, where Ruth and Oliver live, all events in the novel are shown to have a global impact. For example, the September 11 attacks cause Nao's father to become even more depressed and the US bombing of Afghanistan causes Nao's menstrual bleeding to resume. 3.11 is also framed as a global disaster that has global causes and implications. The most obvious one is the tsunami's role in linking Ruth's life to Nao's story over time and space, but the novel also points out facts, such as the coast of Japan moving closer to British Colombia by 13 feet and the length of the day being shortened as a result of the earthquake and the radiation fallout causing anxiety regarding foods such as oysters and salmon where Ruth lives.[10] Additionally, a Japanese jungle crow, which seems to be a kind of reincarnation of Nao's great-grandmother Jiko, appears in Ruth's dreams and physically finds its way to Cortes Island by riding on the tsunami debris. Nao's *hikikomori* story makes Ruth uneasy as she realises that she and Oliver are a kind of *hikikomori* as well and Nao's father and Oliver make the same 'pu-pu-pu' sound with their lips as they sleep. The universe of the novel can be described as functioning like an interconnected quantum system, as Ruth implies in the appendix on entanglement in quantum mechanics. In quantum mechanics, particles can become 'entangled'—that is, 'coordinate their properties across space and time and behave like a single system' (p. 583). When two particles are entangled, the behaviour of one particle can influence the other in a way that cannot be explained by classical physics (i.e. the influence even happens at such a distance that the particles would have to be travelling faster than the speed of light to have an impact on each other). Within the world of the novel, Ruth, Oliver, Nao and Jiko have all become entangled through Ruth's act of reading

---

10   There have been real-life examples of tsunami debris, including fishing floats, soccer balls and fuel tanks, arriving on the coasts of North America (Barboza, 2012; Wian, 2012).

Nao's diary. Further, although Ruth is the observer of Nao, creating her story, one could say she is being created by Nao, as Oliver claims, because classical chronological conceptions of time no longer apply in this quantum system. In exploring the theme of interconnectedness through the lens of Zen Buddhism as well as the modern discoveries of quantum mechanics, Ozeki cleverly creates numerous entangled and interconnected layers in her writing, which makes it possible for her to explore Japanese society from various perspectives.

Meditation as a Solution to Suicide

At first glance, the Japan that is portrayed by Ozeki does not appear to be a reliable source of advice on how to *live*—suicide is the most important social issue explored in the novel, both for the plot and because of what it reveals about Japanese society. Many types of suicide are portrayed: Nao's father attempts suicide several times due to his depression and Nao considers suicide as a result of the horrific bullying she is subjected to at school. There is also the mention of the suicide of Socrates, Nick Drake, quantum physicist Hugh Everett's daughter, the Japanese troops and Okinawan civilians in *Tetsu no Ame* (rain of steel; the 1945 Battle of Okinawa), the 9/11 suicide bombers and their victims who opted to jump instead of being burned alive and even the nineteenth-century depiction of the *seppuku namazu*, the Suicide Catfish, committing *seppuku* to atone for the deaths he caused by wiggling and thrashing underground. The issue of suicide is particularly relevant to post-3.11 Japanese society because Ozeki also mentions the post-Fukushima suicide of those displaced by the fallout, as well as the Certain Death Squad (aka Fukushima 50) that remained at the nuclear power plants to prevent a full meltdown (arguably a form of unrealised voluntary death).

Further, the readers' perception of a high rate of suicide in the country is further strengthened by the figure of Nao's father, who internalises foreign stereotypes about Japan as the land of *harakiri* and *kamikaze*. As he puts it in his stilted English, 'Sometimes I think American people cannot ever understand why a Japanese would like to make a suicide. American people have a strong sense of their own importance. They believe in individual self and also they have their God to tell them suicide is wrong' (p. 133). This is contrasted with Japanese Zen Buddhism, which does not explicitly reject the idea of suicide, unlike Christianity. To overcome his Japanese urges, Nao's father attempts to read Western philosophy to find meaning in his life and even emails an old friend psychology professor Dr Leistiko, to ask him to teach him 'a simple American way to love my life' (p. 133). In his email, Nao's father describes that the Japanese have 'appreciated suicide' for 'many thousands of years' (p. 129), using it as a way to (ironically) truly experience life, 'at least just for a moment' (p. 130). This echoes the stereotypical idea in foreign Nihonjinron that suicide is socially accepted in Japan and that 'the Japanese respect for [suicide] allows it to be an honorable and purposeful act' (Benedict, 1946, p. 166).

One of the manifestations of this honourable suicide in modern Japanese society is the Japanese middle-aged workers who lose their jobs due to downsizing and attempt to hide this from their family by spending their days in a park, until they become 'scared and feel ashamed like gomi' (p. 131)[11] and commit suicide, as Nao's father explains. Suicide is also a problem in the modern Japanese schooling system that Nao finds herself in when she returns from the US. According to Nao, Japanese high school exams 'decide your whole future and the rest of your life and even your afterlife' (p. 190), because they determine your choice of university, employment prospects, income, potential partners, the life of your children and whether you receive a proper funeral, allowing you to enter the Pure Land and to not have to come back as a vengeful ghost. It is this kind of singular thought that does not allow for alternatives, which leads to suicide—just like a *rōnin* no longer had a *raison d'être* without his master, the existence of a modern-day *rōnin* (a student who fails their entrance exams and is preparing for the next session) hinges on his success in an examination. Without success, the *rōnin* turns into a nobody in the eyes of Japanese society, similar to Nao's father, who turns into a *hikikomori* after attempting to commit suicide by throwing himself in front of a train. Nao notices that in this state, he looks eerily similar to what she imagines ghosts of workers who commit suicide look like. Even while still alive, Nao's father is somewhere in between the realms of life and death. Nao 'feels like a ghost' (p. 186) after her ostracism at school and after she discovers that no one (even her best friend from Sunnyvale, Kayla) was responding to or viewing her emails and blog posts. Japanese society is shown to be a breeding ground for this kind of half-dead, half-alive outcast class, due to the lack of alternatives when one's life does not go exactly to plan.

---

11   *Gomi* means 'rubbish' in Japanese.

This idea that Japanese society does not provide alternatives is an oft-repeated one in foreign Nihonjinron: in *Japan as Number One*, Ezra Vogel (1979) claimed that the Japanese have a tendency to condemn misfits, causing high suicide rates among those who do not 'enter a place of work that he or his family consider[s] desirable' and that 'suicide rates are high among Japanese youth and those who are discouraged by not making the proper organization may be more depressed than their American counterparts, who will have a variety of later options open to them' (p. 240). In these earlier pages of the novel, Nao and her father reinforce the stereotypical foreign portrayal of the Japanese as people who derive their meaning of life or happiness from a stable career. In this view, residents of the disaster-hit areas who still have not been able to return to their previous occupations would naturally be unhappy, as proven by the example of post-Fukushima suicides. Such a view carries the risk of masking the alarming nature of the high incidence of suicides following a disaster such as 3.11, which throws the lives of many off course.[12] Nao's story is centred around Nao and her father's journey towards rejecting this internalised Nihonjinron idea of suicide and finding their own Japanese way to affirm life.

In the end, Ozeki demonstrates that the Japanese way of thinking points to life and that it may even be more helpful than its Western counterparts in helping people to avoid suicide. Nao's great uncle Haruki (referred to as 'Number One' in the novel because Nao's father is also called Haruki), who was a philosophy student at Tokyo University before getting drafted to the war, is the primary voice Ozeki uses for the comparison between Zen Buddhism and Western philosophy. Haruki chooses to seek meaning in the remaining few moments of his life as a *kamikaze* pilot through his knowledge of Zen Buddhism, rather than Heidegger's philosophy, which he presumably studied at university. Haruki puts Zen master Dōgen's philosophy on an equal footing with those of Western philosophers. He points out that, 'to philosophize is to learn to die' (p. 464), even if there is a difference between East and West in 'the notion of what it meant "to philosophize"' (p. 464). Zen prevents Haruki from becoming despondent thinking about his imminent death and Dōgen's idea that 'both life and death manifest in every moment of existence' (p. 466)

---

12   There were 117 suicides officially reported as '3.11-related' in the Fukushima, Miyagi and Iwate prefectures from 2011 to 2013. However, this figure is likely to be understated as it only includes suicides that could be formally attributed to the disaster (e.g. suicides that took place in evacuation shelters and temporary housing) (Cabinet Office, 2013).

encourages him to live his last moments carefully. Haruki decides to use his last moment to turn his plane off course and to 'end [his] life in watery disgrace' (p. 466), with this knowledge that a single moment can have an impact on the fate of so many.

Although Heidegger and Dōgen both emphasise that a constant engagement with one's death is necessary to live authentically, Haruki compares the thoughts of Heidegger to 'labyrinthine Teutonic chambers', while representing Dōgen's thoughts as 'quiet, empty rooms' in which he finds comfort in the face of death—as Haruki puts it, 'in between the words, Dōgen knew the silences'.[13] Haruki finds 'greater satisfaction in Zen and my own Japanese traditions' (p. 467), which encourage understanding through the bodily experience of *zazen* (seated meditation), rather than words and analysis. In this way, Zen can offer a more direct affirmation of life—*thinking* and understanding in one's mind that one must live authentically is different to *feeling* in one's body that one must live authentically. Therefore, despite what the other Haruki in the novel—Nao's father—initially believes, Zen Buddhism is shown to be a more effective method to find meaning in life than text-based Western thought.

Nao's father also eventually finds meaning in his life through Zen Buddhism, after some exploration of Western philosophy. After turning into a *hikikomori*, Nao's father turns to the 'Great Minds of Western Philosophy', a book series that Nao's mother receives for free from her workplace, as it was not selling well (perhaps an indication that Western philosophy does not suit Japanese tastes). When he finds a philosopher that he does not agree with, he takes their pages out of the books and folds origami insects with them—philosophers that get rejected include Hobbes and Nietzsche. This is particularly interesting because these two philosophers represent differing views on suicide. Hobbes, from his perspective of social contract theory, believed that the desire to commit suicide was irrational (and insane) and, therefore, based on reason, 'a man is forbidden to do that which is destructive of his life, or taketh away the means of preserving the same and to omit that by which he thinketh it may best be preserved' (Hobbes, 1651, p. 64). Although there is no consensus on what Nietzsche's thoughts were on suicide, he never rejected

---

13   Haruki or Ozeki is not the first to compare Heidegger's philosophy to Zen Buddhism. Reinhard May (1996) explored Daoist and Zen Buddhist influences on Heidegger's work (especially his concept of 'nothing') and Steven Heine (1985) pointed out similarities in the conception of time in Heidegger and Dōgen's works (Dōgen's 'impermanence' being similar to Heidegger's 'finitude').

the act, claiming that 'the thought of suicide is a great consolation: by means of it one gets successfully through many a bad night' (Nietzsche, 1909–1913, no. 157). Nao's father rejects both extremes in the Western thought on suicide—outright prohibition, or moral acceptance. The one philosopher that seems to impress him is Heidegger, who would cause him to read passages aloud and interrupt Nao's homework. However, even Heidegger is not entirely helpful, as shown when an even more depressed Nao's father begins to fold a Japanese rhinoceros beetle out of his page. The words of another Western philosopher, Socrates, are used to justify his second suicide attempt: 'I should only make myself ridiculous in my own eyes if I clung to life and hugged it when it has no more to offer' (p. 407). Although Heidegger helps him, he finds the ultimate answer in the Zen Buddhism of his grandmother, Jiko. After all the things he tries, Jiko's final words of 'to live, for the time being' is the only thing that convinces him that *ikiru shika nai* (we don't have a choice but to live), for the time being (as in now, temporarily, but also in the sense that humans are 'time beings', with a time limit) (p. 518). Even though many Western philosophers condemn suicide, the simplicity of Zen Buddhist teaching is what convinces him in the end that life is worth living.

Zen Buddhism also helps Nao live and face her problems in several ways. First, Jiko teaches her to be always respectful and polite to others, no matter how they treat her. There is an especially illustrative and humorous scene when Jiko and Nao go to a Family Mart to buy some rice balls and chocolates for a picnic and they encounter some *yankî* (delinquent) school girls. Jiko calmly returns their nasty words with a bow, which earns her respect and causes them to return the bow. This respect also extends to objects (which are also beings, according to Zen), as shown by the careful re-using of 'every rubber band or twist-tie, every piece of string or paper or scrap of fabric' (p. 295) at Jiko's temple. Although Nao disagrees with Jiko that 'our original nature is to be kind and good' (p. 262) and remarks that 'many of the Great Minds of Western Philosophy back me up on this' (p. 262), spending time with her great-grandmother gives her the ability to forgive. Second, Jiko helps Nao to find calm and peace within herself through *zazen*, which to her is like 'a home that you can't ever lose' (p. 264). This is particularly significant for Nao, who 'never had a home except for Sunnyvale, which [she] lost' (p. 264). After moving back to Japan, Nao feels 'like a foreigner living in that stupid Tokyo apartment with these strange people who said they were [her] parents but [she] barely even knew anymore' (p. 199). Finally, and perhaps most importantly, Zen

Buddhist ideas on time and impermanence are what ultimately stop Nao from ending her life. The Buddhist teaching of impermanence, as Ozeki shows, does not point to a nihilistic view of human existence; instead, it teaches Nao to cherish life precisely because it is fleeting. As Nao says when she is reflecting on her decision to end her life, 'There's nothing like realizing that you don't have much time left to stimulate your appreciation for the moments of your life' (p. 476). Zen Buddhism allows Nao, who grows up surrounded by adult lies and cover-ups, to eliminate her fears for life by allowing her to think about death and face it squarely for the first time.

At first, Nao believes that there are certain suicides that are more controlled and dignified (Haruki) than others (Nao's father)—as Nao points out when she confronts her father, Haruki's suicide was 'totally different', because 'he wasn't a coward' and 'he flew his plane into the enemy's battleship to protect his homeland' (p. 377). However, as Nao later finds out from reading Haruki's secret French diary, Haruki had flown his plane deliberately into the sea instead of the battleship to avoid causing any casualties. Even in the case of a forced suicide like Haruki's, we can still be in control of our own death—every moment of our existence counts, up to our last one because each moment contains numerous possibilities. Dōgen divided the snap of a finger into 65 moments to remind himself of this and, as Haruki puts it, 'in even a fraction of a second, we have the opportunity to choose and to turn the course of our action either towards the attainment of truth or away from it' (p. 466). With this realisation, Nao learns to cope with life by living each moment to the full, while being fully aware of the limited time we have, as time beings. Through the journeys of the main characters, Ozeki shows that despite Nao's father's belief that suicide is a Japanese phenomenon, the Japanese tradition of Zen Buddhism points to life.

Ikigai

Another way of finding happiness in life that is explored in the novel is to become a superhero with one's own superpower (or 'SUPAHIRO-!' and 'SUPAPAWA-!' as Jiko pronounces them)—the terms are first mentioned by Jiko after Nao tells her about her bullying at school and Jiko decides to give Nao instructions on how to sit *zazen*. Jiko's Zen superpower is a kind of enlightened state, which gives people the strength to live their life by becoming superheroes. Interestingly, Heidegger also uses the term hero, a concept that Haruki mentions in his diary. In *Being and Time*, Heidegger (1996) refers to man's possibility of choosing one's 'hero' (p. 385)—a great example of a human being—in the struggle to live authentically. Haruki Number One becomes Nao's new hero when she finds out about him through Jiko and this also helps her to live her life. However, what she does not realise yet at this stage is that her own father is also 'a total superhero' (p. 555) who was fired from his job for standing up for his beliefs—refusing to apply his fun and addictive computer game interface to weapons technology, which would facilitate soldiers to carry out destructive bombing missions. It is through the examples of these two Harukis as well as Jiko that Nao learns what it is to live authentically.

According to both Zen Buddhism and Heidegger, anyone has the potential to be a (super)hero and have superpowers. Your superpower is what you do best, your *raison d'être* or *ikigai*, which you must focus on, accompanied by the knowledge that life is fleeting. Once Nao's father decides to live, with the help of Zen Buddhism, he gets his superpower of programming back and delves into the world of quantum computing.[14] Getting inspiration from Nao's bullying, Nao's father devotes his time to developing an online encryption and security system called 'Mu-Mu Vital Hygienics', which involves using a web crawler to sanitise personal information on the internet. The crawler uses two methods, one mechanical and the other a much more complicated method involving the use of quantum computing to 'collaborate between worlds and switch possible pasts' (p. 549). As for Nao, she finds her *ikigai* in the 'superpower' of writing—on the last pages of her diary, she announces that she will write the story of Jiko's life next and decides that 'at least until I finish writing her story, I absolutely don't want to die' (p. 558).

Through the concept of radical interconnectedness as well as quantum entanglement, Ozeki asserts Ruth's right to care about Nao and other potential 3.11 victims and makes the case for the global relevance and importance of the Japanese disaster. Ozeki suggests that the solution to Japanese problems such as suicide have been contained in the Japanese tradition of Zen Buddhism and that post-3.11 Japanese society needs to reclaim its traditional thinking to overcome these problems of modernity. Ozeki's critique of Japanese society is not directed towards its social problems per se, but rather towards the fact that the Japanese have

---

14   Quantum computers are in development at the time of writing and may soon become a reality, as Galchen (2011) explains in her *New Yorker* article (which Ozeki consulted for her book).

internalised foreign stereotypes about themselves and have ignored their own traditions. As a transnational author, Ozeki provides a view from the outside on what traditions make Japan unique.

Ozeki's focus on Zen Buddhism is particularly interesting in light of the fact that authors and commentators in Japan focused more on Shintō and animistic beliefs, such as the idea of earthquakes as divine punishment, as a spiritual framework for post-3.11 Japan (e.g. Wagō and Kawakami). Ozeki, an ordained Zen Buddhist priest who lives outside of Japan and who has consequently witnessed the popularity of Zen philosophy in the West in recent years, suggests that Zen Buddhism rather than Shintō, is the philosophy that has the power to remain relevant in the post-3.11 world. Japanese Zen philosophy is shown to be a particularly helpful tool for maintaining a positive attitude towards life and accepting changes to one's life plans. Although all the thought systems explored in the novel—Zen Buddhism, Heidegger and quantum mechanics—embrace multiplicity and teach us to cherish our present in the face of impermanence, Ozeki concludes that *zazen* and writing are especially effective ways to experience this. *A Tale for the Time Being* is Ozeki's expression of her continued belief in the power of fiction as well as Zen Buddhism in the post-3.11 world.

While *otaku* scholars such as Morikawa Kaichirō and Takekuma Kentarō (see Chapter 1) predicted the downfall of Japan's cool culture following 3.11, *Shin Godzilla* and *A Tale for the Time Being* affirm Japan's continuing cultural and technological relevance to the world, albeit in different ways. These works both demonstrate that, with some searching, Japanese people can find the solutions to their post-3.11 problems within their own culture, whether it is the *otaku* mindset, *ikigai* or Zen Buddhism.

6

EXOTIC JAPAN

Mirroring the high level of interest in the Fukushima disasters in the French media, French-language authors were quick to respond to the Japanese triple disaster and were focused on the nuclear aspect, like many of the English-language authors. Early cultural responses such as Daniel de Roulet's (2011) short book *Tu n'as rien vu à Fukushima* [You saw nothing in Fukushima], which takes the form of a letter addressed to a young Japanese woman living in Tokyo, or *Après Fukushima—recueil de haïkus du cercle Seegan* [After Fukushima—a collection of haiku by the Seegan group], edited by Seegan Mabesoone (2012), echoed the heightened attention towards nuclear power that dominated the media response to the disaster in France. Poet and Medievalist scholar Armelle Leclerq's (2014) poetry collection *Les équinoxiales* [Equinox writings] continued this exploration of nuclear power by juxtaposing her writings on arbitrary, man-made nuclear disaster exclusion zones and radiation exposure limits against her pre-3.11 exploration of natural beauty in everyday Japanese scenes. In a similar way to Kawakami Hiromi's *Kamisama 2011* (see Chapter 2), the invasion of nuclear radiation into the everyday life of the Japanese, in which people must now protect themselves against rain, air and even food, is captured in her verse, producing a melancholic effect combined with the beauty of her earlier writing. Christophe Fiat (2011) produced his *Retour d'Iwaki*, as well as the radio fiction series *Sur les traces de Godzilla* (2013) on *France Culture*, both of which recount an author's visit (Fiat in the former and a character called Guy Commerçon in the latter) to Tokyo and Tōhoku following the disaster, in which he is tormented by the cries of Godzilla and the history of Hiroshima. These responses demonstrate that Fukushima has become embedded in the French imagination of Japan in a similar way to Hiroshima. Fiat's Godzilla metaphor is particularly apt because in much of the French literary imagination, Japan is now associated with an omnipresent and ominous shadow of the nuclear, despite its appearance of normalcy.

Many of the cultural responses to 3.11 in the French language are examples of insightful writing that attempt to challenge the mainstream discourse surrounding the disaster, including Richard Collasse's (2012a) *L'océan dans la rizière* (see Chapter 3), as well as Michael Ferrier's (2012) *Fukushima: Récit d'un désastre* [Fukushima: the tale of a disaster], Nadine and Thierry Ribault's (2012) *Les Sanctuaires de l'abîme: Chronique du désastre du Fukushima* [Snatched Away to Darkness: The Story of the Fukushima Disaster] and Philippe Nibelle's (2011) *Journal d'apocalypse* [Diary of the apocalypse]. Written by French residents of Japan, these three latter works carefully trace the everyday issues experienced by those living in Japan at the time, such as the lack of information on radiation levels following the disaster, inaccurate media portrayals of disaster-hit areas by outlets based in the capital or overseas and the complicated nature of the Japanese nuclear power industry, making it possible for French speakers to gain an insight into everyday life during and after the disaster in Japan.

However, it is clear that *japonisme* is present in many French literary works, which continue to portray Japan as being fundamentally Other to the West. Interestingly, recent works seem to be harking back to the original, aesthetic *japonisme* of the late nineteenth century, in that they tend to portray Japan as a dreamy land of exotic beauty, rather than the typical late twentieth-century techno-Orientalist portrayal of the Japanese 'as if they have no feeling, no emotion, no humanity' (Morley & Rovins, 1995, p. 172). Perhaps the perceived weakening of Japan's political and economic power following the triple disaster makes the country less threatening compared to the image of 'ants' working tirelessly for world domination, famously popularised in 1990s France by the then prime minister Edith Cresson. For example, Belgian French-language novelist Amélie Nothomb (1999) played a role in spreading exoticising portrayals of Japanese corporate life with her *Stupeurs et tremblements* [*Fear and trembling*]. This book traces the degrading experiences of Amélie as a young employee at a rigidly hierarchical Japanese company, filled with workaholic robot-like Japanese. However, Nothomb's post-3.11 writings retrieve some of the gentler aspects of her stereotypes of Japan, found in *Métaphysique des tubes* [*The character of rain*] (2000) and rebrands the country as a heart-warming and beautiful place of childhood and nostalgia. Nothomb published a special edition of *Stupeurs et tremblements* three months after the earthquake, which was accompanied by the short story *Les myrtilles* [The blueberry trees], the proceeds of which were donated to the Japanese operation of the Doctors of the World organisation. Unlike the book cover of the previous *Livre de Poche* edition (2001), which features a terrified-looking Nothomb against a backdrop of three Japanese men bowing in their suits, the 2011 book cover presents a beautiful red kimono pattern with the title and the author's name in an Asian-style font. The disaster is markedly absent from *Les myrtilles*, a short and simple retelling of Nothomb's heart-warming encounter with a man on the Asama Mountain, where she goes to find blueberry trees, reinforcing this idea of an exotically beautiful Japan.

In this chapter, two more works in this category of *néo-japoniste* fiction are explored to answer two questions: What exactly about Japanese people is still perceived as different and exotic by these French authors? If such a trend exists post-3.11, is it any different to the *japonisme* of yore?

Exotic Precarity in Thomas Reverdy's *Les evaporés*

French author Thomas Reverdy's (2013) novel *Les evaporés* [The evaporated], shortlisted for the Prix Goncourt 2013, was written during his six-month stay at the Kujōyama Villa in Kyoto from January to August 2012, as part of an art residency program associated with the *Institut français du Japon-Kansai*.[1] The novel is the second of Reverdy's recent noir-style works, preceded by *L'Envers du monde* (2010), set in post-9/11 New York and followed by *Il était une ville* (2015), set in Detroit following the 2008 financial crisis. Although Reverdy had the idea to write a novel on the phenomenon of *jōhatsu* (evaporation; disappearances without known causes) prior to 3.11, the novel is based on this experience of living in post-3.11 Japan that the Kujōyama residence gave him. Reverdy's work is rare in that it focuses on the margins of Japanese society, such as the *jōhatsu*, the day labourers of San'ya and the homeless, who are not usually associated with the Western image of Japan as a wealthy and egalitarian country. However, Reverdy's novel is not a

---

1   Renowned French author Eric Faye also took advantage of the program in 2012 and published *Malgré Fukushima* [Despite Fukushima] (2014), which was a personal journal and record of the beauty that remains in the country, despite the nuclear disaster.

work of social criticism. Reverdy does not attempt to invite his readers to pity these marginalised social groups, but portrays them in a dignified light, at times even giving them an exotic, noir-style allure. Rather than questioning the myth of a homogenous Japan through the portrayal of its margins, Reverdy displays that the margins of Japanese society contain the essence of Japanese culture. Although Reverdy is aware of the not-so-pretty side of living in the margins of post-3.11 Japanese society, he opts to portray them in this romanticised way as part of his defence of the dreams, imagination and fiction that fuels our lives, which runs like an undercurrent throughout the book. Reverdy presents a vision for post-3.11 Japan that continues to have an exotic appeal, despite the issues of social inequality that exist in the country.

In this novel, Richard B, a private detective based in San Francisco, spends his days pining for his Japanese ex-girlfriend Yukiko, who left him a year earlier. He is saved from his solitude by a phone call from none other than Yukiko, who asks him for help in looking for her father Kazehiro, who has 'evaporated'—he has intentionally disappeared without a trace, for reasons unknown. Still very much in love with her, Richard B agrees to accompany Yukiko and search for her father in Japan, a country he only knows in relation to Yukiko and the snippets she introduced him to: Japanese cuisine, Zen meditation and Buddhist vegetarianism. Meanwhile, Kazehiro (now known as Kaze) finds Akainu, who is a lonesome 14-year-old boy in San'ya, Tokyo, where they establish a business specialising in removals of all types (mostly unpleasant ones that no one else wants to be involved in). Kaze had decided to evaporate after being fired from his job at an investment company and being threatened by the *yakuza*, for reasons he believes are related to knowing too much about their shady involvement in the post-3.11 reconstruction effort. Following an encounter with a pair of *yakuza* in San'ya, Kaze and Akainu flee to the disaster-hit areas, where Kaze finds employment at the nuclear power plant and later establishes a business specialising in aiding people to evaporate. Akainu, who fled from Tōhoku following the tsunami, believing his parents to be dead, is reunited with his father. Richard B also miraculously manages to arrange a meeting with Kaze, but he does not attempt to persuade Kaze to come back to Yukiko and her mother. In Reverdy's words, 'in a French novel, they would have never been able to find her father and in an American novel, they would have been able to bring him back home. But this was the end of a Japanese story' (310)—hence the subtitle of the book, *Un roman japonais* [A Japanese novel].

The other inspiration for the novel that can be deduced from the subtitle is Richard Brautigan's *Sombrero Fallout: A Japanese Novel*. He quotes extensively from it (as well as Brautigan's other works), with extracts in italics throughout the novel. Brautigan's Yukiko is characterised by her 'long and Japanese' hair, which is described obsessively by her ex-lover, the 'American humorist'. Reverdy's 'Richard B' is a combination of the 'American humorist' and the real-life Brautigan. 'Richard B' is a private detective but also a socially awkward, whisky-drinking poet, much like Brautigan the author (many of Brautigan's poems are presented as being Richard's in the novel). This intertextuality is heightened by the fact that Brautigan's novel is inspired by another Japanese novel, Tanizaki Jun'ichirō's *Sasameyuki* [*Makioka Sisters*]. Yukiko is the name of one of the main characters of *Sasameyuki*—an ostensibly quiet, typically Japanese and beautiful woman, who is unmarried at the age of 30. It is clear that Reverdy draws inspiration from Tanizaki's Yukiko as well as Brautigan's version. There are many parallels between the three texts, including the lack of a father figure (due to death in Tanizaki, suicide in Brautigan and *jōhatsu* in Reverdy) and her portrayal as the epitome of old and beautiful Japanese tradition, which is juxtaposed with the free and independent temperament of her younger sister Taeko in Tanizaki's novel. The result is the complex situation of a French author drawing inspiration from an American author who drew inspiration from a Japanese author, with all three writing about Japan.

The main undercurrent common to these three authors is their exotic portrayal of Japan, centred on the depiction of Yukiko as a desirable, beautiful Japanese female figure, who is lost in life, unmarried, unattached and waiting for the right man. Out of Tanizaki's *Makioka Sisters*, it is not the Westernised and individual Taeko but the frail-looking and typically Japanese Yukiko that Brautigan and, subsequently, Reverdy choose to portray. There is a strong desire to portray Japan in an exotic manner on the part of the two authors. In Brautigan's case, he chose to write about a Japanese woman despite the fact that the novel was inspired by a real-life break-up with his *Chinese* girlfriend, Siew-Hwa Beh. Reverdy, however, defends his decision in his endnote: 'what we call the imaginary—the Japanese imaginary of *nô* or genre films, but also the occidental imaginary of Japan—are part of the reality of things. They shape our world. Without it, a forest will only ever be the sum of its trees' (p. 314). In his view, both images and representations of Japan have value in themselves, regardless of how inaccurate they are, and he is not ashamed of contributing to this exoticism. Reverdy also writes that 'everything that is told here is true', commenting on the truth of fiction and of imagination—once we think of something, it inevitably becomes part of our reality and starts to shape our view of the world. It is no surprise that Reverdy was inspired by Brautigan's *Sombrero Fallout*, in which the American humourist's imagined and absurd story starts to take a life of its own in his rubbish bin. Just like we can indulge in Brautigan's tale of a below-freezing-point sombrero falling from the sky, there is nothing inherently wrong, in Reverdy's view, in enjoying the exoticised portrayal of a beautiful, unchanging Japan that only exists in our imaginations.

Through the eyes of Richard B, who is visiting Japan for the first time, Reverdy explores Western stereotypes surrounding Japan as a country of contradictions. Within days of arriving in Japan, Richard manages to encounter 'all the clichés' from *geiko*, Japanese-style gardening and public baths to synthetic drugs sold freely and eating live icefish on his third day (a miraculous feat, considering that many Japanese people would not have seen these in a lifetime of living in Japan), as though Yukiko is determined to show him all that is strange about the country. Richard expected to see what he had seen in *manga*, films and literature on Japan and finds that 'all the clichés about Japan are true, even those that contradict each other' (p. 84). Japan is a blend of the modern and the traditional, Western and familiar in appearance but Other in many ways. Although Westernised and modern in many ways, Japan is also an island nation where things 'do not change very quickly' (p. 268). The men appear to be in control, but it is in fact the women who control their lives (p. 127) and so on.

In some ways, this phenomenon of contradiction is explained by the idea that 'all of Japan today is but a weakened reflection of the tradition' (pp. 102–103). The tradition exists as traces in a country that is modern and Westernised for the most part, giving the impression of contradiction. Just like Tanizaki's Yukiko, Reverdy's Yukiko represents the beautiful dying tradition. In Reverdy's case, Yukiko's traditionally Japanese elements are preserved in time due to her escape to the US. However, Reverdy makes it clear that this is a phenomenon not limited to Japan. Richard is also a specimen from a bygone era, from 'the country of large spaces and trout-fishing' (p. 267). Yukiko and Richard represent the stereotypical exoticised hetero-images of their respective countries and yet they are lost, even at home, as their 'countries don't exist anymore' (p. 267). Nevertheless, unlike Tanizaki's Yukiko or 'the French who think France is a country of literature, even though they only make perfume and Bordeaux there now and the Italians who would talk about opera for hours' (p. 267), Yukiko and Richard are painfully aware of their outdatedness, living in the modern world.

Reverdy also speaks to the impossibility of understanding the Other in a complete manner, through the relationship of Richard and Yukiko. Richard realises that 'during the whole year that they were together, sleeping together at her place—occasionally at first, then more and more frequently and finally virtually every night—he basically didn't know anything about her' (p. 52). Richard's feeling is also underscored by the fact that, although the two were sleeping at 'home', Yukiko only feels truly at home when she returns to Japan—what Richard thinks of as being Yukiko's home is not even her real home. If even lovers who spend all their time together cannot understand each other, then it seems like an impossible notion that one can come to an understanding of a cultural Other, with whom there is little interaction. Even Kaze, a Japanese-born Japanese, has an exoticised view of his own country. It is revealed that his image of Tōhoku is a highly romanticised one, involving rice, sake and solitary pines. Reverdy claims that all Japanese have a *furusato*—'an image tinged by nostalgia which inspires popular songs' (p. 288), involving some traditional and unchanging element, such as a festival, flowers or a bridge. If exoticism is to be defined as the allure of the Other, often involving reductive representations, then it is everywhere around us—we even exoticise our own childhood, selectively remembering what we can no longer experience easily as adults. It is difficult to blame Richard, who, even after his various experiences in Japan, reduces the Japanese to three characteristics: polite, delicate and beautiful (when it comes to women). Reverdy allows his readers to feel comfortable with this and to indulge in Richard's exotic experiences.

Japan is portrayed as a country that continues to have an exotic appeal to the West. This is contrasted with America, which gives people dreams but disappoints them when they get to know the country. Unlike Richard, whose real-life experiences in Japan do nothing to quell his exotic Japanese dream in the form of Yukiko, she cannot love Richard because her 'American dream' involved 'being an actress, marrying a young and handsome man that she meets by coincidence, who would come home at night to eat dinner with her and make love and take her to holidays in Europe' (p. 291). Her dream is irreconcilably different to the reality of the old, overweight and broke Richard. For Yukiko, her experience with Richard makes her realise that this 'American dream' was not for her and she loses all hope for America. She can no longer maintain that dream because she has realised that her life with Richard would never be the American life she envisioned. Convinced that her real home is in Japan, she decides to not go back to San Francisco.

Richard is aware of the negative sides of Japanese society, such as 'the playacting, the misunderstandings, the solitude, the conformism' and insists that there is no need to accept the whole Japanese 'package', even if he appreciates other aspects of Japanese culture (p. 267). At the beginning of the novel, Richard defends his dying profession of private detective by criticising people who would rather set up webcams in their own home and carry out their own detective work than ask for professional help. In his view, private detectives exist for the purposes of shielding their clients from the harsh, bare reality of the images of adultery and to soften the blow of the news. In a similar way, there are many dreams in the novel that are maintained by the characters not knowing or opting to not chase the full reality. These include Richard's hope for another relationship with Yukiko, the dream of the Bubble economy or even the dream that the government protects its citizens. Despite his insistence, Richard, representing the West in this novel, is reluctant to face various truths regarding Japan, opting to turn a blind eye to the social problems in the country to keep his exotic images alive. For Richard, Japan continues to be a mysterious place of alternatives or escape, where anything is possible. Another interesting metaphor is the story of an old gentleman and art lover told by Yukiko, in which the gentleman created an artists' retreat and then went blind, becoming unable to view the beautiful art around him. However, according to Yukiko, the gentleman was able to obtain satisfaction and peace because he believed the art to be beautiful even though he could not see it. Reverdy implies that the West is like this blind man—Westerners are too far away (either by circumstance or will) to know the real Japan, but they believe the country to be beautiful and they derive enjoyment out of this game of imagination.

In keeping with his argument on the merits of constructed images, Reverdy does not explicitly criticise the Japanese way of not always disclosing the full reality, in both the public and private spheres, unlike other authors and intellectuals commenting on post-3.11 Japan. Kaze's evaporation, central to the plot, involves disappearing without telling his wife anything to protect her. Although Yukiko initially struggles with this, she eventually comes to accept that her father now lives a different life (it is unclear whether her mother comes to such an understanding). Yukiko implicitly admits that her mother lying to her during their weekly calls, reassuring her that everything was fine following 3.11, helped her to focus on her own life in the US. In the earlier pages of the novel, Richard reflects on the seismologists who bravely explained that even if it were possible to predict an earthquake a few days in advance, the population would not be told because there is a higher probability of more people dying from the panic than the earthquake itself. Richard asks: 'Why do politicians, experts and journalists depress us with the prospect of catastrophes for no reason, then?' (p. 18). This inevitably brings to mind the delayed public response of the Japanese Government to the Fukushima nuclear disasters. Reverdy appears to be defending their decision to some extent. Similarly, when he meets Kaze at the end of the novel, Richard decides that there is no point in talking to him about his daughter who crossed the Pacific to find him or his wife's sadness because he is now a different man and he cannot return to his former life. Richard simply calls this 'tact', or the 'virtue of poets' (p. 300), and gives logic and reason to what Japanese intellectuals criticised as 'hide-ism', or the 'Japanese sickness'.

Reverdy explores what is usually hidden in Japanese society, as long as it fits in with his exotic hetero-image. The French journalist that Richard meets explains that 'those on the margins … are more reliable when it comes to knowing about a society … If you want to know the country, study its basement' (pp. 223–224). Throughout the novel, Reverdy emphasises the notion that it is in the margins of Japanese society that the essence of Japaneseness is found. Richard notices the way in which the homeless in Ueno Park prefer to take care of themselves by finding food in rubbish bins rather than begging and how they place their shoes outside of their tents, just like those Japanese living under a roof. In the way of living of the homeless, Richard sees the traces of an ancient code of individual and social honour, exemplified by *bushidō* (the way of the warrior). This symbolic centrality of the margins in Japan is also explained through the metaphor of *ukiyo* (the floating world), which is often used to refer to the worldly existence of prostitutes, actors and vagrants of the Edo period (as in *ukiyo-e*), but has its roots in the typically Japanese concept of impermanence—the idea is that because the world is impermanent, it made sense to Edo-era Japanese to spend their lives seeking pleasure and these marginal figures were necessary. It is important to note that this image of the 'floating world', exemplified by woodblock prints, was also a staple of the *japonisme* movement, which was how Japan was culturally introduced to many in Europe. Richard (and Reverdy) incorporate Japan's margins into their dream of an exotic Japan—the margins represent a typically Japanese space, which does not contradict all the stereotypical clichés about Japan, but rather exemplifies them.

Japan is often described as a wealthy nation, composed entirely of the middle class (*ichioku sō chūryū*)[2] and only in recent years has there been any attention paid to the country's poor or its social margins, especially in the Western media.[3] One explanation for this lack of attention is philosopher Maruyama Masao's metaphor of Japanese society as being a collection of octopus pots, quoted by Richard (p. 123), which suggests that these marginal social groups are isolated from each other as well as from mainstream society, like the octopus in different pots, preventing their plight to be known to the world. For example, the *yakuza* traditionally take special care to distance themselves from mainstream society, which they call *katagi* (respectable, honest) and the average Japanese does not know much about them. However, Reverdy's portrayal of the margins does not aim to bring his reader's attention or awareness to their plight. Reverdy is, for the most part, happy for these marginal groups to stay in their respective octopus pots, each with their own social codes and is only interested in them as a source of exoticism within Japan. Reverdy's portrayal of the margins include the day labourers of San'ya, the homeless and the women of the 'lost generation', but his portrayal gives dignity to these groups and at times even romanticises them, rather than denouncing their situation.

The most notable marginal group that appears in the novel is the day labourers of the district, known as San'ya, in the Taitō ward of Tokyo, where they are given precarious and often dangerous jobs in construction or cleaning, if they are lucky. San'ya labourers are of particular interest in the post-3.11 context, when there was an influx of labourers from the disaster-hit areas, as Reverdy describes: 'those who had debts or who lost themselves in trauma came to Tokyo in the hopes of starting a new life' (p. 73). Ironically, in Reverdy's novel, they are then sent back to Tōhoku to work in the decontamination effort or at the nuclear power plant because 'these men were excluded from the statistics that allow normal people to

---

2   The term *ichioku sō chūryū* refers to the idea that all 100 million (*ichioku*) Japanese people believe that they are middle class (*chūryū*). The *Digital daijisen* dictionary (2015) explains that the term came about in the 1960s, when the majority of Japanese began to describe their standard of living as 'middle class' in national opinion polls.

3   In recent years, there has been increased attention on the issue of the working poor. Examples include articles by Fackler (2010) for the *New York Times* and by Kim (2014) for Reuters.

feel safe' (p. 74). It is implied that these men were originally the 'workers, fishermen, craftsmen and farmers' from the disaster-hit areas, forced to live closer and closer to the water (and, therefore, being in a more vulnerable situation in the case of a tsunami) due to their economic position relative to the landowners (p. 188). However, Reverdy remarks that an interesting aspect of San'ya is that the area does not look like a slum. It looks like an ordinary suburb like any other to an undiscerning eye. One really has to know what to look for, which makes it perfect for Reverdy's mysterious, noir-style setting. In the style of French crime fiction, even the urban landscape of San'ya is endowed with a dark, exotic beauty. For example, the recruiting of day labourers on the street is gracefully described as 'a ballet without music or poetry' (p. 71), with the men rolling up their sleeves to show they are not cold, taking off their hats and smiling to show their healthy hair and teeth.

A French ex-journalist in the novel explains that 70 per cent of those living in San'ya are *jōhatsu* (p. 274), which is unsurprising considering the tens of thousands that disappear every year in Japan. As Reverdy reminds us time and again, the police do not typically investigate these cases and the families do not like to discuss the issue either because it is considered dishonourable. Nevertheless, the notion of disappearing and starting a new life seems to hold a romantic appeal to the French, rather than repel them. Lena Mauger and Stephane Remael's (2014) reportage *Les évaporés du Japon* [Evaporations in Japan] was met with enthusiasm by French readers. The book has many factual similarities with Reverdy's work and includes the story of a man who runs a business helping people to evaporate, much like Kaze. The French fascination with the idea of evaporation is likely to be linked to domestic economic factors in France, where unemployment reached record levels in 2015. Perhaps this makes the idea attractive to French readers who dream of starting their life afresh, like the *jōhatsu*.[4] Although Richard initially confesses that he does not understand why anyone would do this in Japan, he eventually comes to a certain understanding of the phenomenon. Introduced by the French journalist, Richard meets a real-life *jōhatsu*, the ex–pink film director Pinky, who was forced to evaporate due to some debt that he incurred from the *yakuza* for the budget of one of his ambitious films. Richard describes Pinky as having a 'certain allure … of an old beauty which has

---

4   This contradicts the idea that Japan is a country in which you are given one chance for everything in life, as observed in Ozeki's work. Although evaporation is living *outside* of normal society and is not truly comparable, it is an indication that stereotypes of Japan tend to exist in contradictory pairs.

preserved its charms' (p. 244); preferring to meet in bars hidden in the upper levels of old buildings and armed with a bragging grin (p. 273), he is undoubtedly a likeable character, despite his past.

People in Japan do not always evaporate for financial reasons. It could be claimed that Yukiko is also a kind of *jōhatsu*. Reverdy seems to encourage this interpretation by calling his novel *Les évaporés*, when the singular *L'évaporé* would suffice to refer to Kaze's evaporation. Yukiko became an adult during the lost generation of the 1990s, when 'the youth never had so little future outlook' and 'there had never been more people committing suicides and running away' (p. 48). Yukiko runs away from home at the age of 18 and starts waitressing at a bar in Tokyo. Although Yukiko was not in debt like many of the other *jōhatsu* in the novel, she escapes from mainstream society and attempts to start a new life, first in the underworld and then in the US. Her Japanese friends are also shown to be precarious, marginal figures, but in a different way; having missed the 'right age' to marry at 25, now they are leftover 'Christmas cakes' that no one shows interest in after the 25th (Christmas Day). Without a stable job, they rely on part-time work and dates with older men to support themselves. However, Reverdy paints their existence in a romanticised light as being beautiful and seemingly without worry, such as snacking and drinking tomato *shōchū* and shiso *tantakatan* in an *izakaya* in Meguro.

Although most Japanese marginal figures are an object of Reverdy's romantic Western gaze, from the labourers of San'ya and the *jōhatsu* to the 'Christmas cake' girls of the lost generation, there is one exception: the *yakuza*, who are often portrayed in a positive manner and exoticised in the West, in a similar way to the Italian mafia. French readers would most likely associate the *yakuza* with Kitano Takeshi films such as *Zatōichi*, in which the chivalrous code of *ninkyō* is respected. Following 3.11, foreign media focused on *yakuza* disaster relief efforts, which were not reported on in Japan (e.g. Adelstein 2011b, 2012; Bouthier 2011). Similarly, in the novel, the *yakuza* are initially described as having had a role in re-establishing order in the disaster-hit areas before the police and reclaiming their 'historic role as the protector of the nation' (p. 177). Yukiko even takes the role of defending the *yakuza* by saying that they make society safer and describes it as 'a company for people who couldn't become salarymen' (p. 266). Reverdy also takes advantage of their seedy mystery on a superficial level, as evidenced by his depiction of the lavish traditional-style abode of a *yakuza* '*shōgun* of the shadows', who lives with a 12-year-old girl dressed in elaborate *maiko* gear and blackened teeth.

However, just like this girl who appears beautiful at first glance but conceals a terrible secret, the *yakuza* is shown to be rotten at the core. Despite the traditional portrayal of the *yakuza* as a Robin Hood–style figure who helps the downtrodden in the spirit of *ninkyō*, Reverdy shows that the *yakuza* in post-3.11 Japan could not be further from this ideal. Kaze was fired from his job because he knew too much about the involvement of the *yakuza* in the reconstruction business in the Tōhoku region. These *yakuza*, as we find out, send the people who have borrowed money from them and the homeless to the disaster-hit areas, where the lucrative reconstruction contracts are, to take a cut. The *yakuza* take advantage of the indebted victims in Tōhoku, whose houses, still under loan, were washed away or devalued close to zero. The bleak and bare villages of temporary housing with plastic bathrooms are the only part of Japan exempt from Reverdy's exoticism, which highlights this contrast between the *ninkyō* ideal and reality.

There is no longer a strict demarcation between normal society and the *yakuza*, as supposedly dictated by their chivalrous code, with the *yakuza* posing as legitimate companies to secure these reconstruction contracts. The *yakuza* are described as being involved in petty crimes and violence from racketeering, beating up Koreans and selling Chinese prostitutes, to threatening people who cannot pay back their debt. They take advantage of those in the margins instead of helping them. Similar to when he describes the temporary housing in Tōhoku, Reverdy's language becomes raw and bare when it comes to these crimes committed by the *yakuza*, which makes his criticism clear. The French ex-journalist underscores this idea that the *yakuza* has lost touch with their chivalrous roots, when he describes their past activities: 'It was more human. It smelled of urine and bitter alcoholic sweat … It was violent, brutal, unfair, tragic, if you will, but fun, noisy, colourful, sensual. It was life' (p. 226). Reverdy speaks through the voice of Kaze, who is disgusted by the world of the *yakuza* and creates his own system of escaping them—*jōhatsu* and *yonige* (skipping town, especially when one is indebted to the *yakuza*), which are undoubtedly precarious forms of living, but at least ones in which you can be in control of your own destiny. This provides justification for the motivation of Kaze's clients, who do not wish to 'be victims for their whole lives' (p. 257). When Richard finally meets Kaze, he does not criticise him for his choice, accepting that this is a suitable way of living for some Japanese.

In Reverdy's novel, almost everything about Japan continues to be exotic, beautiful and different to the West following 3.11, even the indebted, the homeless, the day labourers from Tōhoku and unmarried women in precarious situations. While Reverdy is generally a fan of the exoticised Japanese hetero-image and its artistic value, this does not make him blind to Japanese social issues, which he demonstrates in his condemnation of the kind of petty and unchivalrous crimes against the weak committed by the *yakuza*. Nevertheless, Reverdy returns to exoticism at the end of the novel by romantically portraying the evaporated in Japan as a form of escape from this unpleasant reality. Reverdy's imagination of an exotic and mysterious Japan, as exemplified by Yukiko and her 'long and Japanese hair' is protected, in a demonstration of the strong hold this image continues to have on the French in the post-3.11 world.

Perfectionist *shokunin* in Hubert Haddad's *Le peintre d'éventail*

An important aspect of the exoticised image of Japan in the Western world is that of the Japanese craftsman (*shokunin*). The *shokunin* dedicates his life to the perfection of his technique, in such a way that his dedication, well-practised motions and way of life move the viewer. The *Daijirin* (2006) defines *shokunin katagi*, the 'character of the *shokunin*', as 'a characteristic that is common among the *shokunin*. The tendency to have confidence in one's skills and only completing tasks in a way that one can be happy with, without compromising easily or departing from one's principles for money'. In the West, this *shokunin* work ethic has partly been captured in the term *kaizen*, especially in the context of the automobile industry. Although the term simply means 'improvement' in everyday usage, *kaizen* in a company management context refers to the philosophy of continuous improvement most famously adopted by Toyota and introduced to the West by Imai Masaaki's (1986) book, *Kaizen: The Key to Japan's Competitive Success*. Imai (1986) explained that 'the Kaizen philosophy assumes that our way of life—be it our working life, our social life, or our home life—deserves to be constantly improved' (p. 3). The tradition of the *shokunin*, which is typified by hard work and constant innovation, has been applied to all employed Japanese in Nihonjinron discourse, rather than being limited to those occupations that are involved in manufacturing, as explained by cultural anthropologist Funabiki Takeo (2003, p. 190).

Another derivation of the *shokunin* philosophy is the term *monozukuri*, which is perhaps better known than *kaizen* in France because Renault incorporated the concept into their strategic plan at the time of their alliance with Nissan in 1999. *Monozukuri* literally means 'making things' in Japanese and is used to refer to the spirit of the Japanese manufacturing industry—the realm of the modern *shokunin*. As observed in the Japanese Government's continuing positioning of the country as a *monozukuri taikoku* (the great country of *monozukuri*) through various schemes such as the database of *monozukuri* meisters or the *monozukuri hojokin* (*monozukuri* assistance grant), these ideas of continuous improvement and a strong manufacturing industry (as opposed to service-based economies in the rest of the developed world, such as the UK, Australia and the US) remain an important part of Nihonjinron. Referring to the establishment of the Monotsukuri University/Institute of Technologists in 2001,[5] which is an institution centred on practical skills rather than abstract knowledge, Funabiki observed that this was Japan's challenge to the imported Western concept of the university (pp. 179–180). The ideal of the *shokunin* has even become a source of pride and point of difference for the Japanese, vis-à-vis Western civilisation. As Kita Yasutoshi (2008) wrote in his *Takumi no kuni Nippon* [Japan, a country of artisans]:

> The social influence of the 'shokunin spirit' on the culture of our country cannot be overstated. The mentality of 'making things laboriously', 'learning without giving up' and 'not compromising on quality' has been transmitted among the Japanese as though it is written in their DNA. It is also a generator of the country's power and wealth (p. 70).

This image of the Japanese as being a people who are especially adept at creating practical products, due to their strong work ethic, philosophy of continuous improvement and manual dexterity, is especially interesting to examine in the post-3.11 context because the reconstruction efforts revealed a serious decline in the *shokunin* population (especially those involved in carpentry and construction) that had been occurring prior to the disaster and, due to this, many felt the urgency to preserve and promote this part of Japanese culture. One example of this kind of effort in France was the plan to create a building called 'Takumi Project' in Alsace by the end of 2016, to 'spread the techniques and crafts of the *shokunin* overseas' ('Takumi no waza', 2016). The 2012 documentary film

---

5   *Monotsukuri* is another way to say *monozukuri*.

Jiro Dreams of Sushi by American director David Gelb (also distributed with French subtitles as *Jiro rêve de sushi* by Les Films Séville) was effective at popularising the *shokunin* philosophy overseas, by telling the story of the never complacent 85-year-old sushi master Ono Jirō, who spends every second of his day thinking about how to improve his sushi. For example, he always wears gloves outdoors to protect his hands and experiments with massaging an octopus for 45 minutes instead of 30 minutes. In the following section, I explore Hubert Haddad's (2013a) novel, *Le peintre d'éventail* [The fan-painter], which presents a vision of the *shokunin* spirit rebuilding cultural traditions in post-3.11 Japan.

Tunisian-born French-language author Hubert Haddad is a recognised master of making Other figures accessible to French-speaking readers through his ornate and poetic prose. A prolific author, Haddad has produced more than 70 publications in his career, but he is best known for his 'dictionary-novel', *L'Univers* [The universe] (1999), *Palestine* (2009) and, most recently, *Le peintre d'éventail* (2013a; *Le peintre* hereafter), following which, Haddad received the *Prix Louis Guilloux* and the *Grand Prix SGDL de littérature*.[6] *L'Univers* explored the reconstruction of the memory of an Eastern European man whose family died in the concentration camps, whereas *Palestine* is the story of an Israeli soldier becoming the Other, a Palestinian, after losing his memory and being adopted by a Palestinian family. In a similar way, Haddad brings the post-3.11 story of fictional gardener and painter Matabei Reien to his French readers in *Le peintre*. *Le peintre* was published simultaneously with *Les haikus du peintre de l'éventail* [The haikus of the fan-painter] (2013), which is a collection of *haiku* poems that belong to the novelistic universe of *Le peintre*. Following the success of these books, Haddad also wrote another Japan-inspired novel, *Ma* (2015), which is a story of lovers linked together by the real-life early twentieth-century *haiku* master Santōka.

Haddad's ability to put himself in the shoes of such a varying range of protagonists from different cultures and places is partly due to his erudition and extensive research, but he also fills in the gaps using his imagination. At the time of writing, Haddad had never visited Japan, but was 'fascinated from a distance … by the extraordinary refinement of a civilisation that has based its fragile reality on an awareness of impermanence between

---

6   The *Grand Prix SGDL de littérature* was also awarded in 2015 to Laurent Mauvignier for his *Autour du monde* [Around the world], a collection of individual stories in various parts of the world, linked together by the events of 3.11. This demonstrates the high level of cultural interest in 3.11 in France.

destructive typhoons, or during the long wait until the next earthquake' (2013b). The names of the characters in *Le peintre d'éventail*, such as Lady 'Hison', 'Osue' and 'Enjo', are not names typically considered Japanese within Japan, but rather names that sound Japanese in French. The novel is set in the imaginary Atōra region near the Fukushima power plants, by the Jimura Mountain and close to a village called Katsuaro in the Fubata district (although this is inspired by a village called Katsu*rao* in the Fu*taba* district, Fukushima Prefecture).

In *Le peintre*, Haddad creates an ephemeral and elusive wooden *ryokan* (inn), owned by the retired *geisha* Lady Hison,[7] which attracts 'deserters of everyday life' (p. 60). At this inn is an ever-changing garden of unimaginable beauty, meticulously maintained by the frail master gardener and fan-painter Osaki Tanako. Burmese-Japanese Matabei Reien, Lady Hison's lover and guest, receives some of Osaki's teachings before his death and becomes his successor, devoting his time to Osaki's art of maintaining the garden according to the seasons, then capturing its ephemeral beauty in brushstrokes on a paper fan, using a combination of painting and *haiku*. Matabei eventually creates his own disciple out of Xu Hi-han, Lady Hison's new Taiwanese-Japanese kitchen boy. Following a complicated love triangle involving Lady Hison's beautiful new female guest Enjo, Hi-han flees the inn to attend university in Tokyo. The 3.11-inspired tsunami arrives shortly after, as though to echo this human drama, razing virtually everything to the ground and killing everyone except Matabei, who happens to be taking a walk around the hills at the time. Matabei manages to overcome extraordinary circumstances in the following year to restore Osaki's washed-away drawings and writings on his fans, staying alive just long enough to pass them onto Hi-han, now a professor at the University of Tokyo.

Haddad's Japan is a *japonisme*-style portrait, exotic and beautiful, full of vibrant, colourful flowers that change constantly with the seasons and is studded with beautiful pale women with ink-black hair. The cover of the first edition of the novel features the words *Sublime Japon* (Sublime Japan) in capitals across a bright red border, on the simple black-and-white leaf pattern of the background. It is clear that the publisher, Zulma, felt that

---

7   Lady Hison is only described as an 'ex-prostitute' or 'ex-courtesan' in the text, but French readers are likely to associate this with the word *geisha* (and this was probably Haddad's intention). Putting aside the question of whether *geisha* provided sexual services, Lady Hison's appearance—always wearing a *yukata*, with her hair up high in a bun—indicates that she is a courtesan in the traditional style, rather than a modern prostitute.

this theme of sublime Japan was an essential piece of meta-information for potential readers because they typically use this red banner to display the name of a prize won by the book (rather than information about the book's content). In the early pages of the book, the reader is presented with this description of the sublime nature around the inn, as Matabei recounts his arrival there:

> There were Chinese cedars on the hills, a magnificent ginkgo that attracted pilgrims, blue oaks and beautiful chestnut trees, red maples up to the wooden bridge—not a reliable means to cross the indecisive river—between the Duji lake and the forest of giant bamboo trees covering the southern slope of the first mountain with green shadows. There was also this ash-coloured light that I loved, on foggy mornings, the harmony of the tea plantations off the little paths and the snow that took up residence on our heads from the end of autumn (p. 14).

The *shokunin* in this novel, Osaki and Matabei, dedicate their lives to capturing the essence of this beauty in their art, both in the garden as well as on the fans, relentlessly pursuing a form of perfection that they know cannot be obtained and are never complacent with their level of achievement. As Matabei tells Hi-han, 'the ideal garden is only but a dream', but 'imperfection leads to perfection' (p. 99).

While the *shokunin* philosophy came under the global spotlight following 3.11, there has also been a debate within Japan on whether this kind of elaborate training process is necessary. Livedoor founder Horie Takafumi (2015) started this debate by commenting on his Twitter account that 'only idiots need to train for years' as a sushi chef and that it was possible to learn the essential skills in three months at a 'sushi academy' designed to quickly train chefs, instead of the traditional requirement of *meshitaki san nen, nigiri hachi nen* (three years cooking rice, eight years shaping sushi), or even *shari taki san nen, awase go nen, nigiri isshō* (three years cooking rice, five years adding vinegar and your whole life shaping sushi). Horie argued that this lengthy training developed as a way to decrease competition in the industry, by keeping the number of trained sushi chefs low, rather than out of necessity.[8] Horie criticised the Nihonjinron idea that the Japanese tend to reward effort (*doryoku*) rather than talent—

---

8   'Sushi shokunin no "meshitaki 3 nen nigiri 8 nen" wa jidai okure? Horiemon no zanshin na kangae to wa' [Is the 'three years cooking rice, eight years making sushi' tradition behind the times? Horiemon's unconventional views] (2015).

'not only *doryoku* ("strenuous effort") but *kurō* ("suffering") is expected of a young person who has ambition', as argued by Takie Sugiyama Lebra (1976, p. 75) in *Japanese Patterns of Behaviour*. An example that is often given for this in Nihonjinron is the Japanese examination system, which is designed so that the candidate who does the greatest amount of memorisation and studying is the most successful, rather than those who can think on their feet.

The *shokunin* that we encounter in Haddad's novel, namely Osaki, is a romanticised image of the traditional system that Horie so despises—the dedication and endless quest for perfection in the most extreme circumstances. Osaki and Matabei are prepared to put in all the sweat, blood and tears necessary, prioritising their art over their lives. By the time Matabei meets Osaki at the start of the novel, he already 'seemed to be on the verge of death', 'his hair so whitened and his body so thin that he gave the impression of not belonging to the human race', although Matabei also observes that he was raking the gravel of the paths and climbing trees the previous night (p. 30). Osaki carries himself with his will rather than physical strength because he feels that he cannot depart from this world until his fans are in safe hands. Even at such a dire time he refuses to see a doctor, preferring to spend his last bit of remaining energy teaching Matabei. Osaki's selfless dedication to his art at this last stage of his life leads Matabei to conclude that he was 'without doubt an unrivalled artist, who, reaching the height of artistic achievement, prioritized his watering cans and rakes, hidden behind his paper fans' (p. 71). Osaki's ashes are scattered around the garden as he wished for, 'dispersed throughout the flowerbeds, on the moss and the arrangements of autumnal flowers, chrysanthemums and thriving roses, on the tree roots, through the channels of water and on the boulders, in a gesture similar to the offering of incense' (p. 61). Osaki ends his life by becoming part of his own art, fertilising the flowers and trees that he cherished.

True Japanese *shokunin* are shown to live discreetly in their quest for perfection, unlike some of their flamboyant and eccentric European counterparts, such as Mozart, Picasso and Salvador Dalí. Since they are never satisfied with their art, they are not boastful. Osaki does not seek money or fame in exchange for his art and, in his lifetime, he only ever sells a few paintings to a distant relative. The descriptions of his few material possessions underscore this idea of austerity: in the living room of his hut where he serves Matabei plain boiled water, 'the only furniture there was a rolled-up mattress and a chest, a portable stove next to the sink and a low table with a heater' (p. 37). Living in his humble, hidden-away hut, which was 'caulked like the hull of a boat', Osaki was so invisible that it took Matabei a year to notice his presence (p. 15). Osaki is a hermit, who does not travel outside the confines of the inn because he feels that there is already enough for him to do there. Despite his dedication and achievement, Osaki remains his modest self at his deathbed, expressing regret for not having been able to paint all the fallen leaves. He claims that he painted 'just a few, from one year to another, a few sheets' (p. 43). After witnessing his quiet death, Matabei comes to the conclusion that 'true masters live and die unknown' (p. 54). Osaki becomes the image of the discreet Japanese *shokunin* ideal. Matabei seems to approach Osaki's artistic heights eventually, but only when he sacrifices his health by living alone in the reconstructed hut in the exclusion zone to resuscitate his master's work.

The relationship between Osaki and Matabei and, subsequently, Matabei and Hi-han, is that of master–apprentice, which is typical of Japanese *shokunin*. This tradition is shown to be key to maintaining Japanese cultural traditions in the face of natural disasters and the resultant state of physical impermanence, with Matabei sacrificing his life following the tsunami to revive his master's work, which Hi-han then dedicates his academic career to analysing. This relationship is usually commenced by the apprentice approaching a potential master and undergoing many years of difficult training, before becoming a *shokunin*. However, in the novel it is Osaki who approaches Matabei in search of a successor, due to his failing health. In a style typical of the apprentice system, Matabei does not receive much guidance—exemplified in the Japanese idiom of *mite nusumu* (to see and steal), disciples are expected to 'learn using their bodies', by observing and doing. As Hi-han observes when he is getting started as a kitchen boy:

> A dictionary of season words does not produce the right emotions for a haiku poet and neither do recipe books give inspiration to an apprentice cook. But observing an ancient woman with deformed hands cutting up some raw fish will make you a master in knife skills (p. 67).

When Osaki first invites Matabei to his humble abode, he suggests that Matabei helps him and that he would show him some 'little things' (p. 38). Matabei 'learned customs through his voice and techniques from his hands, by simply walking by his side and helping him more and more as he became weaker' (p. 78), but he mainly learns his art indirectly from the works and the garden that Osaki left.

However, Haddad's idea of a *shokunin* revival in post-3.11 Japan is subversive compared to the aforementioned Nihonjinron conventions, in that he portrays a wide range of characters with this *shokunin* spirit. Although he does not draw much attention to this, Matabei is a foreigner. His father was a rich Burmese who seduced and married a young woman from Kyoto, whose last name he adopted as necessitated by the customs at that time in Japan. Hi-Han, Matabei's apprentice, is also a foreigner, whose parents were among the Taiwanese who were sent to Japan after the war. However, foreigners are not the only atypical *shokunin* in Haddad's novel. Although Haddad's three main characters are male, there are a few female characters who display *shokunin* qualities, such as manual dexterity, hard work and persistence. This is particularly interesting in light of the difficulty for women to be *shokunin* in most fields in Japan.[9] For example, Aé-cha, who is Korean as well as being female, creates various Japanese-style dolls from carved and round-shaped *gosho* to hollow paper-mâché *daruma* for good luck and lacquered wooden *kokeshi*, which are kept in a dollhouse in her room. Although never given a name, the mute and ancient ex–rice farmer maid of the inn expertly carries out her cooking and cleaning duties and moves about with a smile despite her age and fragility. Lady Hison proves herself to be an able *okami* (a female proprietor and manager of a traditional inn) with the spirit of *omotenashi*,[10] and a master of 'the art of presentation', according to Hi-han (p. 68). Although not placed on the same level as Osaki or Matabei, these female characters with strong dedication and work ethic reinforce the idea that the *shokunin* spirit resides in all Japanese.

In *Le peintre*, Haddad portrays post-3.11 Japan as a country in which beauty continues to be found everywhere, created and maintained by humble old masters, who stubbornly chase their unattainable ideal

---

9   Takeuchi (2004) contended that 'the very body of the creator is a corollary to the sanctity of the product. Thus women were automatically banned from certain trades where the notion of pollution by blood would have been sacrilegious' (p. 9). For example, there are very few female sushi chefs, with commonly cited reasons ranging from elevated body temperatures making the sushi too warm to menstrual cycles affecting their sense of taste.
10   *Omotenashi* refers to the Japanese spirit of hospitality, which has gained popularity since TV presenter Takigawa Christel used the term in her speech in 2013, in the successful bid campaign to bring the Olympics to Tokyo in 2020.

of perfection through a lifetime of training. Despite the frequency of natural disasters, manual skills are securely transmitted from generation to generation through a demanding apprentice system. Haddad expands the range of possible *shokunin* considerably from the standard Nihonjiron concept. Even those who are only partially Japanese or women are shown to carry the *shokunin* spirit within them.

In contrast to the recurring stereotype of Bashō, Zen Buddhism and suicide, which were apparent in the English-language texts that portrayed Japan's uniqueness, the two selected French authors focused more on post-3.11 Japan as a source of aesthetic and artistic inspiration, as well as a faraway place of escape and mystery, which appears to be a revival of the *japonisme* of the late nineteenth and twentieth centuries. In these texts, there is limited portrayal of social issues and the literary events occur in traditional settings in Kyoto or Tōhoku, which are considered suitable for the depiction of old Japan. Perhaps the Fukushima nuclear disasters prompted these authors to reflect on what could be at stake if such events were to happen again in Japan and that this encouraged them to focus on what makes Japan exotic and different from the rest of the world. More broadly, parallels can be drawn between the exoticism of these works and the post-3.11 self-Orientalising discourse in Japan, as observed in the promotion of Japanese traditional culture through government initiatives, such as the 'Takumi project' or setting up 'Japan Houses' in overseas cities. Japan's continued exotic appeal in the post-3.11 world perhaps did not grow organically in France, but rather had some of its seeds planted by the Japanese, who wished to draw on Nihonjinron concepts to market Japanese culture overseas.

CONCLUSION

Birmingham and McNeill (2012) summarised the confusion that the Japanese had regarding their identity following the triple disaster:

> Can Tohoku recover? Inevitably, the question leads to an even more fundamental one: What sort of country does Japan want to be? The nation's epic industrialization drive seems to have run out of steam. Its dream of energy self-sufficiency lies in ruins. Its population is aging and declining. Japan's squabbling political leadership seems powerless to stop the nation's slide down the economic league tables (p. 180).

This self-perception took an interesting turn as images of the cool, calm and collected response of the Japanese to the 3.11 disaster impressed the world. These images, which were imported back to Japan along with reactions of non-Japanese viewers, inspired many Japanese to live up to this ideal and restored their pride in a country that had been dwindling in global economic and technological influence during the 'lost two decades'.

Combined with the prospect of the 2020 Tokyo Olympics and the renewed direction and hope brought by Abenomics, Japan has experienced a surge in patriotism and nationalism, which has manifested itself in some cases through extreme xenophobia and hate speech against those considered to be 'anti-Japanese'. Both traditional values as well as modern economic and technological progress were restored as a source of pride for the country. Further, Prime Minister Abe (2013) claimed to have brought the unprecedented nuclear disasters 'under control' and aimed to use the opportunity to build an international reputation for the Japanese as producers and exporters of nuclear reactors and know-how (Kingston, 2013).

At the same time, criticisms against the 'typically Japanese' lack of transparency on the part of authorities in dealing with the Fukushima nuclear disasters and their attempt to suppress dissenting voices through a uniting official discourse (most notably under the slogan of *kizuna*) were what characterised other Japanese images in non-fiction discourses. Some felt that the various habits and attitudes of post-war Japanese society, such as blind trust towards authority and the safety myth of nuclear power, came crumbling down in the aftermath following the disaster. Public intellectuals emphasised that the Fukushima incident represented the end of an era that had lasted 66 years—the time was now *saigo* [post-disaster], as opposed to *sengo* [post-war]—and that Japan should step down from its position as an economic superpower and steer itself into a more sustainable future, appropriate for its ageing society. Authors such as Ōe Kenzaburō and Murakami Haruki, while condemning the response of the authorities, stressed the continuity of Japan from the legacy of Hiroshima and Nagasaki and called for Japan to live up to its identity as a 'no-nuclear' nation.

In many cases, it was this context of conflict between contradictory visions for society that Japanese authors addressed in their writing, rather than the tragedy of the disaster itself. Although cultural responses to disasters such as war literature often attempt to record personal and individual experiences to counteract the dehumanising and generalising effect of the cold facts and numbers of mainstream media, in the case of 3.11, the internet allowed ordinary Japanese citizens to fulfil this role by expressing their first-hand experiences through channels such as Twitter and personal blogs. Instead, what was required from authors was to describe and make sense of the invisible—the nuclear radiation or the general mood in post-3.11 society (*kūki*, to borrow Shiriagari's word)—to help guide their readers, especially those who were not directly affected by the disaster but felt indirectly responsible for the events at Fukushima, to mentally reconstruct themselves and their identity as Japanese citizens. Recognising the need to help resolve tensions between contradictory visions for their society, Japanese authors offered imaginative alternatives in their fictional responses to the disaster.

What Japanese-language authors such as Wagō Ryōichi, Kawakami Hiromi and Shiriagari Kotobuki proposed in their responses was for Japan to proceed by focusing on regaining the traditional, Shintoistic and harmonious relationship that the Japanese have with nature by making use of their resilience, which some public intellectuals had also recommended. While the degrowth theory of economic decline voiced by intellectuals was not commonly accepted in mainstream media, fictional texts, in which these ideas were represented in terms of positive and heart-warming everyday changes, were more approachable and better able to connect with the Japanese public. Other Japanese-language authors, such as Takahashi Gen'ichirō, and the authors of dystopian responses, such as Tawada Yōko, encouraged multiplicity and dialogue by directly portraying the pressure to conform and the lack of discussion in Japanese society. In their own ways, these Japanese-language responses helped to reconcile the ideological polarisation that was observed in Japanese critical discourse following the disaster and aimed to create a future path for Japan somewhere between the two extremes of radical pro-nuclear nationalism and strong criticism of the entire Japanese post-war system. *Shin Godzilla* also embodied a reconciliation of these two camps, in that the work could be viewed both as nationalistic propaganda and a parody of it. The general feeling that one gets from these responses is that the Japanese are a people who will overcome their current state of confusion and domestic squabbling to eventually distinguish themselves from the rest of their world through their philosophy of impermanence and harmonious coexistence with nature, which will lead them to become pioneers in sustainable living. This is because, despite their critical attitudes towards Japanese society, most authors left off their works with a glimmer of hope, be it in the power of words and open discussion, the new generation, a stronger regional Japan, technology or Japanese resilience.

While some Japanese-language authors were backward-looking in their assessment of post-3.11 Japanese society, in many cases evoking nostalgia for 'the good times past', English-language authors were generally more forward-looking in that they focused on valuable cultural, spiritual and philosophical elements found within Japanese culture and how these continued to be relevant in post-3.11 reconstruction, as well as for social issues such as suicide and bullying. There was a particular focus on Zen philosophy, as opposed to the Shintō focus of the Japanese authors, which demonstrated the continued popularity of Japanese-style Buddhism, meditation practices and lifestyle concepts in the English-speaking world. The two chosen English-language texts by Ruth Ozeki and Gretel Ehrlic built on and updated the one-sided post-3.11 media portrayals of *kizuna* and *gaman*, with their nuanced exploration of concepts such as Zen interconnectedness and *wa*, which, in their view, inform the Japanese psyche. At the same time, their elaborate exposition of Japanese ways of thinking helped English-speaking readers to understand how the Japanese deal with devastating disasters and continue rebuilding and also challenged Western conceptions of life and death. The English-speaking world has much to learn from these intangible assets of the Japanese, even though the country has become physically damaged and polluted by nuclear radiation.

Although there were many French-language authors who took similar approaches to the Japanese-language and English-language authors summarised above, Thomas Reverdy and Hubert Haddad (see Chapter 6) focused on the more exotic elements of Japanese culture, such as raven-haired women, the *yakuza*, *shokunin* philosophy or the sublime nature. This reflected the primarily cultural interest many French readers have for Japan and their continued perception of the country, at least in some literary texts, as being a place of beauty, mystery and escape rather than a complex real-life entity with its contemporary social issues. Although the French media showed a strong interest in the Fukushima nuclear disasters, this element of a 'polluted Japan' was not strongly present in the two chosen works of book-length fiction. It seems that nuclear radiation does not hinder French willingness to seek escape and inspiration in Japanese culture, an attitude that may conceal the unwillingness of the French themselves to face up to the issue of nuclear power, upon which their country is heavily reliant.

Many of the Japanese-, English- and French-language responses that were examined can be placed on a spectrum ranging from social criticism to entertainment, in which the Japanese-language responses tended to be the most focused on Japanese social issues, whereas English-language responses dealt with social issues but treated them in an entertaining or educational way for the readers and French-language responses tended more heavily towards exoticism and entertainment, even when they dealt with social issues. This makes sense given that foreign-language authors were not expected to respond to the aforementioned need of Japanese readers to rediscover their identity in the face of increasingly polarised ways in which their country was being represented, as well as to come to terms with their sense of involvement and responsibility for the nuclear disaster. As the examples analysed in this book demonstrate, in a situation in which information came in the form of one-sided views from mainstream media or a vast expanse of self-published individual experiences, Japanese fiction was valued over other media due to its ability to provide imaginative alternatives.

However, reality is never so simple and there are some works that do not comfortably fit on this spectrum, especially when it comes to portraying differences between Tokyo and Tōhoku. In one case (see Chapter 4), the spectrum was completely reversed, with the Japanese-language response *Kimi no na wa* displaying some serious self-exoticisation by the Japanese, whereas the English-language response by Gretel Ehrlich and the French-language response by Richard Collasse were much more socially critical. Both these authors had spent a significant amount of time researching, travelling and living in Japan and possessed more knowledge about the disaster than many Japanese authors. These exceptions go to the very heart of my project—the hypothesis that, in this age of globalisation, when studying events that have an impact on a global scale, such as 3.11, it makes sense to study the responses to the event in a global manner. These two examples, as well as the works of French authors, such as Michaël Ferrier or Nadine and Thierry Ribault, demonstrate the importance of looking beyond national and linguistic borders in the analysis of literary and cultural responses to events. Further, based on this evidence, I expect to see a growing tendency for self-images and hetero-images of nations to converge in the future. As more people travel and live in different parts of the world, differences between what a country's citizens and residents perceive as their national character and what foreigners perceive should become minimal. As authors move freely between countries, with some of them (e.g. Richard Collasse) spending more time in Japan and having more on-the-ground knowledge than an ethnically Japanese author born overseas, it becomes increasingly difficult to label an image as being a self-image or a hetero-image.

However, as shown by the references made to the divine punishment theory by various intellectuals and authors following 3.11, it was mostly Japanese authors who viewed disasters as change agents and an opportunity to reflect on Japanese society, as well as addressing the question of 'who are the Japanese?' As such, Japanese cultural responses to disaster are often critical of their own country, which motivates readers to act in certain ways. Conversely, foreign-language authors are perhaps prompted by Japanese disasters to reflect on what could have been lost and express their solidarity through positive portrayals of the country. The differences may also be simply explained by the fact that it becomes morally difficult for outsiders to criticise a country and its citizens following a disaster, which fosters more positive hetero-images. This could be understood as 'a paradise built in the imagination', which is similar to

Rebecca Solnit's 'paradise built in hell'—the outpouring of sympathy and grief towards victims usually translates to a desire to see the best in these people and to temporarily put aside political differences. To understand the social and cultural construct of Japan's post-3.11 future, it is essential to study hetero-images from a variety of sources, to contrast them against self-images and to determine how they influence each other.

REFERENCES

Abe criticizes increase in hate speech in Japan. (2013, 8 May). *The Asahi Shimbun: Asia & Japan Watch*. Retrieved from www.asahi.com/ajw/

Abe, Shinzō. (2013, 7 September). *Presentation by Prime Minister Shinzo Abe at the 125th Session of the International Olympic Committee (IOC)*. Prime Minister of Japan and His Cabinet. Retrieved from japan.kantei.go.jp/96_abe/statement/201309/07ioc_presentation_e.html

Adelstein, Jake. (2011a). Muenbotoke. In Patrick Sherriff (Ed.), *2:46: Aftershocks: Stories from the Japan earthquake*. London, UK: Enhanced Editions.

Adelstein, Jake. (2011b, 9 April). Mobsters on a mission: How Japan's mafia launched an aid effort. *The Independent*. Retrieved from www.independent.co.uk/news/world/asia/mobsters-on-a-mission-how-japans-mafia-launched-an-aid-effort-2264031.html

Adelstein, Jake. (2012, 21 February). How the Yakuza went nuclear. *The Telegraph*. Retrieved from www.telegraph.co.uk/news/worldnews/asia/japan/japan-earthquake-and-tsunami-in/9084151/How-the-Yakuza-went-nuclear.html

Akasaka, Norio. (2009). *Tōhokugaku: wasurerareta Tōhoku* [Tōhoku studies: The forgotten region]. Tokyo, Japan: Kōdansha.

Akasaka, Norio. (2014, 2 June). Makenai 'shitatakasa' wo: Akasaka Norio san Higashi Nihon Daishisai 4 nenme [We need to be undefeatably tenacious: Akasaka Norio, four years from the Great East Japan Earthquake]. *Asahi Shimbun*. Retrieved from www.asahi.com/shimen/20140602/index_tokyo_list.html

Anderson, Benedict. (2012). 'Kibō' no nashonarizumu [The nationalism of hope]. In Kyōdō Tsūshinsha shuzai han [Kyodo News crew] (Ed.), *Sekai ga nihon no koto wo kangaete iru: 3.11 go no bunmei wo tou—17 kenjin no messeji* [The world is thinking about Japan: We asked about post-3.11 civilisation and 17 intellectuals responded] (pp. 202–215). Tokyo, Japan: Tarō Jirōsha Editasu.

Anderson, Mark. (2006). Mobilizing *Gojira*: Mourning modernity as monstrosity. In William M. Tsutsui & Michiko Ito (Eds), *In Godzilla's footsteps: Japanese pop culture icons on the global stage* (pp. 21–40). New York, NY: Palgrave Macmillan.

Angles, Jeffrey. (2017). Poetry in an era of nuclear power: Three poetic responses to Fukushima. In Barbara Geilhorn & Kristina Iwata-Weickgenannt (Eds), *Fukushima and the arts: Negotiating nuclear disaster* (pp. 144–161). Tokyo, Japan: Routledge.

Applebaum, Anne. (2011, 14 March). If the Japanese can't build a safe reactor, who can? *The Washington Post*. Retrieved from www.washingtonpost.com/opinions/if-the-japanese-cant-build-a-safe-reactor-who-can/2011/03/14/ABCJvuV_story.html

Arita, Eriko. (2012, 8 April). Keene shares his love for Tohoku. *The Japan Times*. Retrieved from www.japantimes.co.jp/news/2012/04/08/national/media-national/keene-shares-his-love-for-tohoku/

As U.S. damage measured, emergency declared in California counties. (2011, 12 March). *CNN International Edition*. Retrieved from edition.cnn.com/2011/US/03/11/tsunami/

Azuma, Hiroki. (2007). *Gemu-teki riarizumu no tanjō* [The birth of game-like realism]. Tokyo, Japan: Kōdansha.

Azuma, Hiroki. (2011a). Shinsai de bokutachi wa barabara ni natte shimatta [The disaster broke us apart]. In Azuma Hiroki (Ed.), *Shisō chizu beta 2* [Thought map beta 2] (pp. 8–17). Tokyo, Japan: Contectures, LLC.

Azuma, Hiroki. (2011b, 16 March). For a change, proud to be Japanese. *The New York Times*. Retrieved from www.nytimes.com/2011/03/17/opinion/17azuma.html

Azuma, Hiroki. (2011c, 5 April). Daishinsai to genron jin: mizukara media 'ni naru' yakuwari [The great earthquake and public intellectuals: Our role of 'becoming' the media]. *Asahi Shimbun Digital (Web shinsho)*.

Azuma, Hiroki. (2012). Atarashii kuni, atarashii seiza [A new nation, a new constellation]. In *Shisō chizu beta 3: Nihon 2.0* [Thought map beta 3: Japan 2.0] (pp. 42–53). Tokyo, Japan: Genron.

Barboza, Tony. (2012, 26 May). Scientists observe 'tragic experiment' of Tsunami Debris. *Los Angeles Times*. Retrieved from articles.latimes.com/2012/may/26/local/la-me-tsunami-debris-20120526

Beech, Hannah. (2011, 14 March). How Japan copes with tragedy: A lesson in the art of endurance. *Time*. Retrieved from world.time.com/2011/03/14/how-japan-copes-with-tragedy-a-lesson-in-the-art-of-endurance/

Benedict, Ruth. (1946). *The chrysanthemum and the sword: Patterns of Japanese culture*. Boston, MA: Houghton Mifflin Co.

Berndt, Jaqueline. (2013). The intercultural challenge of the 'Mangaesque': Reorienting manga studies after 3/11. In Jaqueline Berndt & Bettina Kümmerling-Meibauer (Eds), *Manga's cultural crossroads* (pp. 65–84). New York, NY: Routledge.

Birmingham, Lucy & McNeill, David. (2012). *Strong in the rain: Surviving Japan's earthquake, tsunami and Fukushima nuclear disaster*. New York, NY: Palgrave Macmillan.

Bloch, Marc Léopold Benjamin. (1961). *Feudal society* (Vol. 1). Chicago, IL: University of Chicago Press.

Bo, Meng. (2011). Higashi nihon daishinsai ni kansuru Furansu shakai no hannō [French reactions to the Great East Japan Earthquake]. *Ajiken World Trends*, *189*, 52–54.

Boss, Joyce E. (2006). Hybridity and negotiated identity in Japanese popular culture. In William M. Tsutsui & Michiko Ito (Eds), *In Godzilla's footsteps: Japanese pop culture icons on the global stage* (pp. 103–110). New York, NY: Palgrave Macmillan.

Boudette, Neal E. & Bennett, Jeff. (2011, 26 March). Pigment shortage hits auto makers. *The Wall Street Journal*. Retrieved from www.wsj.com/articles/SB10001424052748703696704576222990521120106

Bouthier, Antoine. (2011, 25 March). La reconstruction après le séisme, un enjeu pour la mafia japonaise [Reconstruction following the earthquake, a challenge for the Japanese mafia]. *Le Monde*. Retrieved from www.lemonde.fr/planete/article/2011/03/25/la-reconstruction-apres-le-seisme-un-enjeu-pour-la-mafia-japonaise_1498556_3244.html

Brown, Alexander James. (2018). *Anti-nuclear protest in post-Fukushima Tokyo: Power struggles*. New York, NY: Routledge.

Brown, Lester. (2012). Seitaikei no kiki to gendai bunmei [The ecosystem crisis and modern civilization]. In Kyōdō Tsūshinsha shuzai han [Kyodo News crew] (Ed.), *Sekai ga nihon no koto wo kangaete iru: 3.11 go no bunmei wo tou—17 kenjin no messeji* [The world is thinking about Japan: We asked about post-3.11 civilization and 17 intellectuals responded] (pp. 158–173). Tokyo, Japan: Tarō Jirōsha Editasu.

Bryce, Mio & Davis, Jason. (2010). An overview of manga genres. In Toni Johnson-Woods (Ed.), *Manga: An anthology of global and cultural perspectives* (pp. 34–61). London, UK: Continuum.

Burgess, Chris. (2011). Japanese national character stereotypes in the foreign media in the aftermath of the Great East Japan Earthquake: Myth or reality? *The Tsuda Review*, 56, 23–56.

Cabinet Office, Government of Japan. (2013). *Higashi nihon daishinsai ni kanren suru jisatsusha sū (Heisei 25 Nen)* [Suicide numbers relating to the Great East Japan Earthquake (2013)]. Retrieved from www.npa.go.jp/safetylife/seianki/jisatsu/H25/H25_jisatunojoukyou_03.pdf, p.11.

Chavez, Amy. (2011, 26 March). Hey, look! No loot! *The Japan Times*. Retrieved from www.japantimes.co.jp/community/2011/03/26/our-lives/hey-look-no-loot/

Chiba, Toshihiro. (2015, 1 February). Shokunin keishi no Nihonjin ga, kensetsu gyō wo dame ni suru [The Japanese disregard for *shokunin* will ruin the construction industry]. *Tōyōkeizai Online*. Retrieved from toyokeizai.net/articles/-/59426

Christopher, Robert C. (1984). *The Japanese mind*. New York, NY: Ballantine.

Chung, Hosung. (2012). Nihon yo, nakanaide kudasai [Japan, please don't cry]. In Kyōdō Tsūshinsha shuzai han [Kyodo News crew] (Ed.), *Sekai ga nihon no koto wo kangaete iru: 3.11 go no bunmei wo tou—17 kenjin no messeji* [The world is thinking about Japan: We asked about post-3.11 civilization and 17 intellectuals responded] (pp. 22–41). Tokyo, Japan: Tarō Jirōsha Editasu.

Collasse, Richard. (2012a). *L'océan dans la rizière* [The ocean in the rice paddy]. Paris, France: Editions du Seuil.

Collasse, Richard. (2012b, 19 March). 'Kizuna wa doko ni?' Chanel Nihon hōjin shachō ga shōsetsu de keirin ['Where is the *kizuna*?' Chanel Japan CEO raises alarm with his novel]. *Sankei Digital*. Retrieved from www.iza.ne.jp/kiji/events/news/130928/evt13092800280000-n1.html

Condry, Ian & Fujita, Yuiko. (2011). Introduction. *International Journal of Japanese Sociology*, 20, 2–3.

Crushed, but true to law of 'Gaman'. (2011, 16 March). *The Australian*. Retrieved from www.theaustralian.com.au/archive/in-depth/crushed-but-true-to-law-of-gaman/news-story/ebb255b141079ee5fc801700b93ca425

DiNitto, Rachel. (2019). *Fukushima fiction: The literary landscape of Japan's triple disaster*. Honolulu, HI: University of Hawaiʻi Press.

Donarudo Kīn san, Nihon kokuseki shutoku: shinsaigo eijū wo ketsui [Donald Keene acquires Japanese citizenship, decided to move permanently after the earthquake]. (2012, 8 March). *Asahi Shimbun*.

Ehrlich, Gretel. (2013a). *Facing the wave: A journey in the wake of the Tsunami*. New York, NY: Vintage Books.

Ehrlich, Gretel. (2013b, 18 March). Embracing impermanence. *The Economist*. Retrieved from www.economist.com/blogs/prospero/2013/03/qa-gretel-ehrlich

Fackler, Martin. (2010, 21 April). Japan tries to face up to growing poverty problem. *The New York Times*. Retrieved from www.nytimes.com/2010/04/22/world/asia/22poverty.html

Fackler, Martin. (2012, 2 November). Lifelong scholar of the Japanese becomes one of them. *The New York Times*. Retrieved from www.nytimes.com/2012/11/03/world/asia/with-citizenship-japan-embraces-columbia-scholar.html

Ferrier, Michaël. (2012). *Fukushima: Récit d'un désastre* [Fukushima: The tale of a disaster]. Paris, France: Gallimard.

Flax, Bill. (2011, 17 March). A contrast in catastrophe: Japan and Haiti. *Forbes*. Retrieved from www.forbes.com/sites/billflax/2011/03/17/a-contrast-in-catastrophe-japan-and-haiti/

Fowler, Edward. (1992). *The rhetoric of confession: Shishōsetsu in early twentieth-century Japanese fiction*. Berkeley, CA: University of California Press.

Fujiwara, Masahiko & Sakurai, Yoshiko. (2011). Nihonjin no kakugo to hokori ni tsuite [On the determination and pride of Japanese people]. *Shūkan Post, 43*(21), 32–36.

Fukuda, Mitsuru. (2012). *Daishinsai to media: Higashi Nihon Daishinsai no kyōkun* [The great earthquake and the media: Lessons from the Tōhoku earthquake]. Tokyo, Japan: Hokuju Shuppan.

Fukuma, Kenji & Wagō, Ryōichi. (2011). Daishinsai no toshi, shi no ima o kangaeru: *Aoi ie*, soshite, *Shi no tsubute* sanbusaku kara [Thinking about poetry today in the year of the Great Earthquake: *Aoi Ie* and the *Shi no tsubute* trilogy]. *Gendaishi techō* [Journal of Contemporary Poetry], *54*(11), 10–23.

Funabiki, Takeo. (2003). *'Nihonjinron' saikō* [A rethinking of *'Nihonjinron'*]. Tokyo, Japan: Nihon Hōsō Shuppan Kyōkai.

Galchen, Rivka. (2011, 2 May). Dream machine: The mind-expanding world of quantum computing. *The New Yorker*. Retrieved from www.newyorker.com/magazine/2011/05/02/dream-machine

Gebhardt, Lisette. (2014). Post-3.11 literature: The localisation of pain—internal negotiations and global consciousness. In Lisette Gebhardt & Yuki Masami (Eds), *Literature and art after 'Fukushima': Four Approaches* (pp. 11–36). Berlin, Germany: EB-Verlag.

Genpatsu taisaku: mondai sakiokuri wo tsuzukeruna [Nuclear power plant measures: Stop postponing the problem]. (2014, 12 March). *Asahi Shimbun*.

Genyū, Sōkyu & Yōrō, Takeshi. (2011). Daishinsai, kokka shusai de 'tsuitō to chinkon' wo [The government should host ceremonies of mourning and repose of souls for the earthquake]. *Voice, 407*, 154–165. Tokyo, Japan: PHP kenkyūjo.

Haddad, Hubert. (2013a). *Le peintre d'éventail* [The fan-painter]. Paris, France: Zulma.

Haddad, Hubert. (2013b). Le manuel du parfait jardin—Hubert Haddad répond à *Transfuge* [The manual for the perfect garden—Hubert Haddad talks to *Transfuge*]. Interview by Ariane Singer for *Transfuge*. Retrieved from www.zulma.fr/livre-le-peintre-d-eventail-572046.html

Hampton, Jean. (1986). *Hobbes and the social contract tradition*. Cambridge, UK: Cambridge University Press.

Hayashi, Yuka. (2013, 16 May). Anti-Korean voices grow in Japan. *The Wall Street Journal*. Retrieved from www.wsj.com/articles/SB10001424127887324031404578482570250163826

Hearn, Lafcadio. (1897). A living god. In Lafcadio Hearn (Ed.), *Gleanings in Buddha-fields: Studies of hand and soul in the Far East* (pp. 1–28). New York, NY: Houghton Mifflin Company.

Heidegger, Martin. (1996). *Being and time: A translation of Sein Und Zeit* (Joan Stambaugh, Trans.). New York, NY: State University of New York Press.

Heine, Steven. (1985). *Existential and ontological dimensions of time in Heidegger and Dōgen*. New York, NY: State University of New York.

Henmi, Yō. (2013). *Aoi hana* [The blue flower]. Tokyo, Japan: Kadokawa Shoten.

Hirano, Kei'ichirō. (2013, 2 April). Jisatsu ganbō wa pojitibu na ishi kara umareru: Hirano Kei'ichirō interview zenpen [The desire to commit suicide comes from positive intentions: Interview with Hirano, Kei'ichirō, part one]. *Cakes*. Retrieved from cakes.mu/posts/1594

Hobbes, Thomas. (1651). *Leviathan, or the matter, forme and power of a commonwealth, ecclesiastical and civil*. Retrieved from books.google.com.au/books?id=L3FgBpvIWRkC

Hoffman, Michael. (2011, 22 May). Extreme nationalism may emerge from the rubble of the quake. *The Japan Times*. Retrieved from www.japantimes.co.jp/news/2011/05/22/national/media-national/extreme-nationalism-may-emerge-from-the-rubble-of-the-quake/

Horie, Takafumi. (2015, 29 October). ？そんなん当たり前やん。そんな事覚えんのに何年もかかる奴が馬鹿って事だよボケ [Tweet]. Retrieved from twitter.com/takapon_jp/status/659652245152260096

Iida, Tetsunari, Satō, Eisaku & Kōno, Tarō. (2011). *Genshiryoku mura o koete: posuto Fukushima no enerugī seisaku* [Beyond the 'nuclear village': Post-Fukushima energy policy]. Tokyo, Japan: NHK Shuppan.

Ikeda, Nobuo. (2012). *Genpatsu kiken shinwa no hōkai* [The breakdown of the 'danger myth' of nuclear power]. Tokyo, Japan: PHP kenkyūjo.

Imai, Masaaki. (1986). *KAIZEN, the key to Japan's competitive success*. New York, NY: Random House Business Division.

Imamura Fukkōshō jinin. (2017, 26 April). *Mainichi Shimbun*. Retrieved from mainichi.jp/articles/20170427/k00/00m/010/128000c

Ishiba, Shigeru. (2011, 21 September). 'Kaku no senzai teki yokushi ryoku' iji no tame genpatsu tsudukeru beki [We should continue with nuclear power, to maintain the deterrent effect inherent in it]. *News Post Seven*. Retrieved from www.news-postseven.com/archives/20110921_31301.html

Ishino, Hikari. (2013, 11 March). Bungaku to shinsai: Takahashi Gen'ichirō *Koisuru genpatsu* to kotoba no chikara [Literature and earthquakes: Takahashi Gen'ichirō's *Koisuru genpatsu* and the power of words]. In *Narajo×bunka 2012 ima wo meguru 20 no hōkoku* [Nara Women's University × Culture 2012: 20 Reports on Current Affairs] (pp. 26–33). Retrieved from koshisuzuki.web.fc2.com/narajyobunka2012/ishino.pdf

Ivy, Marilyn. (1995). *Discourses of the vanishing: Modernity, phantasm, Japan*. Chicago, IL: University of Chicago Press.

Iwamura, Jane Naomi. (2011). Zen's personality: D.T. Suzuki. In Jane Iwamura (Ed.), *Virtual orientalism: Asian religions and American popular culture* (pp. 23–62). New York, NY: Oxford University Press.

J.A.C. Project. (2006). *Nihon gaten: shokuhatsusuru 6-nin* [Nihonga painting: six provocative artists]. Yokohama, Japan: Yokohama bijutsukan [Yokohama Museum of Art].

James, Susan Donaldson & Goldman, Russell. (2011). Japanese, waiting in line for hours, follow social order after quake. *ABC News*. Retrieved from abcnews.go.com/Health/japan-victims-show-resilience-earthquake-tsunami-sign-sense/story?id=13135355

Japan to protest Fukushima-Olympics cartoons in French weekly. (2013, 12 September). *The Japan Times*. Retrieved from www.japantimes.co.jp/news/2013/09/12/national/japan-to-protest-fukushima-olympics-cartoons-in-french-weekly/

Jimenez, Chris D. (2018). Nuclear disaster and global aesthetics in Gerald Vizenor's *Hiroshima Bugi: Atomu 57* and Ruth Ozeki's *A Tale for the Time Being*. Comparative Literature Studies, 55(2), 262–284.

Kaigai 'Nihonjin ni kokoro kara no keii wo': shinsai ji no 'Nihon no tamashii' ni gaikokujin kandō [The world sends their heartfelt respect to Japanese people: Foreigners are touched by the 'Japanese spirit' displayed after the earthquake]. (2013, 5 June). *Pandora no yūutsu* [Pandora's gloom]. Retrieved from kaigainohannoublog.blog55.fc2.com/blog-entry-829.html

Karatani, Kōjin. (2011, 24 March). How catastrophe heralds a new Japan. *CounterPunch*. Retrieved from www.counterpunch.org/2011/03/24/how-catastrophe-heralds-a-new-japan/

Kariya, Tetsu & Hanasaki, Akira. (2013). *Oishinbo 110 (Fukushima no shinjitsu 1)* [Oishinbo 110 (the truth about Fukushima 1)]. Tokyo Japan: Shōgakukan.

Katayama, Morihide & Yamanaka, Hiroyuki. (2016). Ongaku kara fukayomi suru *Shin Gojira*: soshite Ifukube ongaku ga mimi ni nokoru wake [A close reading of *Shin Godzilla* through music: Why Ifukube's music gets stuck in your head]. In *Shin Gojira: watashi wa kō yomu* [Shin Godzilla: This is how I read it]. Tokyo, Japan: Nikkei BP. Available from business.nikkei.com/atcl/opinion/16/083000015/092600025/

Katō, Norihiro & Fujimura, Kōhei. (2016). Gojira wa Anno jishin de ari, gen tennō demo aru [Godzilla is Anno himself and also the current Emperor]. In *Shin Gojira: watashi wa kō yomu* [Shin Godzilla: This is how I read it]. Tokyo, Japan: Nikkei BP. Available from business.nikkeibp.co.jp/atcl/opinion/16/083000015/091300015/

Kawakami, Hiromi. (2011). *Kamisama 2011* [God bless you, 2011]. Tokyo, Japan: Kōdansha.

Kawakami, Hiromi & Numano, Mitsuyoshi. (2012). Sekai wa yuragi, genjitsu to gensō no sakaime mo yuraide iru: nihon bungaku no hon'yakuka tachi to shōsetsu *Kazahana* o kataru [The world is shaking and the border between reality and fantasy is being blurred: Discussing the novel *Kazahana* with translators of Japanese literature]. *Japanese Book News Salon*. Retrieved from www.wochikochi.jp/topstory/2012/04/jbn2.php

Keene, Donald. (2012). Naze, ima 'nihon kokuseki' wo shutoku suruka [Why I am obtaining Japanese citizenship now]. *Bungeishunjū, 90*(5), 274–281.

Kendall, Philip. (2013, 4 April). Pro-Korean, anti-Korean forces face off in Shin-Okubo. *Japan Today*. Retrieved from japantoday.com/category/national/pro-korean-anti-korean-forces-face-off-in-shin-okubo

Kim, Chang-Ran. (2014, 14 May). Japan's working poor left behind by Abenomics. *Reuters*. Retrieved from www.reuters.com/article/us-japan-economy-poverty-idUSBREA4D0U820140515

Kimura, Saeko. (2013). *Shinsaigo bungaku ron: atarashii bungaku no tame ni* [On post-earthquake literature: For a new Japanese literature]. Tokyo, Japan: Seidosha.

Kimura, Saeko. (2018). *Sono go no shinsaigo bungaku ron* [On post-earthquake literature, part II]. Tokyo, Japan: Seidosha.

Kingston, Jeff. (2013, 25 January). 'Abe-genda': Nuclear export superpower. *The Japan Times*. Retrieved from www.japantimes.co.jp/news/2014/01/25/world/abe-genda-nuclear-export-superpower/

Kirishima, Shun. (2013). Nihon de yomenai Murakami Haruki no dengon [A message from Murakami Haruki, that can't be read in Japan]. *Asahi Shimbun Weekly AERA, 6*(3), 30–32.

Kita, Yasutoshi. (2008). *Takumi no kuni Nippon* [Japan, a country of artisans]. Tokyo, Japan: PHP Shinsho.

Knighton, Mary A. (2014). The sloppy realities of 3.11 in Shiriagari Kotobuki's Manga. *The Asia-Pacific Journal: Japan Focus, 11*(26), article 1. Retrieved from japanfocus.org/-Mary-Knighton/4140

Kobayashi, Yoshinori. (2011). *Gōmanizumu Sengen Special: Kokubōron* [Special manifesto of arrogant-ism: On national defence]. Tokyo, Japan: Shōgakukan.

Kobayashi, Yoshinori. (2012). *Gōmanizumu Sengen Special: Datsu Genpatsuron* [Special manifesto of arrogant-ism: On anti-nuclear politics]. Tokyo, Japan: Shōgakukan.

Kōkami, Shōji. (2009). *Kūki to seken* [The 'air' and society]. Tokyo, Japan: Kōdansha.

Kristof, Nicholas. (2011, 11 March). Sympathy for Japan and admiration. *The New York Times*.

Kudō, Yuka. (2016). Shisha tachi ga kayou machi: takushī doraibā no yūrei genshō [The town frequented by the dead: The phenomenon of ghost sightings by taxi drivers]. In Kiyoshi Kanebeshi (Ed.), *Yobisamasareru reisei no shinsaigaku* [The study of the awakened spirituality in the aftermath of the earthquake] (pp. 1–23). Tokyo, Japan: Shinyōsha.

Kunisue, Norito & Hirata, Atsuo. (2013, 13 January). French president of Chanel Japan pens novel about disaster area. *Globe by The Asahi Shimbun*.

Kurokawa, Kiyoshi. (2012). Message from the Chairman. In Fukushima Nuclear Accident Independent Investigation Commission (NAIIC) (Ed.), *The official report of the Fukushima Nuclear Accident Independent Investigation Commission (Executive Summary)* (p. 9). Tokyo, Japan: The National Diet of Japan.

Kurose, Yōhei, Sawaragi, Noi & Azuma, Hiroki. (2012). The 'Bad Place' after 3.11—Tokyo. In *Shisō chizu beta 3* [Thought map beta 3] (pp. 346–374). Tokyo, Japan: Genron.

Kyoto City. (2011, 16 August). *Kyoto gozan no okuribi no torikumi ni kansuru kokoro kara no owabi to onegai* [Our sincere apologies and wishes regarding our undertaking of the 'gozan no okuribi' festival]. Retrieved from www.city.kyoto.lg.jp/bunshi/page/0000106056.html

Lebra, Takie Sugiyama. (1976). *Japanese patterns of behaviour*. Honolulu, HI: University of Hawai'i Press.

Leerssen, Joep. (2007). Imagology: History and method. In Manfred Beller & Joep Leerssen (Eds), *Imagology: The cultural construction and literary representation of national characters. A critical survey* (pp. 17–32). New York, NY: Rodopi.

Maita, Toshihiko. (2015, 27 October). Media he no shinrai do ga takai dakeni yoron yūdō sareyasui Nihon [Japan, a country whose public opinion can be manipulated due to its high level of trust in the media]. *Newsweek Japan*.

Manabe, Noriko. (2016). *The revolution will not be televized: Protest music after Fukushima*. New York, NY: Oxford University Press.

May, Reinhard. (1996). *Heidegger's hidden sources: East Asian influences on his work* (Graham Parkes, Trans.). New York, NY: Routledge.

Mikuriya, Takashi. (2011). *'Sengo' ga owari, 'saigo' ga hajimaru* [The 'post-war' period ends and the 'post-disaster' period starts]. Tokyo, Japan: Chikura shobō.

Ministry of Economy, Trade and Industry, Government of Japan. (2012, March). *Japan's challenges towards recovery*. Retrieved from www.meti.go.jp/english/earthquake/nuclear/japan-challenges/pdf/japan-challenges_full.pdf

Miyadai, Shinji. (1995). *Owari naki nichijō wo ikiro* [Living in 'the endless everyday']. Tokyo, Japan: Chikuma Shobō.

Mockett, Marie Mutsuki. (2015). *Where the dead pause and the Japanese say goodbye: A journey*. New York, NY: W.W. Norton & Company.

Mondale, Walter F. (2012). Hakki sareta Nichibei no pa-tona-shippu [U.S.–Japan partnership brought into full play]. In Kyōdō Tsūshinsha shuzai han [Kyodo News crew] (Ed.), *Sekai ga nihon no koto wo kangaete iru: 3.11 go no bunmei wo tou—17 kenjin no messeji* [The world is thinking about Japan: We asked about post-3.11 civilization and 17 intellectuals responded] (pp. 116–129). Tokyo, Japan: Tarō Jirōsha Editasu.

Morikawa, Kaichirō. (2011a, 21 March). おたく文化は、永続する強固な日常(とその閉塞感)を基盤にして成り立ってきた。80年代のアニメはハルマゲドン願望が大きな柱だったし、オウム事件でそれに傷が付くと、重心を近未来から「近過去」のリセットに移して構築されてきた。ところが今や、永続する日常という基盤自体に亀裂が走っている。[Tweet]. Retrieved from twitter.com/kai_morikawa/status/49697021065560064

Morikawa, Kaichirō. (2011b, 21 March). ハルマゲドンを描くような作品だけの話ではない。コンビニの描き方一つ取っても、意味合いやニュアンスがこれまでとは多かれ少なかれ変わらざるを得ないのではないか。虚構を成立させている基盤それ自体が傾いたのだから、制作に関わっている方々はこの問題に直面していると思う。[Tweet]. Retrieved from twitter.com/kai_morikawa/status/49697129094070272

Morley, David & Robins, Kevin. (1995). *Spaces of identity: Global media, electronic landscapes and cultural boundaries*. New York, NY: Routledge.

Murakami, Haruki. (2011). Speaking as an unrealistic dreamer (Emanuel Pastreich, Trans.). *The Asia-Pacific Journal: Japan Focus, 9*(29), article 7. Retrieved from apjjf.org/2011/9/29/Murakami-Haruki/3571/article.html

Murakami, Takashi. (2012). Geijutsuka no shimei to kakugo: Doha [The artist's mission and determination—Doha]. In *Shisō chizu beta 3: Nihon 2.0* [Thought map beta 3: Japan 2.0] (pp. 84–99). Tokyo, Japan: Genron.

Muroi, Yuzuki. (2013, 26 June). Migi ja nakereba hidari nano? [Are we necessarily right-wing if we're not left-wing?]. *Shūkan Asahi*.

Nakajima, Yoshimichi. (2011). 'Ganbarō Nihon' to iu bōryoku [The violence of saying 'hang in there, Japan']. *Shinchō, 45*, 130–137.

Napier, Susan. (2006). When Godzilla speaks. In William M. Tsutsui & Michiko Ito (Eds), *In Godzilla's footsteps: Japanese pop culture icons on the global stage* (pp. 9–20). New York, NY: Palgrave Macmillan.

Nietzsche, Friedrich. (1909–1913). Beyond good and evil. In *The complete works of Friedrich Nietzsche* (Helen Zimmern, Trans.). London, UK: T.N. Foulis. Available from www.gutenberg.org/ebooks/4363

Nishi, D., Koido, Y., Nakaya, N., Sone, T., Noguchi, H., Hamazaki, K., Hamazaki, T. & Matsuoka., Y. (2012). Peritraumatic distress, watching television and posttraumatic stress symptoms among rescue workers after the Great East Japan Earthquake. *PLoS ONE, 7*(4). doi.org/10.1371/journal.pone.0035248

'Nuclear power' cited the most in Tokyo Governor election tweets. (2014, 5 February). *The Japan Times*. Retrieved from www.japantimes.co.jp/news/2014/02/05/national/nuclear-power-cited-the-most-in-tokyo-governor-election-tweets/

Obama, Barack. (2011, 17 March). Remarks by the president on the situation in Japan. Retrieved from www.whitehouse.gov/the-press-office/2011/03/17/remarks-president-situation-japan

Odagiri, Takushi. (2014). The end of literature and the beginning of praxis: Wagō Ryōichi's *Pebbles of Poetry*. *Japan Forum, 26*(3), 361–382.

Odajima, Takashi. (2012, 23 March). Retteru to shite no Fukushima [Fukushima as a label]. *Nikkei Business Online*. Retrieved from business.nikkeibp.co.jp/article/life/20120322/230156/ (link discontinued).

Ōe, Kenzaburō. (2011, 28 March). History repeats: Japan and nuclear power. *The New Yorker*. Retrieved from www.newyorker.com/magazine/2011/03/28/history-repeats

Ogino, Anna. (2011). *Daishinsai yoku to jingi* [The great earthquake: Greed and honour]. Tokyo, Japan: Kyōdōtsūshinsha.

Oguni, Ayako. (2013, 2 March). Shinsaigo 'kotoba' wa kawattanoka: Tanikawa Shuntarō san kara henshin [Did 'words' change after the earthquake? A reply from Tanikawa Shuntarō]. *Mainichi Shimbun*.

Okada, Toshio. (2000). *Otakugaku nyūmon* [An introduction to otaku-ology]. Tokyo, Japan: Shinchōsha.

Oliver-Smith, Anthony & Hoffman, Susanna M. (2002). Introduction. In Susanna M. Hoffman & Anthony Oliver-Smith (Eds), *Catastrophe and culture: The anthropology of disaster* (pp. 3–22). Santa Fe, NM: School of American Research Press.

Ozeki, Ruth. (2013a). *A tale for the time being*. Melbourne, Vic.: Text Publishing.

Ozeki, Ruth. (2013b, 10 September). I write in order to think. It's the way I ask questions and interrogate the world. It's the way I experience life most fully. Interview of Ruth Ozeki by Lara Touitou. *Feedbooks*. Retrieved from www.feedbooks.com/interview/233/i-write-in-order-to-think-it-s-the-way-i-ask-questions-and-interrogate-the-world-it-s-the-way-i-experience-life-most-fully

Ozeki, Ruth. (2013c, 14 March). Freedom from duality. Interview with Jessica Gross for *Kirkus*. Retrieved from www.kirkusreviews.com/features/freedom-duality/

Ozeki, Ruth. (2013d, 14 October). How the Japanese earthquake shook this novel to its core. Interview with Marsha Lederman for *The Globe and Mail*. Retrieved from www.theglobeandmail.com/arts/books-and-media/how-the-japanese-earthquake-shook-a-novel-to-its-core/article14843683/

Parry, Richard Lloyd. (2014). Ghosts of the tsunami. *London Review of Books, 36*(3), 13–17. Retrieved from www.lrb.co.uk/v36/n03/richard-lloyd-parry/ghosts-of-the-tsunami

Pew Research Center. (2011, 15 March). *Strong public interest in Japan disaster*. Retrieved from www.people-press.org/2011/03/15/strong-public-interest-in-japan-disaster/

Pilling, David. (2014). *Bending adversity: Japan and the art of survival*. New York, NY: The Penguin Press.

Reconstruction Agency. (2012, 29 March). *Zenkoku no hinansha to no kazu* [Total number of evacuees in the country]. Retrieved from www.reconstruction.go.jp/topics/120328hinansya.pdf

Reischauer, Edwin O. (1977). *The Japanese*. Cambridge, MA: Belknap Press.

Reverdy, Thomas. (2013). *Les évaporés* [The evaporated]. Paris, France: Flammarion.

Roan, Shari. (2011, 21 March). Japanese restraint is steeped in a culture of tested resilience. *Los Angeles Times*. Retrieved from articles.latimes.com/2011/mar/21/health/la-he-japanese-quake-culture-20110321

Saitō, Minako. (2011, 27 April). Yūki wo tamesareru hyōgensha: genshiryoku mura to bungaku mura [Authors are having their courage tested: The nuclear village and the literary village]. *Asahi Shimbun.*

Saitō, Tamaki. (2011, 11 December). 'Kizuna' renko ni iwakan [Feeling uneasy with the repetition of 'kizuna']. *Mainichi Shimbun.*

Sakamoto, Rumi. (2011). 'Koreans, Go Home!' Internet nationalism in contemporary Japan as a digitally mediated subculture. *The Asia-Pacific Journal, 9*(10), article 2. Retrieved from www.japanfocus.org/-Rumi-SAKAMOTO/3497

Sakamoto, Rumi. (2016). Kobayashi Yoshinori, 3.11 and *Datsu Genpatsu Ron.* In Mark R. Mullins & Koichi Nakano (Eds), *Disasters and social crisis in contemporary Japan: Political, religious and sociocultural responses* (pp. 269–287). New York, NY: Palgrave Macmillan.

Sakurai, Yoshiko. (2014, 23 May). Heito supīchi wa Nihonjin no hokori no ketujo ga gen'in [Hate speech is caused by a lack of pride in Japanese people]. *News Post Seven.* Retrieved from www.news-postseven.com/archives/20140523_255470.html

Samuels, Richard J. (2013). *3.11: disaster and change in Japan.* Ithaca, NY: Cornell University Press.

Satō, Tokujin & Kawaguchi, Kentarō. (2012, 8 January). *Edanomics v. maeharanomics: konmei minshu no 'tairitsujiku'* [Edanomics v. maeharanomics: The axis of conflict in the DPJ]. *Asahi Shimbun*, p. 1.

Shiono, Nanami & Andō, Tadao. (2012). Hisaichi no kodomo tachi ni 10nen bokin wo! [Let's have a ten-year charity fund for the children of the disaster-hit areas!]. *Bungeishunjū, 90*(5), 318–327.

Shiriagari, Kotobuki. (2004). Chosha intabyū: itsumo mannaka ni tama wo otoshitai [Author interview: 'I want to always be dropping the ball in the middle']. *Issatsu no hon* [Just one book], *9*(6), 14–17.

Shiriagari, Kotobuki. (2011a). *Ano hi kara no manga* [Manga since that day]. Tokyo, Japan: Enterbrain.

Shiriagari, Kotobuki. (2011b). Tachisukumi, kao wo age … Shiriagari Kotobuki san [Stunned, but looking up … An interview with Shiriagari Kotobuki]. *Ōkoshi Kensuke no 'ima wo miru'* [Ōkoshi Kensuke's 'looking at now'], NHK. Retrieved from www9.nhk.or.jp/nw9-okoshi-blog/cat6311/97789.html (link discontinued).

Shiriagari, Kotobuki. (2011c). Manga dakara dekiru koto ga aru [There are some things only manga can do]. *Neppū, 9*(10), 19–23.

Shiriagari, Kotobuki. (2011d, 21 August). 'Shōjiki, jibun ga uketa shokku no hyaku bun no ichi mo kakete inai'. Shiriagari Kotobuki ga mita 3.11 to manga no kanōsei ['To be honest, I haven't even been able to express a hundredth of the shock I received'. The possibilities Shiriagari Kotobuki saw in 3.11 and manga]. *Nikkan Cyzo*. Retrieved from www.cyzo.com/2011/08/post_8253.html

Shushō: 'fūhyō ni kuni to shite taiō' Oishinbo byōsha [PM: the government will respond to the infliction of 'reputation damage'; portrayal in *Oishinbo*]. (2014, 17 May). 47NEWS. Retrieved from www.47news.jp/CN/201405/CN2014051701001481.html (link discontinued).

Silenced by Gaman. (2011, 20 April). *The Economist*. Retrieved from www.economist.com/node/18587325

Sukhenko, Inna. (2014). Reconsidering the eco-imperatives of Ukrainian consciousness: An introduction to Ukrainian environmental literature. In Scott Slovic, Swarnalatha Rangarajan & Vidya Sarveswaran (Eds), *Ecoambiguity, community and development: Toward a politicized ecocriticism* (pp. 113–129). Lanham, MD: Lexington Books.

Sushi shokunin no 'meshitaki 3 nen nigiri 8 nen' wa jidai okure? Horiemon no zanshin na kangae to wa [Is the 'three years cooking rice, eight years making sushi' tradition behind the times? Horiemon's unconventional views]. (2015, 10 April). *Syoku-yomi*. Retrieved from job.inshokuten.com/foodistMagazine/detail/8

Suter, Rebecca. (2016). Beyond Kizuna: Responses to disaster in the works of Murakami Haruki. In Mark R. Mullins & Koichi Nakano (Eds), *Disasters and social crisis in contemporary Japan: Political, religious and sociocultural responses* (pp. 288–308). New York, NY: Palgrave Macmillan.

Tabuchi, Hiroko. (2009, 19 July). Why Japan's cellphones haven't gone global. *The New York Times*. Retrieved from www.nytimes.com/2009/07/20/technology/20cell.html?_r=0

Tachibana, Akira. (2012). *(Nipponjin)* [(The Japanese)]. Tokyo, Japan: Gentōsha.

Takada, Jun. (2011). Fukushima wa Hiroshima nimo Chernobyl nimo naranakatta: higashi nihon genchi chosa kara mieta shinjitsu to Fukushima fukko no michisuji [Fukushima did not become Hiroshima or Chernobyl: The path to Fukushima's reconstruction and the reality I observed during on-site research in Eastern Japan]. The fourth 'True Interpretations of Modern History' essay contest winner. Available from agora-web.jp/archives/1433511.html

Takahashi, Gen'ichirō. (1998). *Bungaku nanka kowakunai* [I'm not afraid of literature]. Tokyo, Japan: Asahi Shimbunsha.

Takahashi, Gen'ichirō. (2011a). *Koisuru genpatsu* [A nuclear reactor in love]. Tokyo, Japan: Kōdansha.

Takahashi, Gen'ichirō. (2011b, 29 September). Genpatsu no yubisashi otoko [The pointing man of the nuclear power plant]. *Asahi shimbun*.

Takahashi, Gen'ichirō. (2012a). *Ano hi' kara boku ga kangaete iru 'tadashisa' ni tsuite* [What I've been thinking about 'correctness' since 'that day']. Tokyo, Japan: Kawade Shobō Shinsha.

Takahashi, Gen'ichirō. (2012b, 7 January). Genpatsu jiko ga mochifu no ishoku shosetsu wo kanko Takahashi Gen'ichirō shi ni kiku [Interview with Takahashi Gen'ichirō, who has published an unconventional novel with the nuclear incident as a motif]. *Nikkan gendai*. Retrieved from gendai.net/articles/view/book/134530 (link discontinued).

Takeda, Tsuneyasu. (2012). *Kore ga ketsuron! Nihonjin to genpatsu* [This is the conclusion! The Japanese and nuclear power]. Tokyo, Japan: Shōgakukan.

Takekuma, Kentarō. (2011). 'Owari naki nichijō' ga owatta hi [The day the 'endless everyday' ended]. In *Shisō chizu beta 2* [Thought map beta 2] (pp. 148–159). Tokyo, Japan: Contectures, LLC.

Takeuchi, Melinda. (2004). Introduction. In Melinda Takeuchi (Ed.), *The artist as professional in Japan* (pp. 1–16). Stanford, CA: Stanford University Press.

Takumi no waza wo Furansu de hasshin: nen nai nimo kōgeihin shūfuku kyoten, shokunin kōryū mo [Propagating the art of craftsmen in France: A 'repair base' for crafts and interaction between craftsmen planned for this year]. (2016, 7 January). *Asahi Shimbun Digital*. Retrieved from www.asahi.com/articles/DA3S12148710.html

Tamogami, Toshio. (2013, 20 March). Fukushima genpatsu no jiko kara 2nen tatte [Upon the passing of two years since the Fukushima nuclear power plant accident]. *Tamogami Toshio official blog: kokorozashi ha takaku, atsuku moeru* [With high ambitions burning hotly]. Retrieved from ameblo.jp/toshio-tamogami/entry-11494727117.html

Tanikawa, Shuntarō. (2012). Words. In Elmer Luke & David Karashima (Eds), *March was made of yarn* (pp. 7–9). London, UK: Harvill Secker.

Tawada, Yōko. (2012). Fushi no shima [The island of eternal life]. In Elmer Luke & David Karashima (Eds), *March was made of yarn* (pp. 11–21). London, UK: Harvill Secker.

Tawada, Yōko. (2014a). *Kentōshi* [The messenger of light]. Tokyo, Japan: Kōdansha.

Tawada, Yōko. (2014b). Tawada Yōko X Robāto Kyanberu Taidan [Robert Campbell talks to Tawada Yōko]. *Tawada Yōko Kentōshi Tokusetsu Saito* [Special Website for Tawada Yōko's *The Emissary*], Kodansha Book Club. Available from kodanshabunko.com/kentoushi/#Talk

TEPCO. (2011, 13 March). Jukyū hippaku ni yoru keikaku teiden no jisshi to issō no setsuden no onegai ni tsuite [On the enforcement of planned blackouts due to pressures in supply and demand and a request to save electricity even more] [Press release]. *Puresu rirīsu*. Retrieved from www.tepco.co.jp/cc/press/11031315-j.html

Thompson, Christopher S. (2011). Japan's Showa retro boom: Nostalgia, local identity and the resurgence of Kamadogami masks in the nation's northeast. *The Journal of Popular Culture, 44*(6), 1307–1332.

Tokyo Metropolitan Government Election Administration Commission. (2014, 10 February). *Heisei 26 nen Tōkyōtochiji senkyo kaihyō kekka* [2014 Tokyo Metropolitan Government election results]. Retrieved from archive.is/20140210010234/http://sokuho.h26tochijisen.metro.tokyo.jp/h26chi_kai.html

Tsunehira, Furuya. (2011, 28 May). いつかは地震や津波で破滅が来ると薄々感じながら、自分の担当の時代にはたぶん来ない、いや来ないで欲しいという希望的観測が、問題の先送りを行ってきた元凶。竹島も尖閣もパチンコも四島も拉致も全部同じ構図。原発は「問題の先送り・棚上げ」という戦後日本体制そのもの。[Tweet]. Retrieved from twitter.com/aniotahosyu/status/74167842764881921

Tsuruoka, Masahiro. (2011, 12 April). Sekai no 'kizuna' ni kansha: shushō, kakkoku yūryokushi ni messēji kōkoku [Thanking the world for their 'kizuna': PM sends message advertisement to major international newspapers]. *Asahi Shimbun Digital*. Retrieved from www.asahi.com/special/minshu/TKY201104110475.html

Umehara, Takeshi. (1994). *Nihon no shinsō—Jōmon/Ezo bunka wo saguru* [The depths of Japan: Exploring the Jōmon Ezo culture]. Tokyo, Japan: Shūeisha.

Vogel, Ezra. (1979). *Japan as number one*. Cambridge, MA: Harvard University Press.

Wagō, Ryōichi. (2011a). *Shi no tsubute* [Pebbles of poetry]. Tokyo, Japan: Tokuma Shoten.

Wagō, Ryōichi. (2011b). Pebbles of poetry: The Tōhoku earthquake and tsunami. *The Asia-Pacific Journal, 9*(29), article 4. Retrieved from japanfocus.org/-Jeffrey-Angles/3568

Wagō, Ryōichi. (2011c). Hito to chikyū ni torubeki katachi o anji seyo: *Shi no tsubute* to iu basho kara [Suggesting to people and the earth how they should be: from a place called *Shi no tsubute*]. *Gendaishi techō* [Journal of Contemporary Poetry], *54*(8), 128–138.

Wagō, Ryōichi. (2011d). Chosha ni kiku: Wagō Ryōichi *Shi no tsubute* [Ask the author: Wagō Ryōichi *Shi no Tsubute*] *Chūō kōron* [Central Review], *126*(8), 246–248.

Wagō, Ryōichi & Hiroki, Azuma. (2011). Fukushima kara kangaeru kotoba no chikara [Thinking from Fukushima about the power of words]. In Azuma Hiroki (Ed.), *Shisō chizu beta 2* [Thought map beta 2] (pp. 186–193). Tokyo, Japan: Contectures, LLC.

Wagō, Ryōichi & Kamata, Minoru. (2011). Taidan: 'ganbarō' de naku 'akiramenai' [Interview: 'don't give up' not 'hang in there']. *Fujin kōron* [Women's Review], *96*(25), 58–61.

Wagō, Ryōichi & Sano, Shin'ichi. (2012). *Kotoba ni nani ga dekiru no ka: 3.11 wo koete* [What can words do in the aftermath of 3.11?]. Tokyo, Japan: Tokuma Shoten.

Weisenfeld, Gennifer S. (2011). *Imaging disaster: Tokyo and the visual culture of Japan's great earthquake of 1923*. Berkley, CA: University of California Press.

West, Ed. (2011, 14 March). Why is there no looting in Japan? *The Telegraph*. Retrieved from blogs.telegraph.co.uk/news/edwest/100079703/why-is-there-no-looting-in-japan/

White, Garry. (2011, 26 March). Car makers hit by Japan's disaster. *The Telegraph*. Retrieved from www.telegraph.co.uk/finance/newsbysector/transport/8408865/Car-makers-hit-by-Japans-disaster.html

Whiting, Robert. (1990). *You gotta have wa*. New York, NY: Vintage.

Wian, Casey. (2012, 23 May). Flotsam from 2011 Japan tsunami reaches Alaska. *CNN*. Retrieved from edition.cnn.com/2012/05/22/us/alaska-tsunami-debris/

Willacy, Mark. (2012, 25 June). Experts warn of another disaster awaiting at Fukushima. *7.30 Report* (ABC Australia). Retrieved from www.abc.net.au/7.30/content/2012/s3532725.htm

Yamada, Marc. (2011). John Lennon v. the Gangsters: Discursive identity and resistance in the metafiction of Takahashi Gen'ichirō'. *Japanese Language and Literature, 45*(1), 1–30.

Yanagida, Kunio. (2013). *Owaranai genpatsu jiko to 'Nipponbyō'* [The ongoing nuclear accident and 'sickness of Japan']. Tokyo, Japan: Shinchōsha.

Yanagita, Kunio. (1940). *Yukiguni no haru* [Spring in snow country]. Tokyo, Japan: Sōgensha.

Yoshikawa, Naohiro. (2010). *Garapagosu ka suru Nihon* [The 'galapagosization' of Japan]. Tokyo, Japan: Kodansha.

Yoshimoto, Takaaki & Takahashi, Gen'ichirō. (2005). Kotoba no genzai [The 'now' of language]. In Takaaki Yoshimoto (Ed.), *Yoshimoto Takaaki taidansen* [Yoshimoto Takaaki *taidan* collection] (pp. 293–333). Tokyo, Japan: Kōdansha.

Yoshimura, Man'ichi. (2014a). *Borādo byō* [The bollard disease]. Tokyo, Japan: Bungeishunjū.

Yoshimura, Man'ichi. (2014b, 1 June). Shincho *Borādo byō* kankō kinen intabyū: 'roshutsu suru kakō no sekai' [An interview for the occasion of the publication of a new book, *Borādo byō*: The imaginary world that is revealed]. *Kyōto daigaku shimbun* [Kyoto University Newspaper]. Available from www.kyoto-up.org/archives/2008

www.ingramcontent.com/pod-product-compliance
Lightning Source LLC
Chambersburg PA
CBHW050927240426
43670CB00023B/2964